HUMAN VALUES IN MUSIC EDUCATION

by

JAMES L. MURSELL

Professor of Education
Lawrence College,
Appleton, Wisconsin

SILVER, BURDETT AND COMPANY

NEW YORK   NEWARK   BOSTON   CHICAGO   SAN FRANCISCO

Printed in the United States of America

Contents

Foreword

Why should music be taught in our schools? This basic question always confronts the general educator, the administrator, the music teacher, and the public. It becomes of even greater urgency in relation to the entire curriculum, particularly at a time like the present, when every subject is being evaluated either for its retention or removal from "the enlightened way of living," which it is the function of the school to mediate to our boys and girls.

For some time music teachers, supervisors, and general educators have been seeking a comprehensive and convincing answer to this fundamental question, by which music could be justified in the curriculum both for its positive contributions and in reply to the objections that have been raised against it. These objections, however, can be shown to have been based upon incomplete information, ignorance, and even prejudice.

This book attempts to formulate a statement in behalf of music, and to offer an interpretation of its values in terms of a social philosophy of education. It is hoped that such an undertaking may prove serviceable in several directions. Music teachers and supervisors have, no doubt, often felt that progressive educational conceptions had important and fruitful bearings on their work. It may be, however, that in many cases they have not fully recognized the extent to which music education may exemplify such conceptions. Moreover, the application of a social educational philosophy to music carries with it very far-reaching practical consequences, and these have not always been clearly appreciated. Again, general educators, even when sympathetic to music, do not always perceive its complete educational possibilities or the opportunities for advance which it offers. One of the chief arguments of this book is that the music program can exemplify, here and now, the sort of education and the sort of schooling which we all desire and toward which we are moving. This in itself constitutes an exceedingly strong defense for the place of music in the program of studies.

The topics considered in this book are, in a sense, more fundamental than those arising out of educational psychology and the psychology of music, which I have discussed elsewhere. Psychology is the foundation for our educational techniques. But our problem here is the problem of ultimate educational values. A psychological treatment assumes that music will be taught. A philosophical treatment asks why it should be taught. This, in brief, indicates the relationship of the present work to my former *Psychology of School Music Teaching,* written in collaboration with Miss Mabelle Glenn. In this book also I am indebted to her for numerous suggestions relating to the ways in which procedures and practices in school systems throughout the country—in fact, too numerous to mention in detail—exemplify the human values in music education through their own school music achievements.

Finally, it is my hope that this book will help all of us to make more significant the musical experiences which we should bring into the lives of our boys and girls. For music can, when properly directed, exemplify what education should be at its very best. And it can discharge the great and central mission of all education, which is to raise the level of human quality.

James L. Mursell.

CHAPTER ONE: INTRODUCTION

Music, Education, and Human Values

EDUCATION AND HUMAN VALUES

To all who love music, and believe with passionate conviction in the richness and worth of its mission to mankind, the era of social, economic, and political change through which civilization is passing is a challenge and an opportunity. Forces far beyond our control have made it impossible for us complacently to go on as we have been in the past. We cannot take our ease in Zion, or unthinkingly follow a familiar routine. We must re-think our ideals. And we must inexorably test all our procedures by the touchstone of those ideals. All the values of life, all the values of education, have been winnowed by a great wind. Nor have the values of our own enterprise escaped. With a cogency such as few of us have ever known, it is being demanded of us that we give a reason for what we believe, and a justification for what we seek to do. Yet our hearts need not be troubled. For we are the guardians of a jewel of inestimable worth and beauty, the servants of a potent and beneficent magic. In order to succeed more amply, perhaps, than we could have thought possible, all that we need do is to let the lustre of that jewel shine forth, and the strength of that magic be felt. This is no moment for despair, for the backward look, for taking the hand from the plow. The times in which we live require, above all, that we re-examine, courageously and fundamentally, every particular of our undertaking, and then express, in constructive action, the ideal nature of that enterprise, as we have come to understand it. We must show the significance of our work, as teachers of music, in education, and in life. We must organize music in education for the sake of human values.

All valid educational values are human values. Education exists wholly and solely for the sake of life. Anything in it which does not serve the ends of better and fuller living in no way deserves its place. We cannot ask any more cogent, searching, practically important question than this: Why should teachers teach, and pupils learn, any given subject? Why is it important that children master history, or literature, or science, or mathematics, or reading? What are the values which accrue from such things? There is only one possible answer. Any particular study is valuable only in so far as a mastery of it enables one to live more richly and completely; to be a stronger, better, happier, more coöperative person; to succeed more fully in the great business of being human. If it fails in this, it fails completely, and should be rejected as a detriment to true education. We cannot define the educated man in terms of any list of things he ought to know, and of skills he ought to possess. We can define him only in terms of the life he ought to live. No knowledge is worth anything at all, merely for the sake of having it. No skill, whether of mind or body, is in itself intrinsically desirable. No subject, however venerable its traditional place in the scheme of schooling, or however superficially attractive and plausible its claims may seem, has, *in itself and for itself,* any value at all. All such things are worth having and worth mastering only in so far as they enable boys and girls, and men and women, to live stronger, more satisfying, more worthy lives; only in so far as they release human and spiritual quality.

This is the thought which must inform our work, furnish the touchstone of our self-criticism, and be made the foundation of the edifice of our constructive enterprise. It is of the highest, the most crucial practical importance. Forget it in theory, deny it in practice, and we condemn all our procedures to sterility. Nothing at all—no skill in teaching, no refinement of administrative techniques, no amiability of personality—can then rescue us from the educational valley of dry bones. On the other hand, bring subject matter into relation with life issues, teach with a central emphasis upon human values, and it is amazing how little else really matters. Education, like goodness, is an essence of astonishing simplicity. Yet that simplicity also has a subtlety which easily eludes us. We cloud our work with a mass of irrelevant complexities, largely because of our own dullness of mind and spirit.

The great reason why so much that is taught and learned in the course of conventional schooling is sheer and obvious dust and ashes, is simply that it is out of touch with the true source of all educational values. The whole manner of treatment of many a subject obviously depends on the assumption that it is valuable for itself alone. It is broken up into a series of lessons, each to be assigned to the pupils under duress and threat. The course as an entity is organized about a number of tests; and learning the subject adequately comes to be a matter of "passing" these tests. And all the teaching procedures are supported by, and directed with respect to, an intricate scheme of credits and demerits, which provide about as artificial a motivation as one could well imagine. Many a teacher in the past, and some even yet, when challenged to defend the place of his subject, will say that it is of value because it trains the pupils' minds. He cannot contend that he is giving them anything designed to be useful to them in the daily concerns of their daily living. So he falls back upon the doctrine of a mysterious inner virtue, a value possessed by subject matter in its own right, a disciplinary value. The assumption will not bear analysis. It is a sheer excuse for educationally indefensible practice. It is the impossible belief that a deadly routine may, somehow, have a living issue. Educational values are not to be understood or explained in any such way. Latin, algebra, geometry, English, French, music, and history, for instance, have in and of themselves no strange, mysterious inner magic to transform and strengthen the human mind. Their values can be comprehended only in terms of an enlightened common sense. They must be made useful, and learned for the sake of using them. Otherwise they are useless. Such is the obvious, yet often forgotten, logic of our work. A subject must live in the learner's life. Otherwise it is worth nothing to him. Subjects are tools of living. In this all their values and their power reside. They must be handled with this thought ever before us. We are to apply this doctrine to music.

We have here far more than a point of theory. A comprehensive, far-reaching program of action is involved. The entire business of teaching any subject must be organized, through and through, for the achievement of human values, or it will fail to achieve them, and to justify itself. Every one of the great traditional subdivisions of the curriculum—science, history, mathematics, literature, and all the rest—are rich with boundless possibilities. They are the very stuff of enlightened living. Yet all too often they seem to the learner just so many unprofitable messes of stale husks and dusty chaff. Why should this be so? Not because it is inevitable. Rather because of an educational failure in their presentation. Educational procedures exist for one purpose only,—to bring subject matter to life. Unless they achieve this, they stand condemned. Every great subject is rife with possibilities for raising the level and enhancing the significance of behavior. The task of the school, the teacher, and the pedagogical device is to convert those possibilities into actualities. Education must be organized as a great and conscious act of the highest salesmanship. Always it must seek ways and means of revealing progressively to the learner the human values of what he learns.

What is true of education in general, and of subject matter in general, is of course true of music. We must not merely assent to the proposition that music ought to subserve human values. We must use it as a blueprint to guide all our building. We must come to an understanding of what it means to organize a program of music education for the sake of human values. We must apply our philosophy in concrete decisions and a scheme of positive action. We shall find that it touches every detail of our work. In particular, it applies far more widely than to classroom procedures and techniques alone. Indeed, we shall find that this thought carries us beyond the limits of our subject itself, and brings both us and it into contact with the entire range of schooling and of education. To explain the program involved is the aim of this book. And the particular purpose of the balance of this chapter is to show what general outcomes we may hope for from a scheme of music education organized for human values.

THE MUSICIAN AND HUMAN VALUES

To capture, express, and render beneficently potent the human values of music is an enterprise which should command the enthusiastic support of every musician. It offers an inspiring and greatly needed reinterpretation of his work and way of life. Musicians have all too often been betrayed into following false ideals and serving false gods. They have thought of success as an affair of shining in the firmament of the concert stars. For this goal terrible sacrifices have been made. Years of grinding toil have been devoted to its achievement. A narrowing concentration has been accepted, which has cut the worker off from many of the richest things in life, and indeed in art itself. Hardly earned money has been squandered. Moral integrity has been set aside, and moral values prostituted by base and envious commercial scheming and jockeying for position. In the vast majority of cases, the inevitable end has been failure and frustration, and all the misery which follows from these things. Now all this is essentially irrelevant to and incompatible with the great simplicities, the beautiful realities of a life dedicated to music. That life should be a singularly happy one, filled with inner, spiritual satisfactions, whatever its material rewards. Much of the sense of sterility, of misdirected effort, of personal frustration, which it so often yields, is directly due to entertaining a false, destructive notion of success.

The truth is that music exists to serve human values, and to glorify human life. The successful musician is he who serves those values best. Let us see what a musicianship founded upon this ideal will mean.

1. First, a musicianship founded upon human values will be a valid musicianship. It is not too much to say that the great curse of the present-day musician is the insensate worship of virtuoso display. This is a false ideal, both in the narrower artistic and the broader human sense. Musicianship is an affair of the mind and the spirit, not of the fingers, or the lips, or the vocal mechanism. Von Bülow once stated the three requirements of music as technique, technique, and again, technique. In those words he uttered the great heresy which vitiates much of our musical life. That heresy has lured many a young student into the misguided ambition to copy, in himself, the example of Paganini, or the weakest, least significant aspects of the personality of Liszt. Even where it can be attained, this is no adequate aim. And usually it cannot be attained at all. The essentials of musicianship are the ability to feel and the ability to understand, rather than technique and facile display. They should be held up as ideals for every young musician in place of the prevalent, pestilent virtuoso complex.

2. A musicianship founded upon human values will be a broad musicianship. There is something palpably wrong, something almost degrading, in speaking of a man as primarily a pianist, or a violinist, or a vocalist. To have such an aim in life is surely to compress and narrow the compass and richness of human nature. To want to be merely a pianist, or violinist, or vocalist is almost like wanting to be a very superior kind of juggler. Along such lines as these, a man cannot express all of the best he has, or realize his highest and broadest possibilities. And so it is that true success in living the musical life may well mean a sacrifice of the sort of narrow, intense specialization which is the entrance price of the great lottery

for concert fame, for the sake of a broader, more humane, more satisfying ideal.

3. A musicianship founded upon human values will be a cultured musicianship. The power and meaning of the art of music does not lie at all in any kind of dexterity, however wonderful. It is significant because it is a creation and expression of the human mind, and a vital element in the culture of our race. So it is that the broadly humane musician will become, through his music, a broadly educated man. To understand and know music means also understanding and knowing many other things. To be sensitive to music is to be sensitive to a wide range of cultural and spiritual phenomena. Music has never existed in isolation in the course of human social evolution. It cannot properly exist in isolation in the individual mind. So here again we come at the idea of a sacrifice of specialization for something more truly humane and satisfying.

4. A musicianship founded upon human values will be a musicianship of service rather than display. John Erskine, the President of the Juilliard School of Music, has insisted that one of the great needs of American musical life is decentralization. He tells us that talented students flock to the Juilliard School with the ambition never to return permanently to their home communities. And, in effect, he pertinently asks how, under such conditions, that great institution can do what it should do for music in American life. Now the point for us is this: A humane musicianship, built upon the rock of human values, will not be obsessed with the longing to rush off to New York to join the bread lines and besiege the agencies. It will seek fulfillment and success in quite other channels. It will entertain a far more valid and

dignified aim. It will hold up, as the ideal of a successful musical life, simply being an apostle of beauty. Such a success can be achieved anywhere. It is as valid, as solid, as satisfying in the smallest and most obscure community as in New York or Paris. This is so because it is based upon true rather than false notions. Here is what we must have if the musician is to achieve a truly professional status, comparable to that of other great professional groups, the prevailing meaning of whose lives is clearly service, rather than rejoicing in the status of a superior trapeze artist.

5. A musicianship founded upon human values will be a fructifying musicianship. A notable coincidence in the history of music is that the rise of the virtuoso and the decline of the composer have taken place simultaneously. It is hard to believe this a mere accident. When all the activities of an art come to be dominated by a narrow and limited aim, when the ideal artistic type becomes secondary and derivative, then surely that art is headed for the shallows, shoals, and quicksands of an increasing triviality. The man whose musical life is founded upon human values will find in musical expression the great and obvious essential. His chief and most significant and prevailing impulse will be to say things to people in music, to utter a musical message, not to astonish and impress by display. Whether or no he achieves the heights, he is the true spiritual kin of the great creative spirits, the men who have uttered a musical message of commanding power. It is out of such musical living that the great composer is born.

In the past, professional musicians have often felt impatience, hostility, and contempt towards the aims and procedures of a democratic scheme of music education as offered through the school curriculum. Or else they have been blankly indifferent to the whole business. More recently many of them have sought jobs in the schools, though often without much understanding of, or sympathy for, the purposes of the program. On the other hand, music educators have often retorted with an equal impatience, hostility, and contempt directed towards professional musicians. It is a pernicious and destructive dilemma. The point is that both camps are partly right. The musician has been conscious of much that is inadequate and artistically unworthy in music education. Thus we have the famous and mordant distinction between musicians and school musicians. Meanwhile, the educator has been aware of the narrow, anti-human ideals of too many "professional" musicians. The issue of such mutual criticism must not be a parting of the ways, but a creative synthesis. Music education must earnestly seek the highest artistic standards, for only in these reside the human values of the art. The musician must learn that his pathway towards fulfillment and success in his chosen way of life does not lie towards commercial reward and virtuoso display, but towards an apostleship of beauty. We are in the presence, not of a conflict, but an identity of aim. Musicianship cannot fulfill itself until it realizes the best possible artistic values. I believe that the philosophy to be presented in these pages can heal the breach. We must seek, find, and exemplify the human values of the musical art, and so, each in our several spheres, do what in us lies to promote the cause of music among men.

THE TEACHER OF MUSIC AND HUMAN VALUES

To capture, express, and render beneficently potent the human values of music is an enterprise which should command the enthusiasm of every teacher of music. To do so adds enormously to the significance and dignity of his work. It gives him just what he most needs—an informing wisdom and a constructive vision.

The lack of vision of the human significance of music, and of a wisdom concerning how it may be imparted to others, has greatly impaired the whole status of the music teacher. Often we find the private music teacher confined to a dreary round of giving "music lessons." Too frequently such lessons lack any expertness in the matter of directing the learning process, as well as any rich and far-reaching educational significance. They tend to amount to nothing more than the routine "hearing" of scales, exercises, vocalises, studies, and pieces. Such procedures reveal hardly a glimmer of what the teaching of music to a little child ought to mean, and can mean. Indeed they hardly deserve to be called teaching *music* at all. Rather what is being taught is piano, or violin, or clarinet, or voice, or what not. There is no informing and compelling sense of a mission to influence and enrich the life of the child through the experience of beauty. Again, the teacher of music in the elementary school often does nothing more than have little children sing little songs more or less badly. He follows a rule-of-thumb method in developing the notation and various other aspects of the study phase. And he never asks that greatest and most essential of all educational questions, the question: Why? The advanced teacher who does not have a strong feeling for the human values of his work as its supreme values tends inevitably towards the status and point of view of the concert coach. His great hope, for which he chiefly lives, is to find a pupil of such talent that he promises to become a distinguished virtuoso. To him the ordinary, mediocre pupil is just run-of-the-mine stuff, to be endured for the sake of a fee. He has no sense of a central responsibility to bring music, as a releasing and enriching power, effectively into the lives of all his pupils, whether notably talented or not. There can be no manner of doubt that a very great deal of music teaching, both in the studios and the schools, is most seriously deficient in educational significance. The reason is that it is deficient in human significance.

Now the way towards improvement does not consist of an improved expertness in instructional techniques. Of course, teaching procedures can be improved. Again and again, in other fields, it has been proved that if we will apply the principles and findings of scientific psychology to the enterprise of directing the learning process, results can be obtained which are little less than amazing. The teaching of reading, for instance, is a notable example of a set of pedagogical procedures which have been almost revolutionized in just this way. There is no good excuse for clumsy handling of the learning process anywhere. Assuredly there is no excuse for it in music. In another book I have undertaken to show how musical instruction should be organized expertly with reference to the laws of learning, and the psychology of music itself.[1] It is certain, for instance, that the musical techniques can be taught far more rapidly and easily than is ordinarily done. No teacher with any sense of responsibility towards his pupils can afford to ignore such considerations and to jog along in the time-honored routines to which he himself was subjected when young.

But all this, important and necessary though it be, is not

---

[1] MURSELL, JAMES L., and GLENN, MABELLE, *The Psychology of School Music Teaching,* Silver, Burdett and Company, 1931.

enough. A teacher of music who really desires to merit the title, cannot be content just to do better, and with more expert touch, the very things which he would do anyhow. He must perceive the need to do different things, better things, more significant things. He must plan his work always with an eye to bringing music to the little child not as a series of tasks to be performed, or a series of habits to be set up, but as a many-sided cultural experience and an opportunity for self-expression and social activity. This is true whether his work is done in the grade school classroom or the private studio. Whatever its setting, this must be the source of its significance and the ideal which directs all its detail. In the same way, in dealing with the advanced pupil, he must not aim chiefly at creating dexterity as something inherently desirable or as the chief end of the musician. Rather his ambition must be to help such a student to grow in fineness of musical sensibility and responsiveness and in depth and breadth of musical insight and outlook. His mission to the student with vocational intentions in the field of music is in a peculiar sense compelling. A teacher may do a great deal to make or mar the effectiveness and satisfaction of his pupil's musical career. What a person who is entering music as a profession chiefly needs to save him from the disappointments and pitfalls which will surely hedge his pathway, is the point of view of the sincere, self-effacing artist, rather than the would-be concert star. Any teacher who puts his pupil in the way of acquiring such an attitude has laid him under a life-long debt of gratitude, and has done a real job of music education in the highest, most comprehensive sense.

So it is that, when the teacher of music grasps and expresses the human values of his work, that work becomes transformed and enriched. He ceases to be a mere pedagog, and becomes a fruitful witness to the power of music to strengthen and ennoble the lives of men. His status becomes that of a leader, rather than an instructor.

HUMAN VALUES AND THE ART OF MUSIC

It may be that some musicians who read these pages will suspect that, in insisting upon the human values of music as its supreme values, I am advocating some sort of ballyhoo and tending to slight the highest and most exacting artistic standards. I want to make quite clear, at the outset, and in this introductory chapter, that such is not the case. At the present time, many of our standards in music are thoroughly false and inimical to the best and most creative types of activity. And this is so because our art has become, to some real and dangerous extent, divorced from the service and the lives of men. Just in proportion as music is apprehended as a significant type of human experience, which all can enjoy, and in which all can actively participate, does it become possible to avoid false artistic standards, and to substitute true ones. This involves no compromise with shoddy. Just the reverse. Music, as I shall hope to show in our later discussion, and more particularly, in the final chapter of this book, is a naturally democratic affair. And we may believe with good reason that, in a democratic atmosphere, it can come to its highest perfection.

The great blight of music in America, and to some extent in the whole modern world, is an excess of what I suppose I must call "spectatorship" (for "auditorship" is a clumsy word), as contrasted with participation. This is the obvious logical counterpart of that virtuoso spirit and intent of which

I have already spoken. The typical musical situation is one where a person performs with a sort of inhuman brilliance and dexterity, while a great many other people sit passively listening. This thing has grown upon us little by little until it threatens to swamp and stifle many musical values. We find it in the drawing room, when someone plays a piece or two, as an amiable and decorative interlude to contract bridge. It is strikingly exemplified in the great, formal public concert, where we have a type of spectatorship different, to be sure, in manners but not so very different in mental and spiritual attitude, from that of the audience at a circus or a prize fight. At the opera we see musical spectatorship carried to its highest point, and reduced, indeed, to an absurdity, for often the fashionable auditors seem to do everything but listen. Now we have the radio, which can be turned on like a faucet, out of which gushes a stream of tone, to furnish an obbligato for the conversation. Such situations as these are highly unfavorable to exacting and valid artistic standards. They are inimical to any deep and wide understanding love of music, because they do not bring it to us as something uniquely and intimately our very own. To the mere auditor, music is something external, a performance carried on by someone else, not an experience in which he shares, and of which he owns a part.

Now a humanized musical art will not, of course, exclude listening. But it will put it in its proper setting. For the typical musical activities will become the actual making of music for one's self, for others, and with others; and also the writing of music for one's self, and for others. Much of this amateur music will not, perhaps, be of the first quality. It will lack the perfect polish of the concert platform. If our musical life can be transformed in terms of its human values, there may be an actual diminution of the supply of virtuoso perfectionism. But that will be a very small loss in comparison with a marked gain in the dissemination of musical ideas, knowledge, insights, sensibilities, and attitudes. Such things are not generated merely, or typically, by listening, but rather by performance and creation. And consider the effect which a musically intelligent and sensitive public will have upon the concert artist. To such a public, his performance will be something quite different from a show. It will be something in which they can, in their own measure, creatively share. The excellence of an audience cannot be defined in terms of the excellence of its manners, but in terms of the amount of musical activity which it represents. And the artist, in the intimacies and rigors of his business, needs the support of the musical mind of his audience. In his search for the highest artistic standards, he cannot dispense with the help of his hearers, with their sympathetic support of, and eagerness for, the best he can give them, in the way of performance, and in the way of creation. It is surely true that the serious-minded, sincere artist must consider himself not a spectacle to astonish the ignorant, but a leader in the golden realms of beauty. But no leader can lead without followers. The strength and effect of leadership is conditioned by the intelligence, insight, and sympathy of followership. A humanized music will provide, above everything else, a great and growing band of followers, whose active support will make it possible for the work of the artist to be more significant, more artistically valid, more musically sincere, than it could otherwise be.

The thing always to remember is that music in a vacuum, music for itself alone, music as a show, loses enormously in artistic values. In proportion as it becomes woven into the texture of our daily living, it acquires a new artistic significance.

MUSIC AND THE GENERAL EDUCATOR

The attempt to organize music in education for the sake of human values is full of significance and interest for the general educator, the principal, or superintendent. A great many school administrators in this country have educational ideas far in advance of their practice. Of this fact they are well aware. Oftentimes they are imbued with the philosophy of a humane, vital, and progressive education. They are aware that learning subject matter for its own sake—which means learning it for the sake of passing tests and gaining credits—is an exceedingly barren affair. They know very well that what educates human beings is significant experience. They recognize clearly enough that many of the things done in the schools are entirely contrary to such doctrines and their implications. But how to make a change? There comes the rub. The conventional administrative pattern of school-keeping is a gnarled. tough, sturdy growth, not easily to be altered or adapted to new issues. It may seem very attractive to shatter the existing scheme to bits and then re-mold it nearer to the heart's desire. To talk about doing so is easy enough. But as a practical matter it is exceedingly complex and daunting. What, specifically and in detail, will be the aspect of the new machinery? Where shall we look for teachers expert enough and flexibly-minded enough to carry on the new enterprise? Can public support be rallied for anything which departs extensively from the old, accepted, habitual ways? All in all it comes to this. Many school leaders have no great faith in, or enthusiasm for, our present educational conventions. They see that something much better might be done. But actually to do it, suddenly and on a large scale, seems to them virtually impossible.

Now the music program, in many ways, offers an ideal starting point for a reorganization of a school system in accordance with the principles of vital and progressive education. As I shall hope to show in detail as we proceed—and it is a central point in my whole argument—it is perfectly in accord with the doctrine of a socially functioning education. Music is properly taught exactly when it is taught in terms of that doctrine. More readily than almost any other curricular subject it lends itself to thoroughgoing reorganization along genuinely progressive lines. With most other subjects—with science, or mathematics, or history, for instance—we have to do things which at least seem strange, difficult, complex, and questionable. But all that is required in the case of music is that we present it in harmony with its obvious essence and genius, and at once we have a shining example, not only of how music ought to be taught, but also of how real education in general ought to be managed. Hence, any superintendent or principal who wishes to work towards what he has come to believe are sounder and more enlightened practices in his schools may well begin with music. It can afford an entering wedge. Moreover, there is little in the way of hampering tradition. The subject is new. It has not become encrusted with conventions or begun to suffer from educational arteriosclerosis. Teachers are willing to learn and even anxious to institute progressive changes. The public will accept something new here, when elsewhere it might be hostile.

Thus it is feasible for the general educator to regard his

music program as leaven in the educational lump and to treat it as a practical pathway towards progressive school reform.

MUSIC AND THE EDUCATIONAL CONSTITUENCY

The best way to insure the place of music in the schools is to make it humanly significant. There is no subject through which constructive relationships with the constituency can more readily, and also more properly, be promoted and maintained. If we teach music in the schools as a routine, or a chore, or a task; if we make it chiefly an affair of dull and dry lessons on notation and kindred matters; then indeed its place may be challenged. We have deprived it of its obvious appeal and value to the child. In so doing we have left ourselves without any solid argument when the constituency asks whether it is worth having. But we can handle it very differently. Let us try to help the children to learn to sing in school, songs they will love to sing outside. Let us give them authentic and moving experiences in the way of listening to great music. Let us point our program towards the actual making of music by participation in musical organizations, such as bands, orchestras, and choirs. Let us bring to them the joys of bodily freedom, so essential to fine musical perceptions, through creative work in rhythm. Let us encourage them to compose music for themselves and in this manner find new avenues of self-expression. Let us carry on all that we do in an atmosphere of joy in musical achievement. Then we shall enlist the most effective supporters any educational program can desire—the children themselves.

These are the natural fruits of the musical spirit. If parents know that their children are gaining such things from their opportunities in school, public support, in the long run, will hardly be lacking. A truly human program of music education offers one of the finest and most legitimate avenues for effective and constructive school publicity. For it is a publicity not based on large assertions, or statistical claims, but on direct and obvious values, visible to anyone with an eye in his head. Again I wish to remind you that educational values are not dependent on magic. They must be apparent to common sense, or they do not exist. They consist in the palpable effects of our teaching on the lives and actions of our pupils. It does not take an expert, or an "authority," or a person with some sort of esoteric training, to recognize such values. If they exist at all, they should be obvious not only to curriculum builders and administrative officials, but to teachers, to pupils, to parents, and to the general public. If education is really doing its job, it is like the dawn. Whoever looks may see it. In the music program, more certainly than in many other fields, education can really do this job of palpably and evidently molding and improving the lives of the pupils. This is why I say that it provides opportunities for the finest, most legitimate type of school publicity. It may and should constitute a constant testimony for progressive educational ideas, and for the true meaning of what the schools are doing. It provides the necessary, vitalizing link between the school and society.

Suggested Supplementary Readings

Bagley, W. C. *The Educative Process,* The Macmillan Company, 1925, ch. 1.

Bagley, W. C. *Educational Values,* The Macmillan Company, 1913, ch. 7.

ERSKINE, JOHN. "Adult Education in Music," *School and Society,* Nov. 15, 1930, vol. 32, pp. 647-653.

KILPATRICK, W. H. *The Foundations of Method,* The Macmillan Company, 1925, ch. 16.

MURSELL, JAMES L. *Principles of Education,* W. W. Norton Company, 1934, ch. 1.

CHAPTER TWO

Music as an Individual Experience

EXPERIENCE AND EDUCATION

What educates us is significant experience. Here is one of the great and central tenets of progressive educational thought. Only a little reflection is needed to perceive its evident truth. Can it be doubted by anyone that a great many of the routine lessons carried on in school have an absolute minimum of educative effect? The literature of education teems with illustrations which are strongly reinforced by the experience of every one of us. There is the ever-familiar, ever-significant story of the child who, after long and serious drill on arithmetic, went home and reported that she had been studying "the guzintas" that day; and when her parents expressed some slight surprise, explained as follows: "You know. Two guzinta four twice; three guzinta nine three times." We also have the case of the boy kept after school by his teacher for correctional work on a point of grammar and told to write out one hundred times, "I have gone." At the end of his task he left the following note: "Dear teacher, I'm all through and have went home."

These are extreme cases, no doubt, but they illustrate a very general defect. They show us that one may learn and yet not be educated thereby. All too often this happens. In history we learn a string of names and dates, apparently for no reason at all except to forget them again, and miss the absorbing story of the growth of our civilization. In geography we memorize lists of products, names of rivers and mountains, and the capitals of states and foreign lands, and may come out of it with the haziest idea of the great central application of the subject, that of adjustment of man to his natural environment. In geometry we learn by heart the proofs of theorems, but fail to see the application of geometry in many phases of life about us. In language we drill on grammar, but never develop a facility in reading or speaking. In music we hammer away at scales, or spend our time on sight reading with no deepening of insight into, or increase of mastery over, the tonal art. Again and again we find that learning is done without any increase in human values whatsoever. This means that no genuine or worthwhile education is going on.

But the opposite also happens. One reads a fascinating and illuminating book; one goes to see a play; one comes in contact with a teacher of vital personality; one becomes a member of a school team; and forever afterwards, one is changed. Why this difference, so striking, so familiar, yet so often overlooked? In the one case we have a mere lesson; a task of learning assigned without rhyme or reason, so far as the pupil can see; a task performed in a spirit essentially perfunctory because it seems destitute of significance. In the other case, we have a vital and compelling experience. Its detail may be forgotten. But something more important than detail remains. One gains from it an awareness of new things in the world, and new possibilities in one's self; a changed attitude and outlook; a new tendency, which may carry us to far horizons; a revised standard of values; a different feeling for what is worth while in life. This is the very essence of becoming educated. The medium for such a process can never be lessons or assigned tasks, but always experience. So in experience we have one of the foundations of a well-planned educational structure. In organizing a program of musical instruction for human values, our first requirement is to think of it, and plan it, as a program of *musical experience*.

This doctrine that experience is the mode and medium of the educative process is so important that I shall take time to contrast it briefly with three other views, all of them fallacious, yet all of which have influenced educational thought and practice in general, and music education in particular. To do this will help us more sharply to define our own position, and also to recognize, and so avoid, certain fallacies.

1. In the first place it is sometimes explicitly said, and often implicitly believed, that education consists in acquiring and storing knowledge. In setting up a great many courses in school, the first question asked by teachers, principals, superintendents, curriculum-builders, and others in authority has too often been: What items of knowledge, what facts, shall we put into them? What names, dates, chemical formulæ, geometrical theorems, and scientific laws ought we to try to introduce into the pupils' heads if we are to do our duty by them? This very mode of approach is the simple secret of why so many courses in school are educationally sterile, for it involves a very profound fallacy. Because of the very nature of the human mind, knowledge cannot be the chief aim, and its acquisition and storage the chief medium, of education. It is possible to acquire knowledge. But our capacity for storing it is remarkably limited. Probably every reader of these pages has had, some years ago, a course in history, a course in science, and a course in geometry. Very well. Suppose that you were confronted with a subject matter test, based upon the

content of these courses which you took. How well do you suppose you could do with it? What is the date of the battle of Marathon? What is an ohm? How does one prove the theorem of Pythagoras? [1] Perhaps there was a short time in your life when you could have answered these questions precisely and promptly. But can you do it now? If you cannot, and if also you hold that the business of being educated means amassing knowledge, then your forgetting has cancelled all the value of your learning, and your education represents a total loss. But you are entertaining a fallacy. The educated man is not a person who carries about with him a brainful of information. Even the learned specialist often lacks a clear and immediate memory knowledge of many things pertaining to his particular field, and must look them up if he happens to need them. For the human mind is not like an encyclopædia, a storehouse of knowledge. Our ability to store knowledge is amazingly limited. By and large we can only *use* it. We acquire knowledge for use only in and through the medium of significant experience. To have a mastery of science, or history, or geography, or anything else, means being able to find relevant information when, as, and if we need it for some application in our own lives.

This is a consideration of the broadest significance for all education. Assuredly it applies also to music education. Here the temptation to emphasize mere information is not so strong as in some other fields, and the knowledge aim is more palpably irrelevant and ridiculous. But the point needs to be remembered. Knowledge about music is useless for its own sake.

[1] EIKENBERRY, D. H., Permanence of High School Learning, *Journal of Educational Psychology*, 1923, vol. 14, pp. 463-481; and MURSELL, JAMES L., *The Psychology of Secondary School Teaching*, W. W. Norton Company, 1932, ch. 9.

To attempt to stock the pupil's mind with such knowledge is pointless and wrong. Whenever it becomes the keynote of our enterprise, it simply destroys all the values and possibilities of our work. Knowledge about music becomes educative only in so far as it supports, expresses, and renders more significant actual musical experiences and fosters valid musical attitudes. To recite facts concerning the life of Beethoven, for instance, is likely to be lesson learning and lesson hearing of the most futile type. To listen to or learn to perform one of the compositions of Beethoven, in the light of, and with the background furnished by, a knowledge of his career is educationally significant. So in music, as everywhere else, knowledge is secondary, experience primary.

2. The second fallacy which I wish to contrast with our doctrine of experience as the characteristic educational medium is the notion that being educated means essentially the forming of habits and the acquisition of skills. Of course we must understand habits and skills broadly as including both mental and motor abilities. We must include such things as the mental skill of solving a problem in square root as well as a physical skill like penmanship; the feeling for a dominant-tonic progression as well as acquiring the right kind of bowing technique on the violin. But even so we are in the presence of a definite and destructive fallacy. Elsewhere I have contended that the learning process cannot, in any event, be interpreted as a process of habit formation.[1] However, our main concern here is not with matters psychological. The point on which I now wish to insist is this: the acquisition of a skill has ab-

---

[1] MURSELL, JAMES L., and GLENN, MABELLE, *The Psychology of School Music Teaching,* Silver, Burdett and Company, 1931, ch. 3; MURSELL, JAMES L., *The Psychology of Secondary School Teaching,* W. W. Norton Company, 1932, chs. 2 and 3.

solutely no value unless along with it we also acquire a disposition to use it. If I may be pardoned a small piece of autobiography, I once undertook to learn telegraphy and got fairly far along with it. But since then I have had absolutely no opportunity or inclination to use it. The skill, of course, has vanished. But it never possessed any educative value, simply because it had no influence, or almost none, upon the course of my living.

The doctrine that education consists in the formation of habits and the acquisition of skills bulks much larger in the minds of music educators than the notion that its essential meaning is the acquisition and amassing of knowledge. It is, however, just as fallacious. Many music teachers think it their chief business to teach certain types of expertness with the fingers, or the lips, or the arms, or the larynx. But again, these things, in and of themselves, are not educative at all. They are secondary, not primary; means, not ends. They must be acquired in a context of experience which makes the learner disposed to use them. The great central task of music education is to provide that context of experience. Skills, to repeat, are not ends in themselves. They are tools of better living. Experience, not habit formation, is the characteristic medium of education.

3. The third and last of our fallacies is the famous dogma that "we learn to do by doing." Here we have one of the most dangerous half-truths in all educational thought. In a great many cases it is quite obviously false. We *do,* but we fail to learn. College students write a great deal, but their writing rarely grows better. We all walk a great deal without becoming more expert walkers. Such considerations apply to countless instances of human behavior—to driving an automobile,

or typewriting, or dancing, or adding up columns of figures, or remembering names and faces, and so on. They certainly prove that, if we are to believe at all in our dogma of learning to do by doing, it can only be under very great qualifications, and with many reservations and exceptions. What such negative instances prove is really clear enough. They prove that doing, in the sense of a mere mechanical going through of a set of motions, pays no dividends in the way of improvement. The mere, sheer, unadorned deed is, in itself, not educative at all.

Yet our dogma is applied precisely in this sense, and apparently with no feeling for its obvious risks and limitations, in the field of music education. Thus we have supervisors insisting that children simply must read their songs at sight without any assistance whatsoever in order that the naked purity of the deed shall be in no way sullied or compromised. Or again, we have the notion that what is educationally valuable is the quantity of reading material through which a class can plough its way, to the end that an enormous number of songs are learned, only to be sung in a way that makes one wonder why any at all should be attempted!

What is essential is not the deed itself, but its setting, its quality as a significant experience. One single, active, significant experience can change a pupil's whole attitude, and be the starting point of a constructive revolution in all his standards. To be sure, no one can do another person's learning or growing for him. All education is self-education. So much is elementary and obvious. On the other hand, people are not educated just by being turned loose to blunder about in a maze of undirected "doing." It is the experience, not the naked deed, which counts. All education has about it the quality of conversion, and conversion depends upon revealing experience. So the music teacher who relies upon unmitigated "doing" to capture human values builds upon the sand. We must rather strive for progressive, ever-renewed musical conversion, through significant musical experience.

While it is true that experience alone educates, this is far from meaning that all experiences are of equal educative value. To read *Othello* is a very different matter from reading the *Adventures of Jimmy Dale*. To solve chess problems is far less significant than to solve problems in mathematics. Doing needlework is a human activity on a lower level than painting a picture. Playing the harmonica can never yield the values which may be achieved by playing the violin. Certain types of experience are relatively trivial, because they do not bulk significantly in the drama of human living. For the educator this creates a great responsibility, and in two directions.

1. First there is a responsibility for *selection*. The school, and the educator, must choose the most significant types of experience and render them available to the pupils. This is an essential educational task.

To be valuable for educative purposes an experience must have the following three characteristics: (*a*) It must be active rather than passive. The doctrine of experience is far from implying that mere "exposure" in, or to, some curricular field can ever be satisfactory or effective. One learns civics as it should be learned, not by absorbing information out of a book, but by doing something about it—adjusting one's conduct, writing a theme, engaging in a project, working up a play. One acquires science and mathematics for educative ends by using them, not just by assimilating them passively. So everywhere and always the desirable educative experience will be an active experience.

(*b*) Then again, a desirable type of educative experience will be many-sided. This is one reason why the ordinary recitation-assignment type of teaching is so very poor. The pupils are subjected to a highly routinized, very limited kind of experience. Contrast this with working up a topic for presentation in a socialized recitation. One must hunt about for one's material, and in doing so one is likely to make all kinds of contacts and do all manner of new and valuable things. One must set to work to assemble one's findings, thereby involving the experience of organizing and writing them up. Perhaps one must confer with other members of the class in order to make a successful presentation. Then one must appear before the group, tell what one has discovered, and undergo questioning and perhaps criticism. Other things being equal, the more varied, the more many-sided an experience, the fitter it is for educational purposes.

(*c*) Third, a desirable type of educative experience will be culturally significant. That is to say, it will be an experience though which the pupil comes into living contact with the great tradition of human culture as an interpretation of human life. This is the reason why certain kinds of extra-curricular experience are educationally not very valuable. They are active. They are many-sided. These are splendid characteristics, too often and too disastrously wanting in many of the experiences afforded by the curriculum. But they lack cultural significance.

One of the chief claims of music to a place of honor in the scheme of education is the remarkable perfection with which it fulfills all these conditions. As I shall try to show in the balance of this chapter, it offers an almost ideal type case of just what an educative experience ought to be. This is one great reason why it is meet for the uses of an educational scheme founded upon humane and progressive principles.

2. So much for the first of the two responsibilities imposed upon the educator by the fact that experiences vary in significance and educative potentiality. This fact, as we have seen, creates the necessity of selection. But when certain experiences have been selected as the most desirable media for the education of children, the work is not yet completed. Indeed, it is only well begun. Besides this we must mediate to the children these experiences which we desire them to have. We must organize our entire machinery and all our procedures for this purpose. Here is the second great responsibility of which I spoke. It is futile to talk about experience as the medium of education, and to make a choice—even an ideally wise choice —of desirable experiences, only to carry on our school program in terms of lesson-learning and lesson-hearing.

Here again, music offers an almost perfect example of what can and should be done. The content of the music program ought to be a rich variety of musical experiences. The methods and mechanisms of the music program must be designed and operated for the sake of bringing these experiences home to the pupils in all their living force. We must not only select the kind of experiences the pupils should have. We must create an environment and maintain conditions in which it is possible to enter into and enjoy them.

In all this we see the first step to be taken in organizing music education for human values. Significant musical experience must be made the foundation of the program. Here must be our chief emphasis. This is a condition to be rigorously, arduously, and literally fulfilled.

MUSIC AS AN EMOTIONAL EXPERIENCE

The limitations of space in this book do not allow for extended discussions of the psychology of music or of musical æsthetics. So the statement is dogmatically made that music, in its essence, expresses and embodies emotion.[1] I cannot here present the evidence on which it depends, or enter into its far-reaching implications or the fine shades of its meaning. I merely present it to the reader as a consideration of the first importance for music education.

We have a wealth of personal testimony to the emotional power of music. Thus Vernon Lee (op. cit., pp. 98-99) records such responses to her questionnaires as the following: "Music nearly always cheers and soothes. It seems to open the gates of heaven. It seems to belong to all that is deepest and grandest in the universe. Often it comes as a 'vox Dei' "; "Permanently raises the spirits and gives confidence that the general trend of events is toward good. . . . It evokes images intermittently, people and their fate, wars, grand events, crowds"; "Music gives serenity, relief from cares; calms and equilibrizes"; "My enjoyment is of the nature of happiness lifting me out of my surroundings." One of Schoen's subjects (op. cit., pp. 169-170), speaking of his response to music, tells us, "I am usually in a state of muscular tension. . . . . . If I am really in the æsthetic ecstasy, I am absolutely oblivious to my surroundings. . . . The effect stays with me for a day or two.

[1] SCHOEN, MAX, The Æsthetic Attitude in Music, *Psychological Monographs,* vol. 39, no. 2, whole no. 178, 1928; LEE VERNON, *Music and Its Lovers,* George Allen and Unwin, Ltd., 1932, ch. 3; DISERENS, CHARLES, Reactions to Musical Stimuli, *Psychological Bulletin,* 1932, vol. 20, pp. 173-199.

I feel as though I do not want to be interrupted by anybody or anything rough or harsh, in any sense. I want nothing rough or coarse which could not share that state with me."

Music paints no picture, tells no story, stands for no system of articulate concepts. It does not directly symbolize anything at all beyond itself. It is design in sound. Often it seems to be just itself, and nothing else, and to have no outer meaning whatsoever. Yet this is not precisely true. The great creative artist, let us say, has some profoundly moving experience. In his music he does not, and indeed cannot, tell us of its detail. He does not paint for us the sunset, recount the love affair, tell the story of a tragic loss. But he takes the emotional essence of that experience and crystallizes it in tone. Of all the sensory media, tone is most closely connected with emotion. This is a psychological fact. Thus music is the most purely and typically emotional of all the arts. Here we find its essence. This must be our chief clue to its proper educational treatment, for it is the central secret of its human appeal and its power in the lives of men. Education in and through music must mean, first of all, participation in noble and humanizing emotion.

Now this gives music a place of peculiar significance and value in our scheme of education. It can fill an aching void. School work is directed, almost exclusively, to the intellect. But surely, if education has to do with the whole man, and is to issue in better and happier living, to ignore feeling is to ignore something of the utmost urgency. Yet it has been done. In the ordinary class, and the ordinary course, emotion comes as a strange visitor. We have been anxious, and rightly so, that children shall learn mathematics, and science, and history, and language. But we have abandoned the whole, or almost the whole, of emotional development to casual agencies; and only too often this has meant turning it over to the detective story, the gangster play, the sex novel, and the cheap motion picture. Are these the kind of experiences from which may come strong and healthy living, and well-balanced personality?

What then must we do? How can we set about educating children for emotional stability and permanent happiness? By providing avenues and opportunities for emotional experiences as valid and worthy as the intellectual experiences which we furnish. And I am convinced that music offers us ways and means for this very thing, more readily available, and more practically manageable, than any other medium. To have been stirred by the mysterious potency of great compositions, to have spent hours of loving labor in refining and polishing to the highest degree the beauty of some noble theme which one wishes to perform, to have sunk one's narrow self in the onward sweep of choral song, to have known the joy of participating in finely wrought instrumental ensemble, to carry with one as a permanent possession the triumphant pæan with which Beethoven closed his Fifth Symphony, some ineffable pure mystery distilled by the genius of Palestrina, or that "crying voice above the thunder which is the Revolutionary Etude"—surely we might desire such experiences as these for all young people for whose best good we are concerned. Just because of its commanding power over human emotion, music is one of the foundation stones in the building of the good life.

Our most central plea for music in the scheme of education comes to this. Music is a refuge for the spirit, a wellspring of water in the thirsty land which many of our pupils must traverse. In sorrow, in fatigue, in distress, one can turn to it, sure that one will not be disappointed. Why deny our pupils such a gift? Again we have rich testimony that music, to a unique degree, is capable of taking one outside one's self, and translating one into a realm of harmonious fairness. To quote once more from Vernon Lee: "Music vivifies the spiritual centers"; "The highest draws me up into an atmosphere above time, place, and circumstance, and all the smallnesses of life"; "It isn't very often that life gives such emotion as for instance a Mozart piece. . . . Music sets one right with the world, sets one in perspective" (pp. 98-99). These are but a few gleanings from what many have said, and more have felt, concerning our art. When we open a doorway into such a realm as this, then indeed we have done something worth doing to lead our pupils toward better and fuller living.

But we must translate our conception into the practicalities of school management and teaching. What does it mean, put in such terms? In general, any and every kind of musical undertaking will be educationally significant in proportion as it offers an avenue of emotional experience. This is a doctrine which I wish to follow into its concrete implications and applications.

1. First of all, it reminds us that the voice is the primary agency for musical development. It is the direct and natural avenue for emotional expression. When music is sung, we feel its emotional power and pull with a unique intimacy. Moreover, vocal music offers a natural avenue for artistic emotion, precisely because here there is a relative absence of technical barriers and problems. So it is that we believe that everyone should begin music with vocal experience, and that the desire to sing should be fostered, as a chief means of musical

development. When a child is introduced to music through any instrumental agency whatsoever, great limitations are at once created. We may go further than this and say that a non-vocal musicianship is almost sure to be a crippled musicianship. The primary musical experience should be the experience of song, and this first and foremost, for its emotional values.

2. The singing of songs by children should be made, above everything else, a means of emotional experience, expression, and release. When we use school singing chiefly as an opportunity for drill on notation and for practising reading, we pervert its central purpose and meaning. Yet a great many teachers sincerely believe that this is the central, solid, educationally valuable core of school singing. "What is the good of singing at all," they naïvely ask, "if the children don't learn to read?" Such a question shows an obtuseness to the obvious which is positively baffling. Manifestly it comes from that worship of the intellect so characteristic of school education. Nothing can be worth while unless it has direct intellectual significance. Such is the manifest assumption. But this is entirely and utterly wrong, and we cannot say so too emphatically. The emotional value of a song is worth a thousand times as much as an educative force than the notation in which it is written. To make a beautiful and appealing piece of music a chance for a sort of modified arithmetic lesson would be like using a poem simply as a fine opportunity for teaching grammar.

In just the same way, we should not make school singing chiefly an opportunity for voice culture and voice training. This is often done. We have anxious discussions about the use of the "head voice," about proper posture and breathing, and what not. Such matters are often made primary. Again we have a fallacy, a falsification of human and educational values. The reason is that teachers believe education must consist in the forming of habits and the acquisition of skills. Such matters, to be sure, are far from being negligible. As we shall see later on, technical progress is a real and essential part of musical development. But the moment they are placed in the center of the picture, everything is out of line, and our procedures become sterile. Zanzig tells of an incident which perfectly clinches the point I wish to make.[1] He says that he once visited a class of foreign-born children who sang for him some of the folk music of their native land. The tone was not what a supervisor would, perhaps, call "good." The light, pretty "head voice" was not much in evidence. But there was an emotional intensity and sincerity, and a feeling of real musical utterance about the whole performance, which was deeply impressive, and which contrasted sharply with the technically much better singing of an American group. I do not see how anyone willing to consider such matters with an open mind can reasonably doubt that the great educative value of school singing lies, very largely, in its emotional sincerity as an active experience.

3. We must deliberately seek to have our pupil groups feel what they sing and sing what they feel. That is to say, the attitude with which a group of children approaches the singing of a song is all-important and has a determining effect upon the educative value of the experience. Thus we should seek and find the means for building up the emotional background of the songs we propose. Time spent in developing such a background, so that the song is not an affair of mere

[1] Zanzig, Augustus D., *Music in American Life,* Oxford University Press, 1932.

notes, nor even an affair of mere phrases, but an emotional expression, is time spent on making the song educationally effective. Again, we should deliberately lead the children to seek for, and endeavour to create expressive effects when they sing. The notion entertained by many supervisors, that expression is impossible with little children, is very largely an alibi for their own inability to develop it. Once more, we should not be unduly concerned with note errors, and with a vocal placement which may not altogether please us, so long as there is a real and sincere musical intention in the undertaking. Finally, and above all, do not allow the spirit of the conventional school to make you or your pupils in any way ashamed of deep emotion. For it is the very breath of life in music education.

4. Evidently, we must select songs for the children with an eye, chiefly, to their emotional value, and their emotional sincerity. Among our more progressive music educators there is a widespread belief in folk songs as almost the only proper material for school use. Now there is not the least doubt that many folk songs do furnish splendid opportunities for musical experience of the highest value. Yet we need not erect their use into a sort of fetish. We may perhaps consider the folk song as a particular instance of a general principle. What we must have are songs which are emotionally valid, emotionally alive. The disproportionate use of the drill song, as such, is quite enough to parch away all the educational and human values of our work.

5. From the very first we must organize our instrumental instruction in terms of emotional experience. There is, of course, a peculiar difficulty here, owing to the barrier of technique. Indeed, the technical obstacle is so exceedingly serious

that oftentimes the entire enterprise of music education for many children comes to shipwreck upon it. This is, in part at least, the secret of that extraordinary, obviously false separation between the vocal and instrumental work which is a most serious source of weakness in some of our otherwise very admirable programs of school music. How the technical barrier can be circumvented—as indeed it can—I shall endeavor to explain in a later chapter. Here I am concerned to insist that it must be circumvented, unless we are to admit that elementary instrumental instruction cannot be educative at all, and that it can only be regarded as preparatory for more advanced work. If this is so, then its place in the schools is a dubious one. In order to justify it, there is one condition which must be met. We must make the child's experience with the instrument an experience in creating beautiful, appealing, and significant musical effects.

6. Our listening lessons must be fundamentally emotional experiences. This means several things. (*a*) It means that we must avoid in the early stages the emphasis upon facts, or upon the technical aspects of musical form, resorted to, perhaps unthinkingly, by many teachers. The school-minded person is apt eagerly to seize upon the experience of listening to music as a chance to do a nice job of intellectualistic teaching. Such depredations must be repelled both in others and in ourselves. (*b*) The use of story material, or of material from the life of the composer, or the period or place in which the composition was written, is entirely proper and altogether desirable. It should never be used for its own sake, but to enhance the significance of the music, and to bring home the point of its emotional significance. (*c*) The way in which the composition is introduced may be crucial in determining

its educative effect. To present music to the listener is a real work of art. One must choose the right things to say. One must handle the entire situation with skill and tact. (*d*) The entire broad setting, mental and physical, of the experience of listening is of genuine importance. The suggestive effect of a proper classroom atmosphere, of careful preparation so that everything goes without hitch, of reasonably good equipment, and so on—all these are things which will be given due consideration by anyone who really understands where the educative value of the experience of listening is to be found, and how it may be evoked.

7. Our projects in the way of creative music—and more particularly in the way of actually composing songs in class—must be regarded always as experiences in expressing feeling in tone. They are wrongly used when they are made chiefly opportunities for developing the notation, or for teaching musical "theory." The very antithesis of the proper use of creative experience is the copybook writing out of musical notation for the sake of learning key signatures, clefs, lines, spaces, and note lengths. This is the teaching not of music, but of grammar.

8. Everywhere and always we must remember that an emphasis upon emotional values, such as I have advocated, does not in the least mean a slighting or lowering of artistic standards. It is all a question of the kind of standards we wish to develop. The contention of these pages is that art depends far more upon sincerity than upon technique. Technical perfection of musical utterance must be developed as the best recognized way of saying something we want to say. To have a message, to feel a musical impulse, is the great essential. Our whole musical life is in danger of drying up

precisely because we are educating people in reverse order, as it were. We try very hard to give them the means of saying something or other. But we make no effort whatever to see that they have something to say.

Music as an Active Experience

Music offers a natural opportunity for active, dynamic experience, that is to say, the experience of actually doing, actually achieving something. Our program of music education, therefore, should be organized to capitalize such possibilities. Active, dynamic experience is valuable in two ways, musically and educationally. Musically it is valuable because only the person who makes music, however humbly, can fully and intimately understand its inner essence. The ideal listener is the listener who also performs or creates. Even limited experience along this line may, if properly directed, have a very powerful effect in the way of musical development. Moreover, any natural opportunity for active, dynamic, self-expressive experience is of extreme value educationally. Far too much of what is done in school is done *to* the pupils, rather than *by* them. Far too much of the work is organized on the plan of passive exposure and passive absorption. Modern educators almost unanimously preach the importance of activity on the part of the pupil, rather than merely on the part of the teacher. It is pointed out that learning, to be effective, must be treated as an active, not a passive, process; an affair of dynamic response, rather than of having something imprinted upon the blank tablet of the mind. In most subject-matter fields, however, this is a condition none to easy to fulfill, though of course it is very far from being impossible. Music, on the other hand, offers an almost perfect opportunity to put it into effect, and to give the child the experience of actually doing things in his own right.

One of the points most frequently insisted upon by Dr. John Erskine, in his addresses to musicians and music students, is that performance is of far more importance than listening. With this I would strongly and emphatically agree. But I am inclined to think that the point, stated in just this way, is hardly put with sufficient generality. To capitalize the opportunities offered by music for active experience certainly means a very strong emphasis upon musical performance. But it means a great deal more besides. Let us try to understand its practical meaning and its bearing upon the program of our work.

1. First of all, it means that we must rid our minds of the notion that long and laborious preparation is necessary before any sort of genuine musical self-expression can safely and properly be attempted. There are some teachers who will set up drills on the difficulties involved in a new song before giving the children either any chance to try to sing it or any sense of what the song is intended to express. There are others who argue that one must go through a long preparatory process, devoted to establishing the right kind of vocal action, before one should attempt to make music with the voice. Others again there are—and their claims are perhaps more reasonable—who think that the proper approach to any instrument must be a course of formal technical study. Still others feel that, without a thorough grounding in the grammar of music, any attempt to compose or create is bound to amount to unmitigated futility.

Now I would by no means argue for the entire elimination of all formal drill. But I would insist that it must be concomitant with, rather than preparatory to, the actual experience of musical performance and musical creation. When this is not done, when much time is spent in preparing for an enterprise of which the learner has not yet had the least taste, the drill itself yields a minimum of returns. The learner loses some most valuable and important elements of experience. This is one of the very best plans for stifling the creative impulse and hampering all freedom with music.

It is astounding how much can be accomplished by a sort of reasoned impudence, a willingness to "try anything once." It is not only the fool who sometimes rushes in where angels fear to tread. The pedagog mind finds it hard to believe that such things can be so. But they are true, just the same, and in many other fields besides music. I believe that the music teacher is most unwise when he keeps a piano pupil very long at practising strokes on the bank. The thing to do is not to throw him into the water, but to encourage him to enter it and try to swim, and not to mind if he does a great deal of floundering. Conventional education has filled many of us with inhibitions and inferiority complexes, and has undermined our trust in ourselves. Let us create in our pupils a confidence that of course they can sing beautifully if they will really try under guidance; that of course they can master the intricacies of an instrument; that of course they can express a mood by the creation of a musical composition. It may be that we shall feel some astonishment at how very often such confidence is amply justified by the outcome.

I want to point out particularly that the value of thus going ahead and positively tackling a significant undertaking is not due to the necessity of some hypothetical "trial and error" phase in the learning process. All that is a very questionable piece of psychology. Nor is it the "learn to do by doing" routine in disguise. The point is that educative learning is learning instinct with human purpose. The experience of purposive striving to accomplish a desired end is one of the most valuable any individual can have. It is the setting in which he is most likely to achieve that end. Children in school need—indeed we all need—opportunities to dare, to do, to try. Pupils in school have a right to demand that such opportunities come to them in the music program.

2. In the second place, to capitalize music for opportunities for active experience means re-thinking and rearranging the entire class situation. I believe that a most fruitful point of view for a teacher to maintain with respect to the management of groups of pupils is that he is not teaching a class, but creating a social situation in which individuals can engage in significant activities. The classroom should be made into a place where the child can adventure and dare, rather than one where he marches along in a dismal lockstep with his fellows. All the implications of this idea I cannot now discuss, but I shall return to the topic later. For the moment I will just throw out two suggestions. One should encourage both the activity of sub-groups within the class group as a whole and individual contributions.

3. What of the child who has difficulty in expressing himself musically, the so-called monotone? Here two comments seem relevant. (*a*) First of all, do not regard him as in any sense a musically hopeless case.[1] This is exceedingly improbable. There may be all kinds of reasons for his difficulty. It is the teacher's business to explore the situation until he finds the

[1] MURSELL, JAMES L., and GLENN, MABELLE, *The Psychology of School Music Teaching*, Silver, Burdett and Company, pp. 31-32, 1931.

particular obstacle in this particular case, and then to break it down and free the musical impulse. Many a child who perhaps might come under the unfortunate classification of the monotone is really a genuinely musical being. He may have an intense love of music and gain both pleasure and self-fulfillment from his endeavors. By all means encourage him rather than discourage him. And use whatever expert insight you possess to help him to do better. (*b*) Never deal with a musically impeded child as though the ideal for him were to become a young virtuoso. This is not the true musical ideal for any child, and for him it is peculiarly atrocious. He is a human being with a human need for music and the great developmental experiences it offers. Music has much for him. It should mean to him the opportunity to achieve and to do. See that he is not deprived of it.

4. Do not be too much afraid of compositions somewhat beyond the range of your pupils. Of course you must use ordinary common sense. One will neither assign a Scriabine sonata to a young pianist nor attempt the B-Minor Mass with a raw choir. But it is a serious fallacy to think that one must always limit one's self to compositions which our pupils are able to perform perfectly. What will happen if children attempt to sing or play music which is a bit "too difficult" for them? Certainly they will not achieve a perfect result. But perfectionism is not our ideal. From such an experience they may well gain much: new musical insights, courage, a willingness to attack difficulties, and a sense of their own limitations, not as something daunting and chilling, but as a challenge to further consecutive effort. "But," you may ask, "will not children form bad habits if they tackle unduly difficult music?" Not if you know your business. When school music

teachers have often complained that materials have been too difficult, the fault has not always lain with the songs or with the children, but with the teachers themselves. To be sure, difficult music is harder to teach than easy music. But there may be a very definite value and advantage in teaching it from time to time. I do not mean that we should do this consistently. But I do mean that difficulty should not be made an arbitrary and absolute limitation. Moreover, there is a fallacy lurking in this whole doctrine of the formation of "bad habits." Remember, for one thing, that all education consists of *unlearning* as well as *learning*. It may be highly illuminating to have tried a wrong way and found out that it will not work. Remember, too, that a positive attitude and a significant dynamic experience outweigh many bad habits. Indeed, if we have such an attitude, bad habits hardly matter, for they are very transitory. Some teachers are so afraid of the bogey of bad habits that they dare undertake almost nothing really significant. This is wholly wrong. By all means let children try to do something, if they desire to make the attempt. Use your expertness to help them through. If it is in singing an unfamiliar song, sing with them rather than let the musical values be spoiled by a halting performance. Make it possible for them to learn even by their failures so that those failures become, not disasters, but challenges. Cultivate in them an aggressive, conquering attitude of mind and heart. Freedom from a cramping sense of inferiority, willingness to attack difficult undertakings,—these should be one outcome of having studied music.

5. Do not think of, or organize, listening as mere passivity. Merely passive listening is bad. Conservatory students some-

times respond to musical performances with a sort of adolescent criticism which their instructors may find irritating. But after all, this is in the way of learning. It is better than being just a humble sponge. Here we have the illustration of a point of universal applicability. Music education must institute procedures designed to induce, incite, and encourage the listener to respond actively to the music which he hears, even if that response is very far from being perfectly judicious or ideally wise. In this way the experience of listening yields its full quota of educational fruitage. I should be inclined to believe that Dr. Erskine's criticism of listening would be valid chiefly as against a listening of the merely passive kind.

How then can we go about making the experience of listening an active experience? Here are a few suggestions which may stimulate you to think of others.

Associate listening with physical movement.[1] This can readily and naturally be done in the setting of the elementary school. Do not compel the children always to sit quietly when music is being played to them. Encourage them to express its mood and its motion in rhythmic response. Let them create their own patterns of rhythmic movement in response to what the music tells them, and direct their responses gradually into organized activities if you would have the experience significant and not just a diversion. Do not, however, convert such activities into something dictated to them from above.

Again, associate listening with what has been called "æsthetic discussion."[2] By this I mean encouraging the group to

[1] McConathy, Osbourne; Miessner, W. Otto; Birge, Edward B.; Bray, Mabel E., The Music Hour, *Elementary Teacher's Book,* Silver, Burdett and Company, 1929, ch. 2.
[2] Glenn, Mabelle, and Lowry, Margaret, *Music Appreciation for Every Child,* Intermediate Manual, pp. x, 41.

talk over the music they have heard; to tell one another what they have enjoyed, or disliked, in it, and why.

Again, associate listening with analysis and recognition. In the elementary grades the phrasewise study of songs lays the foundation for the recognition of repeated and contrasting phrases as an important part in structural and tonal beauty. From time to time, beginning in the intermediate grades, have the children listen for the return of a theme, for the emergence of a second subject, for repetitions and contrasts. This should not be done always or on every occasion, nor in the spirit of technical analysis. But it has a very genuine value in stimulating a positive rather than a merely receptive attitude.

Lastly, associate listening with choice. If the listening program fails to build up preferences, it has gone wrong somewhere. The child should be helped to develop musical likes and dislikes. They will not, of course, be absolutely permanent, or fixed for life. But they represent a most important and entirely natural element of positive activity in connection with the experience.

6. Give an honored place to creative music. But, as I have already insisted in this chapter, make it what its name implies. In its essence creation is re-combining familiar elements in a new way. When children undertake to write music, what should be going on ought never to be a copybook lesson. It should be a definite undertaking to use their vocabulary of tonal elements to say something musically, to express a feeling, to create something artistically and humanly significant. But can children create music which has any genuine significance at all? Sometimes they can. Often they cannot. But always it is valuable, musically and educationally, for them to try. To do so is valuable musically, because, even if the enter-

prise comes to no notable immediate success, it has a strong effect in the way of enlarging the artistic vision and deepening the artistic insight. It is one of the best of all ways of helping them to understand and feel what music really means and really is. Such an enterprise is valuable educationally, because it is a significant creative experience. It is an opportunity for the child to find out that he really can do things. It helps to teach him the great lesson that, when he thinks there is a lion in the path, if he advances bravely upon it, oftentimes he will find it is chained. Musical creation on a high level is, indeed, an august and supremely difficult act. But we do wrong to treat it as an awesome mystery.

Music as an Experience Both Bodily and Mental

Music offers opportunity for an experience of a type almost unique,—an experience in which bodily movement and mental and emotional apprehension are integrated. The conventional academic studies furnish experience of an almost purely intellectual character. Bodily movement is entirely, or almost entirely, irrelevant. In the case of mathematics, history, literature, and so forth, this is fairly obvious. Even with science, laboratory work is likely to be largely manipulative, rather than a learning of science in and through acts of physical manipulation. On the other hand, physical training offers experience limited almost entirely to bodily movement, with the intellectual element in the background. With music we have a different situation. It appeals both to the mental and the physical sides of our nature. One cannot learn music properly save in and through mental apprehension. At the same time, one cannot learn it properly save in and through bodily activity. Let us see why this is so.

The obvious thought may seem to be that musical performance inevitably requires physical action. One must use the voice or actuate the mechanism of an instrument. But this is the least important and fundamental aspect of the matter. Our actual grasp of, and feeling for, music as design in tone is profoundly and necessarily dependent upon the movement consciousness. On this point we find wide agreement among students of æsthetics and of the psychology of music. For music is an art which depends upon a great deal more than mere auditory stimulation. Pure visual design, such as that produced by the color organ, does not and cannot have the significance and effect upon us possessed by auditory design. The reason simply is that our whole bodies—our whole nervous and muscular systems—respond uniquely and directly to tone in a way that they do not respond to visual forms. The human body itself is the supreme instrument and agency of music; and the power of this art lies precisely in its physical influence upon us. For instance, we apprehend the rise and fall of pitch, to some considerable and important extent, as an actual physical rise and fall, a reaching up and a sinking down.[1] A sequence of harmonies, advancing towards a cadence, affects us as a wave of tension, followed by relaxation. Melodic phrases, too, are felt on this wave of motor tension and release. Rhythm, in all its complexity, depends absolutely upon the motor consciousness,—the feeling of the play of our musculature. So the psychologically correct approach to music is by way of free and full bodily response. We do not under-

[1] LEE, VERNON, *Music and Its Lovers,* George Allen and Unwin, Ltd., 1932, ch. 5; DISERENS, CHARLES, Reactions to Musical Stimuli, *Psychological Bulletin,* 1923, vol. 20, pp. 173-199; WELD, H. P., An Experimental Study of Musical Enjoyment, *American Journal of Psychology,* 1912, vol. 23, pp. 245-308.

stand and enter into music simply by hearing it with our ears. We do not understand and enter into it as we should until our whole bodies are attuned to it and responsive to it. Without the movement consciousness, music would not be a great art, but merely a kind of tonal mathematics. To arouse the movement consciousness in connection with music is one of the great tasks of a system of music education founded on correct psychological principles.

This at once explains why such a plan as the Eurythmic Method of Jaques-Dalcroze is so entirely sound, and why it is capable of producing such very remarkable results in the way of arousing a fine and discriminating musical feeling and of expediting the acquisition of instrumental techniques. It is the great and valid argument for introducing rhythmics into our program of school music. It shows us why primitive music-making has always been so closely associated with the dance in particular, and a wide range of physical activities in general. Moreover, psychological investigations have shown us that when listeners are asked to introspect upon their experiences when they hear music, they nearly always report some kind of movement imagery aroused by it. This suggests and even goes to prove that one of the greatest defects of our conventional music pedagogy is its far too great emphasis upon sitting still, and confining one's self only to small movement, if to any rhythmic response at all. Such a pedagogy ignores one of the most important requirements for the proper apprehension of tonal design. It compromises musical feeling. It unduly slows down the acquisition of technical facility. And it impairs the pupil's grasp of rhythm.

Now it is clear that the foregoing considerations indicate that music may be an educative agency of extraordinary value.

One of the chief criticisms of conventional school work is that it puts far too great a premium on sitting quietly and absorbing knowledge out of books. We talk about education dealing with the whole of human nature, but we tend to treat children as though they were disembodied intelligences. How can an education which does not concern itself with the body pretend to appeal to the entire personality? Moreover, when we do introduce physical activity into our school programs, it is not given its rightful place. It is treated as a sort of reward, or alleviation. The real business of education is supposed to be going on only when the children are glued to their desks. In music, however, extensive physical activity is an essential and constructive part of the actual business of learning. The children become musical-minded by acquiring musical bodies. In this respect it is almost unique among all the subjects of the curriculum.

The moral of our argument is not hard to understand. If we wish our music program to yield its full educational and human values, if we wish to justify it in and through its own exceeding worth, then we should teach music in an atmosphere of motor freedom. Notice particularly that such a condition is by no manner of means fulfilled by the use of such conventional devices as the children's beating time, tapping with the foot, or pointing with the finger at the notes as they are read. For one thing, such devices set up types of response which are treated as mere adjuncts to musical learning, whereas what we require is to have such learning carried on in and through the medium of physical action. The child must be led to feel the music actually in the response he makes to it. For another thing, such movements as time beating, tapping, and note pointing are small and involve only a few of the voluntary muscles. What we need, rather, is free, co-ordinated physical movement, creatively expressive of the meaning, mood, and detail of the music. Such activities can be carried on in connection with almost any kind of musical project. Listening to music may be made vastly more significant if children are encouraged to create patterned rhythmic responses to it, expressive of their feeling for it. Performance, both vocal and instrumental, can benefit if we precede it with, or interpolate into it, such rhythmic activities. Whenever children are being encouraged to create music, they should not be set just to making a tonal pattern, but a structure significant in terms of bodily response. For instance, one phrase can be gracefully stepped, another skipped, and similarly and appropriately expressed in repetitions and contrasts. What we desire is to free the body for the sake of freeing the mind. To do so is of enormous value and aid in musical development. Moreover, it tends to render musical development educationally and humanly valuable also.

Music as a Culturally Significant Experience

Music offers constant opportunity for experience which is culturally significant. In this lies much of its human and educative value. Our program of music education must be organized to take advantage of these opportunities.

But at the outset, there is a misunderstanding which, if not avoided, leads to fatal results. The word "culture" is one of the most misused in the language. Very often we think of it as standing for the merely ornamental, the conventionally decorative. If we are to think of music as just a sort of amiable decoration, a "parlor trick," to use that devastating phrase, we cannot hold it in very high esteem as an element either in education or in human life. As a matter of fact, this is a very great error. It is most assuredly not what we ought to mean when we talk about music as belonging to human culture. The culture of our race means the sum total of knowledge, skill, insight, attitude, and ways of feeling and doing which has been created by the mind of man. It is that great treasury of intellectual goods which man has accumulated in the adventure of living. It is what is sometimes called our social heredity. So far from being merely unessential ornament, we could not, in its absence, live a truly human life at all. The culture of any individual means simply his own personal share of this vast ancestral wealth. Its acquisition should always be regarded as an act of inheriting. From the point of view which I am now developing, music is of value for two reasons. In the first place, it has a place of great importance in the intellectual wealth which our race has created and accumulated, and which constitutes the corpus of human culture. In music man has found it possible to crystallize his attitudes towards and insights into life with a certain unique perfection and appropriateness. Goethe once said, and with much truth, that next to literature, music is the most important element in human culture. And secondly, music is of value because it provides a unique medium through which the individual may be brought into the intimate possession of his ancestral cultural wealth and may be taught to enjoy and use it as his very own. Let us examine this notion in detail and consider some of its practical consequences.

1. Every musical composition worth performing or hearing is the utterance of a personality, reacting to circumstance. Great music is, indeed, an emotional interpretation of life. It is the function of the performer to feel and convey this

emotion, or his performance is merely the outer shell and not the substance of music. Always great music is the resultant, the outcome, of many influences. It is in this sense that we are justified in calling it culturally significant. When we teach it, whether for performance or listening, we should make the learner aware of the circumstances of its creation. It should not be treated as an abstract pattern of tone, still less as just a series of technical problems. Rather it should be regarded as the utterance of a personality and the product of an age. If tonal design were nothing at all but just itself, if it had no emotional meaning whatsoever, how could it possibly be that the music of great musicians is so extraordinarily characteristic of each? We cannot mistake the music of Palestrina for that of Beethoven, or the music of either for that of Debussy. The tonal art is an exceedingly sensitive representation of character and personality. This fact should be recognized in our work as music educators. When a composition is learned, either in the way of listening or of performing, immeasurably more should be done than learning its notes. The learner should be brought to apprehend it on a background of human development, and as the utterance of a personality. In this way the learning of it becomes culturally and humanly significant.

2. The act of learning a musical composition should be considered and treated as an act of cultural inheriting. By this I mean that it should be an entry into a certain directness of communion with the composer. Because this is possible, music is a most admirable agency for conveying culture to others and for enabling them to possess it.

Our schools often attempt to convey culture through the agency of knowledge. One learns, for instance, about the Ren-

aissance, or about nineteenth-century Germany, or about the
facts of the life of Shakespeare. This is wrong in principle.
The reason is that it is a *learning about* rather than a direct
inheriting. What one really needs is to catch the spirit of the
Renaissance, or to feel the inspiration of the libertarian ideals
of early nineteenth-century Germany, or to make a direct
acquaintance with the mind of Shakespeare. When we merely
learn *about* such matters, the raw material of culture is there.
But it is like iron in the ore, or food unprepared for human
use. It is not in form for assimilation. It is not adapted, as
yet, intimately, directly, and powerfully to influence and transform the individual. It is not presented to him as his own.
Now music makes the fulfillment of these difficult conditions
possible. When I learn a Beethoven sonata, I ought to be
brought in touch with an unexampled intimacy and directness, with the very mind and heart of the composer.[1] When
I listen to, or participate in the singing of, some beautiful
folk melody, I should be in tune, not only with the notes,
but with an exotic way of life, and its aspirations, and hopes,
and fears. While recognizing the value of this sympathy, we
are also face to face with one of the great questions of musical
æsthetics. Does the performer or the listener really feel what
the composer felt? I do not see that we must answer this question with an unqualified affirmative (which would probably
not be true) in order to maintain our point. It is obvious
enough that great music is great, precisely because it is the
utterance of a great spirit. This is enough for us. In music
one comes in touch with the spirit, and sees somewhat of the
vision, of the composer himself.

[1] ROLLAND, ROMAIN, *Beethoven, the Creator,* Harper & Brothers, 1929, pp.
19-22.

This same sort of thing is possible in literature, and elsewhere, too. We may meet Shakespeare in his plays, Shelley in his poems, and catch some intimations of other ways of life in the writings of Tolstoy. But as a matter of practice, the temptation to obscure such values with factual teaching is too strong for many teachers of literature effectively to resist. With music, on the other hand, such a temptation is far less pressing. Here a direct inheritance of culture, by living contact, is perhaps easier to achieve. When a pupil has studied a Bach fugue, or participated in a Bach chorale, he should have a new, a lively feeling for the life Bach lived when he lived it, and an awakened sensitiveness to all its circumstances. When one has listened to the Eroica Symphony, the personalities of both Beethoven and Napoleon should take on a new aspect of intimacy and possession. When one has experienced Tschaikowsky's 1812 Overture, the Moscow campaign, and its human meanings, should have forever a new significance, as well as the circumstances which gave the composer an opportunity to express his patriotism.

This means, of course, that our chief emphasis must be upon the emotional and expressive aspects of music, rather than upon its technical content. In this way only will it become a potent agency for the inheritance of culture. Such experiences are of great and essential value in education precisely because they are the means of bringing knowledge to life in the mind of the learner. Knowledge for its own sake should never be the aim or the medium of education. But here it may play its true part in supporting experience, and from that experience, reciprocally, be rendered vital and truly educative.

3. If we wish to organize a program of music education in

such a way as to capitalize the possibilities for culturally significant experience which it can offer, this will imply many things with regard to our choice of material. (*a*) Perhaps the first and most obvious point to have in mind is that we must use only artistically worthy music. Material made to order, for the sake of illustrating, or affording drill upon, some technical point, cannot, in the nature of things, have any cultural significance. As music, it is essentially meaningless. For it is precisely not a direct emotional expression on the part of the composer. This is quite different from having the child discover in a valid, artistic song that is familiar to him an element which he needs to apprehend and apply at this stage of his all-round musical development. (*b*) Another important consideration will be to plan our work in such a way as to bring our pupils into contact with a wide range of musical literature, both in the way of listening and of performance. One of the frequent defects of music education is extreme narrowness. It is intensive exclusively, rather than extensive. Usually this is due to a concentration on technical masteries, or on some fetish such as folk songs as the only road to "salvation," rather than upon a broadening of musical insights. It is one of the deficiencies produced by the virtuoso complex which is the Moloch on whose altar many human values are sacrificed. An explicit aim which was entertained in the organization of the famous *a cappella* choir at Flint, Michigan, was to acquaint its members with a broad range of great choral music. This is a fine illustration of what ought to be done. If we think of music as valuable, in part at least because it makes possible significant cultural experience, the validity of such an aim is obvious. (*c*) More than this, we shall seek to mediate to our pupils a catholic selection of worthy music.

We shall not limit ourselves, for instance, to folk music exclusively, or to "classical" music exclusively (by which I judge the public loosely designates the "highbrow" music of the period from Bach to Brahms). We may not have the highest opinion of modernistic music. We may regard the work even of the best moderns as vastly inferior to the great classics. But this will not prevent our using it, within the bounds of reason. We want our pupils to understand and feel music as the expression of personal temperaments, and the outgrowth of social and historical conditions, and most certainly of their contemporary civilization. The use of "modernistic" material, which attempts (how successfully I will not here consider) to express and convey the emotional aspects of present-day experience, may have a decisive value in this respect.

4. When we attempt to organize a program of music education for the sake of culturally significant experience, this will have important bearings upon the order in which our material is presented. Often the order in which music is presented to the learner is determined by one factor only—the technical problems it contains. For us this is clearly inadmissible. It is not desirable educationally. It is far from being the best plan for the promotion of increasing musical insight and sensibility, and for the inculcation of proper attitudes toward the art. There is a vast world of music significant in the lives of children which they can learn to sing through the imitative process and by listening to it before they can perform characteristic examples through sight reading either vocally or instrumentally.

The cultural setting of a composition should have no small influence upon the sequential order in which it is brought to the pupil. This does not mean making chronology our guide.

A music program should never be regarded as furnishing a series of illustrations for history, chronologically taught. History teachers themselves are coming to understand that this is by no means the ideal order of presentation. Rather what we must seek is an order in terms of human interest and of cultural and emotional relevancy.

CONCLUDING COMMENTS

In bringing this chapter to a close, there are a few comments which still remain to be made.

1. The characteristic medium of music education is not the "music lesson." This is directly implied in all that has been said. Rather that medium is significant musical experience. The formal music lesson must tend toward this, and must always be carried on in such a setting, if it is to initiate a type of learning truly educative. Only so do we derive human values from music education.

2. The doctrine that it is experience which educates does not mean that the teacher can afford to let things slide or to *allow* anything to happen which does happen. Experience must be definitely and carefully *organized* on sound principles. We must see that the right *kinds* of experience are provided. What this means in concrete detail, I have tried to show. How they should be presented will be discussed later under Method.

3. Music education founded upon experience is the proper ideal, not only for those who have no vocational interests, but also for those intending to enter the field as professionals. The education of the professional tends to be far too narrow and limited. The drive to secure technical competence at the earliest possible moment is dangerously strong in both vocal and instrumental music, in the school and in the studio. There

can be no doubt that many values are wantonly sacrificed to this desire, and that the development of many a promising pupil is very seriously warped.

Suggested Supplementary Readings

DISERENS, CHARLES. *The Influence of Music on Behavior,* Princeton University Press, 1926.

FINDLAY, J. J. "Rhythm and Education," *School and Society,* 1923, vol. 17, pp. 1-10.

HOSKINS, E. F. "Correlating Literature with Music and Art," *Peabody Journal of Education,* 1929, vol. 7, pp. 136-138.

JAQUES-DALCROZE, E. *Rhythm, Music, and Education,* G. P. Putnam's Sons, 1921.

PUFFER, ETHEL. *The Psychology of Beauty,* Houghton Mifflin Company, 1905.

SCHOEN, MAX. "The Æsthetic Attitude in Music," *Psychological Monographs,* vol. 39, no. 2, whole no. 178, 1928.

CHAPTER THREE

Music as a Social Opportunity

MUSIC A SOCIAL ART

One of the most striking and essential characteristics of music is that it is a social art. It implies social situations. It tends to create social patterns of very diverse kinds, and it realizes itself properly in only a social environment. All this is true of music to an extent which holds of no other art, and indeed of hardly any other human occupation.

1. The performance of music is normally a social act. This is true in two senses. It is social, first of all, in the sense of being an act of *utterance,* a saying of *something* to *somebody.* The listener, as well as the performer, is an essential part of the complete picture. Even the solo playing of an instrument to an audience is never properly done unless it has about it some of the quality of oratory. Manifestly the greatest artists have this sense of their work. But it is also something which can be, and should be, possessed by persons who are by no means great artists. When anyone appears before others to discourse music, he cannot achieve what he should if he maintains an attitude of shutting himself in behind a sort of invisible barrier and creating tonal effects as though no ears other than his own were hearing them, and no other hearts than his responding. Some performers do exactly this, partly because of their constant dread of forgetting; and here is one

argument against always playing without the score.[1] For the artist greatly needs the sense of the audience, not as something to be dreaded, but as a group to be led with him into the high places of beauty. When this feeling for the social quality and meaning of musical performance is lost, much of its artistic validity and power is likewise dissipated.

In the second place, there is strong reason to maintain that the most characteristic type of musical performance is the cooperative performance. This is the other sense in which it is social. In our worship of the great soloists, we have tended to lose sight of the vitality and significance of ensemble performance, although the growing interest in chamber music and in orchestral and choral music seems like a recession from what may well be regarded as a freak development in musical history. In comparison with the whole course of musical evolution from primitive times, the deification of the virtuoso soloist has been an affair of only a moment. May we not regard it as an aberration, a wandering from the main stream, a falsification of values? Ensemble performance seems like the natural vehicle of musical utterance.

2. Listening to music is normally a social act. The best kind of listening is promoted in a situation where one enters into a genuine and rich communion with one's fellow hearers, and also with the performer or performers. The concert audience usually furnishes about the poorest and least promising condition for effective listening. The occasion is formal. Everyone behaves, with decorous precision, in just the same way. Instead of having an interacting group, we have an aggregate of separate individuals, social only in the meager and limited sense of

[1] MURSELL, JAMES L., and GLENN, MABELLE, *The Psychology of School Music Teaching,* Silver, Burdett and Company, 1931, pp. 78-80.

being all together in one place. The ideal social pattern in listening should be that of a group of individuals brought intimately together through the sharing of an experience, each one of whom finds the significance and richness of his own experience reinforced and enhanced by that of others about him. This implies informality. It implies, for instance, opportunities to talk over what one has heard with other listeners and with performers too. It renders possible a supporting and inspiring sense of togetherness, of sympathy, with the artists. It is the condition of creative social listening.

3. Creating music is profoundly social in its implications. I do not mean that the great composer literally and consciously writes for a definite audience. Such a proposition certainly could not be maintained. But he writes with the sense of having something to say—something to say, perhaps not to any particular audience, but to the ears, and minds, and hearts of all men. This social aspect of musical creation is a necessary moment in it, whether at its highest or its humblest. It is just what differentiates musical composition from the writing of exercises in harmony and counterpoint. Valid composition is the delivery of a message.

The Social Value of Music

This characteristic, constant, flexible, diversified social reference, which music naturally possesses, is the reason why it has always played so great a part in the institutional life of man. It can be used in an enormous number of widely differing group situations and occasions. It can furnish an appropriate element in a vast range of group activities. It can add to the significance and enhance the effectiveness of such activities. This is a point of the utmost importance for music education.

It is one of the chief arguments for teaching music, at public expense, in the schools. Not only does it give us a reason why we should teach it, but it also goes far towards showing us how, and with what emphasis.

Some very important educational thinkers contend that, in the course of social evolution, music has come to occupy a place of steadily decreasing significance in the doings and affairs of mankind. They point to anthropological data which seem to indicate that music played a far greater part in primitive life than it does in modern civilized life. (*a*) In primitive society, music was very closely associated with work activities. The various economic occupations of the tribe had their appropriate songs whose rhythms held the working group together and increased the energy of their labors. In his book, *Arbeit und Rhythmus*,[1] Karl Buecher has presented an idyllic picture of a "world of happy labor," where toil was transformed into a pleasure by the magic of rhythm. It is pointed out with much force that today only vestiges of such musical applications remain, in the chanteys of sailors, the songs of cowboys, and so forth. Just how much of these interpretations belong to what might be called the romantic school of anthropology I am not prepared to say. Perhaps we need not accept them without question. But it is certainly true that in the modern world we have a marked divorce between music and productive labor. (*b*) In primitive times, music was very closely associated with warfare. Certain songs inspired the warriors; others celebrated the passage of the brave into the Great Beyond; still others were hymns of victory. W. H. R. Rivers [2] has told

[1] BUECHER, KARL, *Arbeit und Rhythmus*, 5th Ed. Veit, Leipsic, 1919.
[2] RIVERS, W. H. R., *Instinct and the Unconscious*, Cambridge, The University Press, 2nd Ed., 1922.

us that, in Melanesia, even within recent years, tribes were capable of carrying on an organized fight, apparently without any leadership, simply because the groups were held together and directed by the rhythms of their battle music. Although in our own time music is still used as an embellishment to formal military display and can serve as a relaxation for the men behind the lines, it is no longer such a paramount element in warfare. However, one cannot somehow dissociate music from marching men. Anyone who has had the experience of long, forced marches knows what a tonic and revivifying effect comes from the band's stirring precision. (*c*) Music was a very important and necessary element in primitive religion. Certain types of music were supposed to have magical potency. No doubt they did have a very deep and moving effect upon the worshippers. Whether music has a comparable place in modern religious life, and more particularly in Protestantism, is a question susceptible of considerable study. (*d*) It is suggested, though with a good deal less warrant, that in primitive societies music played a significant part in controlling and directing love-making and mating. Erotic music is said to have been valuable in sublimating the grosser sexual impulses, and in leading to superior sexual selection. All these latter contentions, however, seem a trifle far-fetched.

The conclusion drawn from this entire line of argument is that, while music was once a controlling factor in social life, it has now declined to the status of a mere recreation. Possibly it is a very worthy recreation for those who enjoy it. But, like embroidery, or football, or golf, or stamp-collecting, it is an activity carried on largely for its own sake; and its contribution to and influence upon social life in the large has become very much diminished. Clearly this strikes at the root of any proposal to teach music in the schools, at any rate to all the children. We might retain it as an elective, if funds permit. Whereas it was once a necessity, it has now become a luxury. It must submit to the status which this implies in the scheme of public education. So it is incumbent upon us to examine this argument very carefully, not in any captious or dialectical spirit, or for the sake of scoring debating points, but for the sake of understanding the truth of the matter and ascertaining the soundness of the foundation upon which our enterprise rests.

1. We may begin by admitting frankly the validity of the foregoing contentions, in so far as they indicate that there has been a very great change in the place of music in the social order, though as to the precise nature of that change and the inferences to be drawn from it, certain questions will arise. One of the most impressive phenomena of social evolution is what is known as *specialization*. A great many activities and interests which, in primitive times, were carried on by the group as a whole, have been increasingly delegated to special institutions. For instance, at one time there were no schools. Education was a function of society as a whole. Once the division between religion and politics was extremely nebulous. The chief ruled by divine commission, and in obeying him, men obeyed their gods. Religion, politics, and economic activity were not always sharply separated from one another. Men hunted game, sowed the fields, harvested the crops, and ground the grain at the time and in the manner indicated by the divine providence. Only in highly evolved societies is the practice of medicine in the hands of a special class. Exactly the same kind of evolution has happened to music. Folk music was a function, a product, an expression of the general social

life. Inevitably it was very closely integrated with that life. Art music is a specialized social product, and its relationship to social life is of a different order.

Merely because a certain function undergoes social specialization, this change by no means proves that its social value is impoverished. Naturally this change creates a problem, but it is one of the most characteristic and universal problems of modern life. How can the church, or the school, or the medical profession, or the political state, or the industrial system maintain itself as a specialized institution and still continue to serve the body politic? Exactly the same problem confronts music. We cannot turn back the hands of the clock. We cannot go back to a primitive, undifferentiated social order in which the distinctions between religion, politics, education, medicine, and economic activity are ill-defined or practically non-existent. Neither can we abandon art music and go back to folk music. We must have specializations. But we must find the way to make such specializations promote the general good. This is the crux of the argument outlined above. How can we make an art music, which is inevitably a specialized music, effectively promote general social values? This is the key problem of music education.

2. From being a necessary concomitant of work, war, religion, and love, music increasingly tends to become an end in itself. In this process, something is undoubtedly lost. But also something is gained. This always happens in the course of social specialization. Medicine, finance, industry, and education could never have developed high grade techniques until they came into expert hands. Until this took place, they could never give us the service they offer today, or which they promise for the future. Again, the same is the case with music. Social

specialization is the necessary condition of a great musical art. Whenever we speak of a great musical art, what do we mean? Surely we mean that it can offer a type of individual experience much richer and fuller than would be conceivable for folk music. In particular, we mean that it becomes able to embody and express human emotion with an amplitude, a power, and a creative insight that are unique. There is, moreover, an enormous gain in technique. But this phase is not the central factor. The essential change is one of inner significance, inner enrichment.

Art music does not lose its social potentialities by becoming a specialized social and cultural product. The reason for this, which I pointed out in the first section of the present chapter, is that it *remains* an essentially social art. It still requires the working collaboration of listeners, performers, and composers. It still expresses itself characteristically in group situations. So far as its general form as a human activity goes, it is still just as capable as it ever was of fitting into the social patterns of human life. Only its place there is likely to be different.

From this we draw two conclusions for music education. (*a*) It must be our aim to interest the child in the best type of art music. This by no means precludes an approach by way of folk music, insofar as we may find such an approach desirable. Folk songs are the foundation of art music; and they often have a freshness, power, and direct sincerity of feeling which make them admirable material. But we cannot go backwards in social evolution. We cannot recapture the social meaning of music by a sort of regression to primitive conditions. What we must seek to do is to have art music serve modern man, in the stresses and strains of civilized living, with the same uplifting power which folk music had for his ancestors.

(*b*) We must bring music to the child in such a way that he shall become both able and anxious to fit it into the social patterns of his life. This leads us to ask what these social patterns may be into which we consider it important to introduce music.

3. We must seek to bring music into contact with the increasingly important social patterns of leisure time. I need not waste words in insisting upon the familiar fact that leisure time is on the increase. But here arises a point both serious and important, which has by no means received the attention it merits. For, it may be asked, if a man has leisure, does it not simply mean that he has *carte blanche* to do whatever he likes? If we begin to urge upon him what we consider the "worthy use" of his opportunity, have we not spoiled it for him? Have we not even deprived him of it? Are we not once more forcing him to do things which he will not, of his own accord, desire to do? Why, then, should we talk about educating people for leisure? And why, in particular, should we undertake to foist music upon the world simply because the amount of leisure is on the increase?

In all this there lurks a capital fallacy. The actual social meaning of increasing leisure is more time away from the job. But time away from the job is not a mere opportunity for futility, or for emulating the old darky who said, "Sometimes I sits and thinks, and sometimes I just sits." It is an opportunity for living a better life. It has a positive, not a negative, significance. A man who must work twelve hours a day, six days a week, has little chance to be effective in his domestic or civic relationships, or to enjoy the richness of the world. Human beings have a reasonable and proper desire for more freedom from the routine of earning, not because they wish to loaf, but because they wish to live. Leisure with nothing to do is a curse, not a blessing. It is like solitary confinement. Turn a child loose without occupation, and he will bore himself and pester you. He needs to learn how to use his time. And the same is true with adults. Satisfaction does not come unsought; it is not achieved by the ill-regulated, ill-equipped personality. And increasing leisure constitutes a valid challenge to music education simply because musical accomplishment is one of the great techniques of a happy and effective life.

(*a*) Music stands out as a uniquely valuable activity to occupy leisure time, because of its very great individual significance. This I have endeavored to explain in the preceding chapter. Music is an individual possession of the highest value. As we shall see later on, it is a possession which can be enjoyed in large measure by all. (*b*) Music stands out as a uniquely valuable leisure-time activity because of its very great social possibilities. A leisure activity need not be, and should not be, something cut off from all the rest of life. We sometimes talk and think as though this were the case. But it is not true. A man may employ his leisure in playing jackstraws, or pitching horseshoes, and they are harmless enough pursuits. But they are not particularly valuable, and we would not think of putting them into the school curriculum, partly because they lack individual significance and also because they lack social reference. What is worth while for leisure is an activity which will shape up many social contacts, which will mold life towards greater effectiveness, which will determine the social personality. All these values are possessed by music. I shall give my reasons for this claim in a moment, but before doing so, there is one more comment to be made.

We must weave this idea of bringing music into touch with leisure time into the very texture of our program of music education. If our work does not create patterns of social action for the individual, if it does not arouse in him the desire to seek avenues of social activity involving music, and if it does not show him the way towards accomplishing his desire, then it is largely a total loss. Yet music is very often taught in a sort of social vacuum, where the pupils are treated as though all that mattered in their lives were the activities carried on in the school. When one observes the music programs of some school systems, one cannot help wondering what sort of influence the director supposes the work under his leadership should have upon the lives and doings of the children. No subject is more completely dead than music formally taught. Conversely, no subject is more instinct with life than music taught in terms of human values and for the sake of human activities. Here is the touchstone by which to try all our procedures. Are we putting pupils in the way of actually desiring to use music for enjoyment? Are we organizing it into the texture of their lives, so that both now and later on it will seem natural to them to seek and find pleasure in musical activities?

I have said that leisure should be interpreted as an opportunity to live a better, happier, and more effective life. It is an opportunity to meet more adequately the problems of our civilized social existence than is possible without it. And specifically, I now propose to argue that when a man learns to devote a portion of his leisure to music, it may further social effectiveness in five ways. It may offset the baneful effects of routine employment; it may fundamentally improve his democratic attitudes and aptitudes; it may enrich his domestic relationships; it may bring him a new wealth of religious experience; and it may provide him with valuable means of informal social enjoyment.

4. Music can do much to meet the social needs and the personal problems created by the growth of routine jobs. The ideal vocation involves activities in which the worker finds satisfaction and self-expression. As we all know, our machine civilization has made necessary a great deal of work inherently incapable of meeting or even approximating such a condition. Much of the pain of the world is due to men being compelled to earn their living in ways in which it is impossible for them to find any human significance at all. Experience has shown that an ample wage, in and of itself, does not adequately offset such a lack. Authorities tell us that it is one of the primary causes of industrial unrest.[1]

If we can give music an effective place in a man's life, it can do a great deal to offset the effects of routine employment. It is one of the human occupations best adapted to such a use because of its great personal richness as an individual experience, and also because it can be enjoyed on such a wide variety of occasions. Here is a strong argument for promoting music for the worker's leisure. To do this requires a program of education. Otherwise he will not be able to realize the possibilities it offers, and any hopes he may entertain will be disappointed. The fact that many industrial workers spend considerable sums of money for the means of mechanical music indicates a need and an opportunity, but nothing more. Without guidance a man will not be able to listen well or to derive anything like maximal enjoyment from listening. Moreover, if we can open the way towards amateur performance, and, so far as

[1] FITCH, JOHN A., *The Causes of Industrial Unrest,* Harper and Brothers, 1924.

possible, towards creation, music can become a source of rich, lasting, and satisfying values. It is quite true that music has lost its direct connection with productive labor. That it has ceased to have any necessary or possible contact with the social patterns created by industry, however, is entirely false.

The music teacher should always bear in mind that a great many of his pupils are sure to be condemned to lives of routine toil, and therefore should shape his work to serve them. To mention only two communities, Flint, Michigan, and Bethlehem, Pennsylvania, afford examples of how a program of music education may be organized to meet this particular social need. A great many of the people living there are industrial workers who are able to find in both festival and school music projects agencies for the enrichment of their lives. This is brought about quite simply by organizing music in terms of actual, expressive, artistic enterprise primarily, rather than in terms of the acquisition of musical skills for which no effective outlet is provided. The communities mentioned in this paragraph and many others are beginning to foster community choruses, orchestras, and ensemble groups where boys and girls may continue their musical interests after their schooling has been completed. We cannot understand too clearly that just the teaching of skills is never enough. All that we know forbids us to believe in any magic agency of transfer which will carry such skills over into their life uses. These alone make skills educationally and humanly valuable.[1] We must have a program of music education which is consciously and deliberately directed toward the promotion and maintenance of significant, satisfying social activities.

[1] MURSELL, J. L., *The Psychology of Secondary School Teaching,* W. W. Norton Company, 1932, ch. 4.

5. Yet another social trend in the modern world with which music must be brought into contact is the growth of sharp divisions among men. I have already commented upon the tendency toward specialization in any highly developed society. This has an effect of constantly creating new social classes and stratifications and erecting barriers between human beings. In an industrial community the subdivisions between jobs and between the various levels of employment constantly tend to harden into social classifications. In one of his romances, H. G. Wells has given us a picture of the culmination of this trend in a society where everybody is trained for a specific occupation and where there is almost no life lived in common, or any mutual understanding between individuals.

It is quite evident that the multiplication of segregated social classes, and the erection of barriers in the way of common understandings, is exceedingly pernicious, and that it threatens the very foundations of the social order itself. One of the great tasks of a vital education—perhaps, indeed, the greatest task of all—is to fashion a common way of enlightened living. What this means, in the concrete, is that education must seek to institute ways of action in which all may share. We need social patterns which cut across the stratified social classes, and in which everyone—rich and poor, tinker, tailor, soldier, sailor—may have an effective part. This is the obvious, common-sense road towards the creation and extension of an effective community of understanding among men. Any use of leisure which promotes such things must surely be counted worthy.

On the basis of these and other considerations, we must not be fantastic in our claims. We cannot believe music capable of solving completely this or any other great social problem.

But the fact remains that it is, in many respects, ideally suited to serve as the foundation of active social groupings which cut across, and are indifferent to, conventional social subdivisions. As I have insisted, it is by nature a social art. It tends strongly towards the creation of social patterns in which men may come together and be happy together. It can give human beings a taste of the ideal democracy. But again, it will not realize its possibilities in this regard apart from conscious, skilled, and sympathetic educational direction and guidance. We cannot just teach music and leave it to the learners to find out how to use it. We must teach them both the mastery and its uses.

6. Music should be brought into greater contact with the social pattern of the modern home. The old-fashioned home was an extremely rich and stable institution with a vast influence on its members; for it was a place of common work for the common good. It produced food, clothing, shelter, and afforded protection in sickness and old age. It was strong as a center of many-sided, vitally important activities. But much of this economic foundation has been removed. The commodities and services needed by the family are no longer produced by their coöperative labors. Hence, inevitably, the importance of the home and the family in the scheme of human living has declined. How can it be recaptured and restored? Only by creating a new cycle of home-life activities, which obviously must be activities in the way of recreation and common enjoyment rather than of economic productivity. Instead of being a center of common labor, the home, if it is to retain and increase its stability and remain a dominating moral force in society, must become a center of common happiness and a place for the enjoyment of personality relationships. Once

more, any use of leisure which favors such ends and tends to strengthen the home must be counted worthy.

In this enterprise of reconstituting the home on a new foundation, it is clear that music may and should have no small or negligible part. But it cannot play that part unless our program of music education is deliberately, consciously, and with sympathetic insight, organized for and pointed towards such ends. Music education must aim deliberately at the home, and regard, as one of its most valuable purposes, the imparting of certain techniques of family activity and family happiness. So I would say to every teacher of music, whether in the schools or elsewhere: Remember that the children you teach have homes now and will be home-makers later on. Your work should be geared and directed towards helping them to achieve better and more effective domestic relationships and activities, both now and later on. Teach music expressly as something which can and should be used in the home. Let this influence your selection of material and all your processes of instruction. Do not teach pupils as though they were so many isolated individuals whose chief need was a purely personal, individualistic skill. Give them songs which they will want to sing in their homes now, to add to a permanent memory song repertoire,[1] and to teach their own children later on. Release in them the power to use their voices as a means of enriching domestic activities. When you give them the experience of listening to music, remember that many of them have victrolas and radios in their homes and adapt your work to a more effective synchronization of interests. If you teach instrumental music, con-

[1] McConathy, Osbourne; Miessner, W. Otto; Birge, Edward B.; Bray, Mabel E., *The Music Hour,* Intermediate Teacher's Book, pp. 21-22, Silver, Burdett and Company, 1931.

sider the possibility of promoting ensemble work in the homes
they represent. Do not let creative music become a classroom
stunt. Give it reality, give it a human outlet, by encouraging the
composition of music for home enjoyment. All in all, do what
in you lies to bring music to the children as a gift to be shared
in the family circle, to its benefit and enrichment.

7. Music should be brought into contact with the social
patterns of our religious life. The status and place of music
in the Protestant Church are subjects far too large to be discussed adequately in the space available. But certain things
seem reasonably clear. Our church music has shown a tendency to develop in the direction of a sacred concert, performed
by a small group of virtuosi. But this professional trend represents its degeneration. Far-sighted religious leaders have pro-
tested against it and have insisted that it greatly impoverishes
the whole act of public worship. Moreover, such a tendency
is by no means inevitable. A humane and wide-awake program
of music education can do a great deal to promote a type of
church music far more in keeping with the devotional aims
of religion. We can develop really excellent congregational
singing, which is all too rare in America, under the leadership
of a volunteer chorus choir, and possibly an instrumental ensemble as well. With our schools and conservatories turning
out excellent musicians who have all too little chance to contribute their abilities through organized community activities,
the extension of such a program would improve church music
standards immeasurably and increase congregational participation.[1]

---

[1] A most promising movement is under way to show what can be done
with more than amateur voices and training by Mr. Marshall Bartholomew's
"Voice Band," of New York City (119 West 57th Street).

The Westminster Choir School of Princeton, New Jersey, under the direction of Dr. John Finley Williamson, has done pioneering work in preparing choir leaders to develop and train chorus choirs recruited from within the church membership and also to work with the congregation for a more satisfying musical performance.

The reform of musical practices in the Catholic Church today depends very largely upon the extent to which the recommendations of Pope Pius X embodied in his now famous *Motu Proprio* (*Motu Proprio of Pope Pius X and Other Papal Documents on Liturgical Music*) are carried into effect in individual schools, parishes, and dioceses. The traditional music of the Church, Gregorian Chant, had almost entirely reverted during the passage of the centuries to be the function of only the choir. Congregational singing of chant had practically ceased. To eliminate concert music and restore chant and congregational singing the Pope recommended the establishment of the necessary training schools, called *schola cantorum,* in both the principal churches and even smaller churches and country parishes. With the recent development also of teaching procedures that accord with accepted principles of learning for little children by which the study of chant becomes an integral part of their school and musical experiences, a way seems opened for participation in the musical services of the Catholic Church by the many rather than by the few.[1]

8. Finally, music should be brought into contact with that wide and loose variety of social patterns constituted by our informal social group life. Here it has many appropriate uses.

[1] SCHREMBS, MOST REV. JOSEPH, and SISTER ALICE MARIE, *The Catholic Music Hour, Gregorian Manual,* Silver, Burdett and Company, 1934, Introduction. WARD, JUSTINE, *Catholic Education Series,* Catholic Education Press, 1920.

To quote almost a truism, many an informal social occasion can gain added significance and enhanced pleasure if it is made an opportunity for producing and sharing music. The quality of the music is an important factor. First, excellent music, and then music well performed, perhaps not with perfect technical finish but with genuine artistic insight, are far more pleasurable and satisfying than musical rubbish however well done. There is no doubt that one reason why we do not have more group singing and playing and more effective and enjoyable listening in our informal social gatherings is simply that people have not been directed how to capitalize such opportunities. To teach them this is no impossible undertaking, but rather a grateful and socially valuable one.

Finally, we must aim at deliberately and directly creating social patterns and maintaining types of social activity through music, if our work is to capture its full human values. This involves a conception of the music program and its nature and responsibilities both different from and very much larger than that entertained by a great many supervisors and general educators. I cannot by any means exhaust all the implications and possibilities involved in our conception. In the balance of this chapter, however, I shall try to indicate the sort of enterprise we should seek to effect.

Social Opportunities Within the School

It is evident that, if music is to function as an effective and important element in the social life of the individual, our teaching must have such a reference. The music program should be organized to include and to promote social activities, social organizations, and social patterns, both transient and permanent, in which and through which music may be made and enjoyed. The obvious place to begin this organization is in the school. For the school provides a multitude of social opportunities which should be capitalized in the interest of music, and which, reciprocally, may be made more significant and more enjoyable by being associated with music. These should be regarded as genuine educational possibilities of the highest value. Music should not be regarded as just another curricular subject. Any subject loses in vitality when it is handled in a water-tight compartment and associated only with the formal system of grades, recitations, tests, and credits. In the case of music, this is particularly unallowable; for, as we have seen, musical values are dissipated when social experience is not cultivated and used. Moreover, it is totally unnecessary because many social opportunities for music are ready and waiting for our utilization.

1. The work of the school music teacher should never be regarded, either by himself or by others, as fully successful unless it relates itself to the informal social occasions which constitute such an important part of the life of the school. For instance, that influence should be felt in club meetings, in rallies, in class socials, in school assemblies, and so forth. It is not an uncommon experience for teachers to find that the pupils resent or at least resist any suggestion or hint of guidance from them in carrying on their social activities; even the music teacher is frequently made to feel *de trop* on such occasions. Surely this indicates a spirit of formalism in the work and should be taken as a danger sign. Music is something to be enjoyed on social occasions. It is one of the few agencies which can make a social event itself more enjoyable. If the music program exerts no influence within the school and allows for no such use as this, can we doubt that there is some-

thing radically, something *educationally* wrong with it? The very last thing we want is to transform a free social occasion into the semblance of a formal lesson. It may be just our school-minded insistence upon the value of formal lessons that is the source of the trouble. Part of the influence of the music program should be a raising of musical standards and a provision for significant musical self-expression in the general social life of the school. If, in their own social groups, pupils never wish to sing the songs we have taught them, surely something must be wrong with the songs we have chosen, or the way we have taught them, or both. If pupils who are conducting a rally, or giving a party, or managing an assembly never even think of calling upon an instrumental ensemble for a performance, surely this casts a shadow upon the vitality of the instrumental teaching. If our work in creative music is doing what it should, then surely a song composed by some pupil might occasionally seem a desirable addition to some free social event or program.

2. It is often found that evening rehearsals help to dissolve the formalism which so easily besets the music program. For instance, the Inter-High School Orchestra at Yonkers, New York, has been in the habit of meeting for rehearsal from seven-thirty to nine in the evenings. The Bangor (Maine) High School Chorus also follows the plan of evening rehearsals. Of course, we should have adequate rehearsals during school hours as well. But the evening rehearsal represents a definite drive towards organizing music as a leisure-time pursuit. Moreover, while it should be disciplined and orderly, like any other serious attack upon serious music, there is no reason why it cannot be given a great deal more of the atmos-

phere and manners of an enjoyable social occasion than is possible in the rehearsal held during school hours.

3. Another admirable, and often very effective plan, is the
cultivation of chamber music groups in particular, and of
small music groups in general. Such experiences have a unique
and very great value, both socially and musically. To have
been a member of a string quartet may well contribute to
learning something eminently worth while, both about art
and about the nature and possibilities of human association.
One of the difficulties in carrying out such a plan is that it
may demand an excessive, and indeed impossible, amount of
the teacher's time. It is often found that this difficulty can be
met by having multiple small group rehearsals. Thus at Flint,
Michigan, where this plan has been adopted, there has been a
multiple string quartet of twenty (five performers to each
part), a brass sextet of twelve, and a woodwind quintet of ten.

4. Our instrumental classes should be used as opportunities
for the enjoyment of ensemble playing. They should not be
treated, solely or chiefly, as chances for mass instruction in
technique. Class work in music should definitely take advantage of the social opportunities provided "ready made"; and
here is one way in which this enjoyment can be gained. It
should not mean merely a device for teaching a great many
individuals the same thing at the same time, and so cutting
costs.

5. In many school systems, music clubs can be organized as
a valuable part of the music program. When this is done, they
should not be regarded as a mere adjunct or appendix. Thus
in the New Trier, Illinois, High School there have been two
music clubs, a junior and a senior organization. Each has a
membership of fifty. A small fee is charged, largely for the

sake of its moral effect. The clubs are responsible for many enjoyable social occasions, valuable both musically and educationally.

6. With regard to larger musical social occasions, such as music competitions of various kinds, school music festivals, and the presentation of operettas, there are several comments to be made. In the first place, and most emphatically, the social aspects of our music program should by no means be confined to such occasions. Many of the artistic, as well as the intimate human values of our work, imperatively demand the small and relatively informal group. This must be the mainstay and staple resource of the social side of our enterprise. Secondly, however, the large, formal occasion is by no means to be despised or abandoned. It may not always seem worth the amount of work we have to put into it. Sometimes it most certainly is not. Its value should not be regarded chiefly as display. Its great reason for existence is the opportunity it affords for natural music-making in a natural setting, and for the creation of a music consciousness in the school system and among the constituency. In the third place, the quality and the artistic sincerity of the work are an absolute condition precedent to any genuine value at all. Supervisors who are satisfied to stage trashy operettas, and then complacently regard themselves as workers of marvels, are self-deceived. Indeed, the amount of time and work expended is not justified if we have developed a socially valuable experience in coöperative endeavor, such as operetta productions are, only to find that the boys and girls have gained nothing worth while musically and artistically by contact with inferior music and text. Such exhibitions are destructive rather than promotional of those musical and human values which it is our business to seek.

Obviously this involves questioning the supervisor's own standards of taste.

7. Social activities along the lines suggested may often provide opportunities for fusing the vocal and instrumental instruction. This is something greatly needed in school music. Completely to achieve it means a great deal more than having an informal instrumental ensemble occasionally accompany a group of singers. Even this much is often lacking. It can be provided with the right kind of tactful and inspiring guidance.

Such are some pertinent and concrete suggestions for taking advantage of the social opportunities provided by the school in the interests of music. Others will probably occur to you. But before we leave the subject let us formulate still more clearly the principles on which all such practices depend.

No music program can be considered complete unless it seeks to develop and promote the musical side of the existing social life of the school. But it must go even beyond this. It must seek also to institute a definite range of social activities centering about music. Work along these two lines is not secondary to the actual processes of instruction. It is part of instruction. It is a most important and valuable means of making music truly educative. It should be taken with all seriousness. Some teachers still cling to the idea that only what is dull, and difficult, and concerned in some direct way with facts or habits, should be considered as really important in connection with education. But this is a capital error. Educational values are life values. If learning does not apply to living, it is worthless. An important, if not the most important, part of the entire educational enterprise is to organize our processes and shape up our entire situation to make it apply.

One special difficulty arises here which confronts the kind of music program I have tried to indicate. It is the problem of credits. What kind of recognition in these terms can and should be given to such a range of activities? I shall return to the whole issue in another connection and there deal with it at greater length. Here two points can be briefly made. (*a*) A vital music program has a strong tendency to maintain itself without the support of extrinsic interest and the motivation supplied by the credit system. (*b*) Everyone will admit the difficulty of evaluating vital musical activities in terms of credits. What is really implied is precisely the grotesque inadequacy of the credit system itself. Our method of educational bookkeeping simply cannot give us a record of the most important values of our work. This is a problem involved everywhere by progressive and vital education. We see it as a particular case, and perhaps with an especial cogency, in connection with the music program.

Social Opportunities Outside the School

No teacher worthy of the name can be satisfied to influence only the activities carried on by pupils as part of their contact with the school. As a matter of fact, what the pupils do in school derives its value precisely from its effect upon their out-of-school living. So it is that the school should institute definite, organized relationships with the life of the community. In some curricular fields this is difficult to accomplish. But music offers many splendid opportunities along such lines. The music program can reach out beyond the school, and must do so in the name of education. Not only must that program be set up so as to create and maintain musical, social activities within the school, but also it must make a contribution, and a considerable one, to placing the school in the position of a community center of culture.

Here again I cannot pretend to discuss exhaustively all the possible procedures which can be set up to bring this about. A few concrete suggestions may serve to make the principle clear, and may be found stimulating.

1. First, one should definitely consider the possibility of promoting musical activity in the home through the agency of the school music program. There should be an attempt made to fulfill the great responsibility of all education for the enrichment of home life. It should not be at all difficult to plan our activities (listening, vocal and instrumental performance, and musical creation) in such a way that they may naturally and normally be expected to function in the home. Once the idea and its importance are adequately grasped, it is something far from impossible to work out in practical detail. Moreover, one should understand that here is an application of the metaphor about casting bread upon the waters and receiving it again after many days. For, if our school music program can give life to musical activities in the homes of the community, a matchless reciprocal benefit will surely be received. What better support for his work could a music educator even dream of than an active, constructive interest in school music from the homes of his pupils?

2. Wherever possible, the program of school music should be brought into constructive relationship with the church and church school music of the community. Often we find that this is done. One of the tests which we might not unfairly apply to the music of any school system would be the extent to which it influences the music of the local churches. In centers where first rate work is being done in music education

that influence can indeed be very far-reaching. Thus we often find the churches of such communities carrying on their music through the agency of unpaid chorus choirs; and on investigation, it appears that the members have found the gift and power of song under the auspices of the public schools. Again, there is a real mission for school music in the way of improving our congregational singing. The diffident person can be helped to join in the singing. The invariably enthusiastic singer can be encouraged to modify his interpretation to accord with the devotional needs of the music. Moreover, if the children are participating in vital and significant musical experiences during the week, one natural and normal outcome will be the choice of artistically as well as devotionally significant material in the Sunday school.

3. Again, the meetings of the Parent Teachers Association open up considerable possibilities for the music program. The aim should not be merely to furnish a little incidental music now and then, but to establish a vital relationship with the work carried on with the children in the schools. One suggestion which has been made is that occasionally the parents might learn one of the children's songs. Consider what this would imply concerning the choice of a song, and how it may influence the children's own sense of vitality and reality in what they are learning.

4. As a final suggestion, it should be possible to promote attendance at concerts by school children as one factor in the music program. As part of their music appreciation experience, elementary school children attend concerts specially given for them by the high school orchestra.[1] This tends to arouse interest in local concerts sponsored outside of school. What

[1] East Orange, New Jersey; Cleveland, Ohio; etc.

we must have is far more than a little propaganda now and then when some musical occasion of unusual interest is about to occur in the community. It must not be an affair of advertising. There should be organized preparation for the occasion in the way of directed listening. The concert itself should be built up in the minds of the pupils as a red-letter event. Afterwards there should be opportunities for the pupils to discuss what they have heard. What we want also includes out-of-school experience and out-of-school contacts to bring vitality and life significance to school learning. In some of our larger centers, instead of the music program being organized into relationship with the general musical activities of the community, there are regularly organized series of special children's concerts. This plan has been effectively carried out in connection with the symphony orchestras in such cities as New York, Boston, Philadelphia, Detroit, Minneapolis, Chicago, St. Louis, Kansas City, Los Angeles, San Francisco, and doubtless many others.

Many other possibilities will no doubt readily occur to the reader's mind. These may well involve constructive relationship with community singing, or with music at the service clubs, and so forth. Whatever the detailed application, the principle is always the same. The educative value of our work lies in the extent to which music actually functions in the lives of our pupils. Hence, we must endeavor to give it an organized place there by integrating our teaching in the schools to a wide range of social activities outside.

THE PROGRAM OF INSTRUCTION IN MUSIC

The reader of this chapter and the last one may have obtained the impression that I am advocating a scheme of music education which involves everything but the daily round of instruction in music; or, at least, that the actual work of instruction must occupy a very secondary place. This is far from being the case. The great principle on which I have been concerned to insist is that the educative and human values of any plan of instruction are life values, and that, if we fail to take care of these, everything fails. The crucial question to ask about teaching is not whether it is expert in itself, but whether it modifies the behavior and enriches the experience of the learners. This transfer, this carry-over into life activities is secured in two ways:—(*a*) by means of a valid inner organization, and (*b*) by means of carefully planned and energetically promoted outer contacts. Both are essential. Nothing that has been said should be taken in the sense of a disparagement of a well-planned scheme of class work. That scheme, however, cannot exist in isolation and still do what it should. It must be regarded as the center of a wide range of social activity, both in and out of school. It must definitely relate itself to such activity. Let us see what must be the characteristics of a scheme of musical instruction capable of sustaining such relationships and of being used as a dynamic agency for the promotion of social activities in terms of music.

Music instruction must be carried on through the medium of three kinds of projects—listening, performing, and creating. These are the three characteristic avenues of musical self-expression. Equally so, they are the three cardinal agencies for musical development. All drill on techniques, on reading, and on the study phase [1] in general, must be carried on with reference to one or another of these three types of projects. We

---

[1] MURSELL, JAMES L., and GLENN, MABELLE, *The Psychology of School Music Teaching*, pp. 52-54.

grow musically by listening to music, by performing music, or by creating music. For an adequate and rounded musical development all of these are necessary. We cannot dispense with any of them. Now our point here is that such musical projects become truly educative in so far as they carry over into life and influence social behavior. Musical instruction organized on some other basis—as, for instance, where it concentrates upon technical mastery as an end in itself—and which does not make its chief end either listening, or performing, or creating actual music, can hardly be expected to function readily in life. One may very probably wish to listen to music, or to play or sing, or to write a piece for one's self. However, even a scheme of instruction based upon these three kinds of projects must still be organized internally for use, if it is going to have a maximum chance of being used. It must be brought into intimate touch with out-of-school and out-of-class social activities and institutions.

1. First let us consider the listening project. We must seek to train the child to listen to music, not as a lesson activity, but as a life activity. This involves several considerations. (*a*) It is necessary to make a very careful choice of musically significant materials for presentation to our classes. Our ideal must be, not a lesson which terminates when the bell rings, and which is happily forgotten when the pupils leave the school house, but a dynamic experience which will make the child wish for more of the same sort.[1] (*b*) Expert direction in listening is very essential. A musical composition is an exceedingly intricate structure. One may concentrate upon many different elements in and aspects of it. We must seek to lead

[1] GLENN, MABELLE, and LOWRY, MARGARET, *Music Appreciation in the Junior High School,* Teacher's Manual, pp. vii-xi.

the child to attend to its significant elements, and primarily these must be the elements of the tonal pattern, to which we attend for their emotional values. Much of the disinclination to listen to music, much of the feeling that one "gets only a little, or perhaps nothing, out of it," is due to poorly directed attention. The inexpert, undirected hearer fails to catch the musical message of the composer, and misses its emotional content and the intellectual appreciation of its structural design. He has only a confusing mass of sound in his ears. (*c*) We must seek to develop the cultural background of the compositions we present, but we must not do this in the spirit or with the intent of teaching facts for the sake of knowing them. Our development of the cultural background of a piece of music— something concerning the life of the composer, the times in which he lived, or the particular circumstances which prompted this particular utterance—must be for the sake of adding significance to the experience of listening, and of directing the listener towards sympathetic and receptive emotional attitudes. (*d*) We should seek to promote listening outside the classroom. A too prevalent conception of listening in organized music education is that it is an activity carried on entirely in the school. With this we cannot agree. Let us capitalize whatever opportunities for listening to music may come to the child in the course of his everyday life—at home, over the radio, in the movies, at concerts, at dances, and elsewhere. Let us have children tell about such occasions in class. In this way our influence upon the child's listening tends to pass beyond the school walls and to affect his general behavior. (*e*) Part of our general program of listening to music, as part of music education, should be the active stimulation of the pupil to seek opportunities to hear music. Effective educational publicity for music in the community, for important radio programs, for particularly fine phonograph recordings, and for concerts is an entirely appropriate undertaking.

To sum up the whole matter in a sentence, *the aim of our work in listening should be to develop an individually satisfying and socially functioning musical taste.*

2. Next let us consider the performance project—that is, the singing of songs or the playing of instrumental compositions. The great aim of the performance project is certainly not the development of technical dexterity. This is a sheer putting of the cart before the horse. Neither can we consider its aim merely the enjoyable experience of singing a beautiful and appealing song, or playing, either alone or with others, a worthy composition. *The aim of the performance project in music education is to create in the learner both the ability and the desire to express himself musically in life.* Here again, to achieve this, a number of points must be considered.

(*a*) The choice of material is of predominant importance. Our only reasonable chance of stimulating an individual in the direction of self-initiated musical activities is to give him compositions which are so interesting, intriguing, and appealing that to perform them to others and with others will be a source of enjoyment. (*b*) A matter not often considered by music educators, but one which I believe to be genuinely important, is the provision of audience situations for the efforts of our pupils. Class singing is nearly always singing *sans* audience. So is much of the playing in instrumental classes. But the audience is a very important factor in the total setting of the musical act. Why not organize our work to provide one? Why not set up sub-groups within a class and have them play or sing to all the others? The best teachers of English composition find the provision of audience situations extremely stimulating. Surely the same idea applies with even greater force to work in music. (*c*) A third point to have in mind is the peculiar interest and value of properly conducted ensemble performance. As an ideal, this does not mean mere mass performance, such as we have when a group sings in unison. It means a musical activity in which each has his own peculiar and individual contribution to make to the whole effect. This typical and very genuine kind of musical enjoyment should have an important place among our performance projects, both vocal and instrumental. (*d*) Our performance projects should be carried on, not in the spirit of assignments arbitrarily imposed on the pupils by an alien will. Rather we should do our best to set them up in terms of an aroused desire to perform music, both alone and with others.

The general moral involved in all the points on which I have touched is this: We must seek to make our performance projects genuine and educationally effective by relating them with life and by setting them up as natural, musical, life activities.

3. Now for a word concerning the creative project, by which I mean the actual composing of music by pupils. As I have already insisted, it is a perversion of the true aims of such an activity to make it chiefly a means of developing a mastery of the score. Far more than a writing lesson is involved. The purpose of the creative project in music education must be to arouse a desire to express one's self musically to others through the actual creation of the music. Our best supervisors and directors of school music are entirely aware of this. Perhaps one point which is sometimes neglected, however, in handling the creative project is the relating of it to social occasions. To

create a piece of music which will never be performed to any group anywhere is, at best, a truncated activity. It has been deprived of much of its natural force and interest. Hence, we should seek and organize opportunities for the actual presentation of worthy efforts in the way of composition by our pupils.

All in all, the program of instruction in music should culminate in a will to be musical. To have the ability to perform or to create, or the instructed power to listen effectively and positively is not enough. It is also necessary to have an effective desire to use that ability. So music education must concentrate upon the musical deed. This depends not only upon the inner organization of the instructional work, but also upon its relationship to social outlets and social opportunities. For the will is not something which exists in a vacuum. It is not a faculty. It is a tendency to respond. Such a tendency is cultivated by presenting the conditions for its operation. So the will to be musical must have a social, an institutional mechanism to support it and render it effective. On this actual use of the abilities which the instructional program generates depends the development of musical values and of educational and human values through music.

The Music Teacher as Social Leader

All this implies a conception of the work of the music teacher very much wider than that ordinarily entertained; for evidently the effective teaching of music requires social leadership of a creative kind, for music, and through music. He is not a teacher of a subject merely, but a creator and sustainer of new patterns of living.

A great many teachers of music do not seem to sense this

opportunity and obligation. The musical and social activities
of the community have no professional meaning to them.
Their idea of the carry-over of their work into life is limited
to a consideration of the number of their pupils who become
professional musicians. They have no sense of social leadership
or responsibilities, either in or out of school. Why is this?
There are, I think, three reasons; and these in turn indicate
three characteristic weaknesses which often beset the music
teacher and threaten the effectiveness of his work.

1. The first of these is a school-bound habit of mind. To a
teacher afflicted with this complaint education means the setting and hearing of lessons. We should remember that in such
an educational philosophy, music plays no vital part. It does
not readily adapt itself to the conventional processes of school
keeping. The traditionalist educator finds it an embarrassment
in the old-fashioned order of things, and is willing to see it even
removed from the curriculum. But in this imputed weakness
is exactly where its educational strength and values lie. What
the subject patently demands of those who teach it is that they
think of their work, not as the giving of music lessons, but as
the effective and persistent promotion of musical living.

2. The second weakness that impairs the effectiveness of the
music teacher is narrow professionalism. It is regrettable if
disappointment at failure to achieve a concert career embitters
him in the mission of teaching. This leads him to regard the
proper kind of music education as a hard and narrow grind,
leading toward virtuosoship, and to look upon anything else
with scorn and contempt. How false and disastrous such a
viewpoint is we have already seen. It completely obliterates all
feeling for the social and human significance of music, which

should be the mainspring of music education. It substitutes a scheme of values which are not even artistically valid.

3. The third great weakness sometimes found in the music teacher is the lack of a genuine, personal, musical enthusiasm. Music must live in the life of the teacher if he is to render it effective in the lives of his pupils. The enterprise of achieving, expressing, and rendering effective the human values of music cannot be accomplished by mechanical means or an external, rule-of-thumb expertness. We cannot tell the teacher just how to do it. He must find for himself the source of inspiration from the very stuff of the art medium in which he works. If the mainspring of emotion is not in him, if he does not find himself possessed with a real enthusiasm for music and for its mission in human life, then indeed it will be impossible for him to create and support a program of music education in which human, social values are effectively realized.

Suggested Supplementary Readings

Bagley, W. C. *Educational Values,* The Macmillan Company, 1913, ch. 13.

Hildebrandt, Edith L. Music Memory Contests, *School Review,* 1922, vol. 30, pp. 300-306.

Mursell, James L. *Principles of Education,* W. W. Norton Company, 1934, ch. 2.

Zanzig, A. P. *Music in American Life,* Oxford University Press, 1932, chs. 5, 9, 14.

CHAPTER FOUR

Music as an Agency for Growth

EDUCATION AND MENTAL GROWTH

Education is the guidance of growth. This is a familiar and pregnant definition. Only those experiences which contribute towards mental and personal growth are educative.

At once we recognize a principle which explains the numerous dead spots which each of us can detect, as we look back over our careers in school. All of us, at one time or another, have taken a course in a subject whose importance in the curriculum is evident enough. In retrospect, however, it seems to have been of no particular value to us, and has not noticeably influenced us as human beings. The reason is that our course of study failed to bring about mental growth. The conditions for such growth, somehow, were not fulfilled. Just where the responsibility lay, it may be hard to determine. Probably the teacher had something to do with our failure. Quite likely we ourselves cannot be absolved from all blame. In any case, an educational failure occurred, even though we secured a satisfactory mark. In the case of music, we find it is a peculiarly admirable educational agency partly because it so readily lends itself to the fulfillment of the conditions necessary to bring about mental and personal growth.

Let us make our idea of education as the guidance of growth clearer by way of two contrasting conceptions.

1. We cannot possibly say that mental growth is the same thing as learning. For it is all too easy to learn something without, in any intelligible sense, becoming educated thereby. A child may learn how to extract cube roots; he may take a course in solid geometry; he may memorize, and undergo drill upon, the rules for Latin conditional sentences; he may practice the F-minor scale on the piano; he may repeat and recite upon the rules against forbidden consecutives. In each one of these cases the educative effect may be nil. Here again, and in yet another connection, we recognize a distinction already drawn, and one of great importance for all teachers,— the distinction between learning and education.

And yet, without learning there can be no mental or personal growth whatsoever. This is obvious without any argument. What must happen, if we are to grow mentally and personally, is that we must learn in a certain manner. We must achieve masteries in a certain setting and with a certain attitude of mind. What we learn must become part of us. It must deeply penetrate and change us. It must make us different people from what we previously were.

Musical learning also may fail as an agency for personal and mental growth. There is nothing magic about music. Just because it is an important subdivision of human culture does not guarantee that any sort of attack upon it will have a beneficial personal effect. If the experience of teachers proves anything, it clearly shows that a pupil may study the most significant subjects and the most momentous topics without any personal educative effect being produced. Many music lessons are a total loss educationally. Whenever this happens, music is not being well learned even for its own sake. We might almost go so far as to say: Whenever music does not operate effectively as an agency for growth, it is not really being mastered at all. For no one can come into living contact with this art and still remain unchanged. So a music education which does not lead to growth is a spurious music education. The business of the music teacher is to take advantage of the human opportunities offered by his field and to fulfill the conditions under which alone mental growth can take place.

2. Again, mental growth is not at all the same thing as amassing a knowledge of subject matter. As we have already insisted, it is always false to think of education as storing knowledge, or acquiring skills, and nothing more. Here is the greatest and most generally accepted error in connection with teaching. Almost unconsciously, teachers will act as though being educated meant nothing but coming to know a list of subjects. Much in our classroom procedures, and our methods of school administration, is directed towards just such an end. Even if it could succeed—even if we could pour subject matter into receptive and retentive minds—the result would be a curiosity shop mentality rather than an integrated and organized personality. But it fails, for the simple and inevitable reason that the human mind is not a storehouse and cannot effectively be treated as though it were.

On the other hand, mental growth is impossible without mastering subject matter. Subject matter is of enormous and indispensable importance. In the course of history mankind has accumulated vast resources of knowledge, insight, skill, ways of thinking and feeling and doing, ideas and conventions. These resources exist in the form of languages, sciences, arts, and the great body of common conventions which control behavior. To say that anyone can be educated, in any rational sense of the term, without assimilating and possessing some measure of these resources is a flagrant and obvious absurdity. Without them, indeed, he can scarcely be said to live a human life. It is only in and through their mastery that his mind can expand, or his personality develop, or his behavior become differentiated from that of the lower animals.

Only when we treat these intellectual resources, out of which we build our curriculum, as matters to be learned for their own sake, do they become educationally valueless. This, most assuredly, was not the reason for their creation. Cæsar did not write his Commentaries for the sake of providing lessons for schoolboys. Nor did Beethoven compose his sonatas to furnish drill material for music teachers. Our intellectual heritage was brought into being for the sake of making possible a more triumphantly human way of life. And no one really shares in it effectively, or makes a part of it truly his own, unless it influences and elevates and renders more effective the whole of his conduct. The content of the curriculum might almost be called the food of the mind. But food cannot be stored up in the body. It must be assimilated into the tissues and used up in maintaining the functions of the human mechanism, if it is to do its work. In the same way, curricular content must be taught for assimilation and for use; and learned for these purposes also, if it is to fulfill its educational purpose and play its true part in human life. It must be treated and presented as the means by which the human mind is nourished and made able to grow.

Once again, music is educationally admirable just because it so readily lends itself to precisely such treatment, and because, in teaching it, one can so easily and naturally fulfill the essential conditions of mental growth. The balance of the present chapter will endeavor to show why this is so and to indicate how we should teach music so as to make it an agency for mental growth.

THE INITIATION OF MENTAL GROWTH: THE SENSE OF A CHALLENGE

The first necessary condition of mental growth is the sense of a significant challenge; the feeling of something which cannot yet be done, but which is worth doing and which one desires to be able to do. This is how the whole process must begin. One great reason why many procedures in school fail of their educative effect is that they entirely falsify this condition. Lessons are arbitrarily assigned. They are learned simply to avoid tribulation and to gain a mark. The pupil feels or displays no awareness that here is something he eagerly desires to master. There is an absence of inner drive.

For many years progressive teachers have sought to break away from such procedures and to fulfill the first condition of mental growth by providing significant challenging situations. In fact this is the chief aim of the project method. We teach science through the construction of a machine; or civics through making a series of "good government" posters or undertaking a community survey; or history through assembling a collection of pamphlets and data. Always the hope is to make the learning real and to connect subject matter with the natural and significant purposes of the pupil's life. The project is designed to come to him as a challenge which he will wish to accept; as an undertaking in the doing of which many relevant things must be mastered.

In general, project teaching has two serious limitations. In the first place, it is difficult to organize in connection with a great many school subjects. In the second place, there is always a risk that the project will become dissociated from the subject matter mastery supposed to be connected with it. When this happens, we have an educative failure just as real and just as sure as if we had handed out subject matter according to the most formal assignment-recitation plan. Often a project may be so artificial, or even so trivial, that, although interesting and appealing for its own sake, it does not lead the pupil into significant learnings. Whenever this happens, it does not provide a starting point for mental growth. Music, however, more than almost any other school subject, naturally arranges itself into significant undertakings, each one of which carries with it a genuine challenge. Its whole genius is contrary to the lesson organization and propitious to the project organization. And musical projects need never be far-fetched or irrelevant to the firm acquisition of solid masteries. Musical masteries, indeed, are only to be acquired in connection with musical projects. Hence, it ideally fulfills the first great condition of mental growth.

I have already set forth, in general terms, the doctrine that instruction in music must be carried on by the medium of musical projects of three kinds. Now I wish to invite the reader to consider that doctrine from a different point of view and to develop another facet of its educational significance, both theoretical and practical. Musical development is always brought about by the mastery of musical compositions. We must always remember that music is not a body of principles and laws regarding tonal relationships, or a body of knowledge about composers and performers and composition and performance, or a body of technical skills. Music is a body of works of art. When we say that a man has a mastery of music, we mean that he has a mastery, limited or extensive, narrow or diversified, of actual musical compositions. We mean that he is able to listen, or to perform, or to create. This meaning is exactly the reason why music education is so admirably adapted for the fulfillment of our first condition of mental growth. It always offers us the chance of presenting to the child diversified and significant challenges which may appeal to his inner purpose and engage his will.

1. First consider musical performance. Here I can put my central thought with the utmost directness and simplicity. I contend that it is educationally very valuable for any child to want to learn to sing a song or to play a piece. This desire provides a natural, direct starting point for a sequence of musical development and of mental growth. It is not a project in any way grafted onto subject-matter learning. It emerges in the natural planning of the learning. And so again I say that if we are to teach music for its educative and human, as well as its musical values, one of the most important things we can possibly do is to make our pupils ambitious to sing songs and to play pieces. It is just as simple as that.

Simple though this central principle may seem, it is not always easy to apply. The arousal of ambition and will is a subtle undertaking which can readily be defeated by crudity, clumsiness, stupidity, and lack of sympathy. Our notion leads us very quickly into all sorts of practical considerations, a few of which we shall now consider.

(a) The first consideration affects the choice of music to be learned. Please notice that I did not say either "the teacher's choice" or "the pupil's choice." For the selection of a composition to be learned must evidently be a coöperative matter, if we are to have any very good chance of using it as a stimulating challenge and of arousing an ambition to master it. Ob-

viously the teacher cannot be content with just saying to himself, "This song would be a fine one for my class to learn";
and then, abruptly assigning it. He is not prescribing a sort of
dose of intellectual medicine which will have an automatic
chemical effect. If the pupils do not like the song, if they do
not want to be able to sing it, then it cannot possibly function
as a challenge, or subserve a truly educational result, even
though it were the greatest masterpiece ever composed. Even
so, it is equally obvious that we cannot shove off the responsibility for choosing upon the pupils. For one thing, they do
not know what songs and compositions are available to choose
from. For another, their choices, without guidance, may be
very unwise and superficial, and amount to no more than
trivial and passing whims.

This situation seems like an *impasse*. What ought to be
done? I think the ideal plan—though indeed it is one not
often adopted—would be somewhat as follows. In the very
early stages—in the kindergarten and first grade, for instance
—the teacher must assume the chief responsibility for choice.
The children are very young; their experience is extremely
limited; and they must be guided constantly. But even so, it
should be guidance and not the imposition of a lesson. First
of all, pick out song material which you have good reason to
believe will be appealing. "Sure-fire" material will be good
melodically and rhythmically, and the verses will be childlike,
not adult, and related to the interests of children. Many moods
can be appropriately appealed to. The words should never be
"silly." Then, wherever possible, give some latitude of choice.
Why not occasionally sing one verse each of two or three songs
to a class of little children and ask them to select the song they
would like to learn? You do not need to stick to the sequence

of any one particular series of school music textbooks. Such a caution is, no doubt, less necessary today than it once was; but it remains important. For, if you ignore it, then no matter how admirable the series, the real choice is not being made either by your pupils or yourself, but by the editors of the texts. As you advance beyond the first grade, organize your work to render possible and induce an increasing latitude of choice in your pupils. Capitalize to the limit their experiences in the way of listening. One of the greatest weaknesses in handling performance projects in music ordinarily is their complete lack of association with listening. Take a hint from the effect of the radio upon the American public. Many, many people have had aroused in them a desire to learn and to sing certain songs by hearing them on the radio. Tie up this natural musical dynamic with your own teaching and make all you can of the listening experiences of your pupils, both out of school and of course in school, where such experiences can be controlled and guided. Do not despise the occasional sentimental ballad or the product of Tin Pan Alley. Remember that standards can be raised only through teaching people to make a choice for themselves and that imposed standards are dead standards. They are usually treated as the Egyptians treated the mummies of their ancestors,—regarded with deep respect and laid upon the shelf! Personal choice, ambition, the engagement of the will,—these are the starting points of every sequence of mental growth. We must deliberately organize our work to encourage them.

(*b*) Then our principle profoundly affects our whole teaching emphasis in handling musical performance. What is it that makes any reasonable human being want to be able to sing or play a piece of music? Surely its beauty, its appeal, its personal effect. We shall put this ideal in the very center of things. When a new composition is presented, one of our chief endeavors will be to give our pupils a musical conception of it,— to let them know what it should sound like. In doing this we may use our own voice, or our own executant skill, or call upon the aid of someone else, or employ one of the devices for mechanical music. Can it be doubted that one reason why a new composition often fails to arouse the musical ambition of the learner, and so fails to fulfill the prime condition of mental growth, is that he has no notion of it as music? We shall not regard it as sufficient to recommend the new work warmly and to lavish on it such epithets as "beautiful," "lovely," "delightful," and so on, although we shall not despise such practices. In the main, however, nothing can "sell" a composition so surely as giving the pupil a chance to hear it well performed.

But does this not preclude developing a new song from the notation? Quite largely. In the lower grades, as we shall discuss later, the notation should be considered distinctly of secondary importance. With the upper grades, it may often be desirable, although the continuation of rote singing is entirely appropriate. Moreover, the extent to which the score is used in any grade, the moment in the learning process at which it is introduced, and the extent to which the pupils are expected to rely upon it independently as their chief guide in singing or playing, will manifestly vary at different levels. Nevertheless, the educative value of a song at any time depends infinitely more upon its appeal to the musical ambition of the learner than upon its use as an opportunity for reading.

Our principle that a performance project in music should be set up as a significant challenge affects our teaching emphasis in many other ways, besides indicating the proper procedures in presenting new material. It means that all through the learning we should do everything in our power to keep the learner conscious of progress towards a desired musical effect. Why should one go through a song on a neutral syllable, or sing it with the *sol-fa* syllables? Why should one try to get a forward voice placement or a head tone? In so far as these are merely assigned requirements, the only answer one can give from the standpoint of the pupil is: Why indeed? They easily seem to him like the peculiar idiosyncrasies of his teacher, and nothing more. But if he finds out that such procedures quickly and certainly give him a better grasp of the melodic line, or a more satisfactory quality of tone—if, in a word, they are recognized as consciously contributory to a valid and appealing musical aim already instituted, then the reason for them becomes self-evident. They are then properly learned—learned, that is to say, in a situation which requires their use.

Again, we shall set up standards, not in terms of avoiding note errors or being able to read the material quickly and accurately, but in terms of the achievement of a desired musical result. We shall seek to make our performance projects as socially significant as we can; for instance, by setting up audience situations. In this way we shall add to their musical significance and stimulate musical ambition. Moreover, we shall avoid one of the besetting fallacies in all education, the belief that quantity, for its own sake, is an important thing. We shall see that what produces mental and musical growth is by no means the sheer amount of material through which we put our pupils. To be sure, we shall not insist upon a deadening perfectionism which keeps them everlastingly hammering upon one or two songs long after desire has failed. On the other hand, we shall recognize that what is educationally essential is the quality, the sincerity, the urgency of effort involved in any project, rather than the extent of ground covered or the number of such projects undertaken.

2. It is clear that the creative project is very well suited to arouse the sense of a significant challenge, of which I have been speaking as the first condition of mental growth. The suggestion to a class that it might be desirable to see whether they could compose a song is one likely to be received with interest and enthusiasm. Beyond this point, it is important that the teacher play the part of guide and helper, and never that of dictator or director. The entire situation needs to be organized and clarified in such a way that the children's personal impulses are given a chance to become effective. How shall one start on such an enterprise as the creation of a song? From the practical standpoint, the children should have advanced far enough to have acquired a tonal vocabulary, through both ear and eye experience, of simple chord and scale figures. If the pupils have never tried to "compose" before, this in itself is quite enough of a puzzle to inhibit all effective effort apart from the guidance of the teacher. We suggest that someone propose a topic or theme. This is the first step in organizing our situation and in pointing up the purposes and activities of our pupils. A number of topics are proposed, and under our guidance one is chosen. What to do with it? One must set to work and make a poem about it. Here is a still further organization of purpose. Then, as one approaches the job of actually making the music itself, one must concentrate on both the emotional significance and the metrical structure of the pattern of words. Throughout we visualize the teacher showing the way, unfolding the possibilities of the situation.

The challenge to compose some music is not left indefinite or permitted to remain hanging in the air. It is reduced to terms of specific and effective planning and writing. Just as it is humanly and educationally valuable for anyone to want to learn to sing a song or play a composition, so it is humanly and educationally valuable for anyone to want to compose music, and to be helped to want it so specifically that actual plans are made, and genuine attempts are carried out.[1]

3. Listening very evidently does not offer such definite and extensive vistas of possible action, or such sharp and effective challenges, as either performance or creation. It should never be a passive experience. The mind should be alert even if the mood of the music is quiet and meditative. In the "listening" experience, the project spirit has its place. For instance, it is entirely possible to inculcate the attitude of wanting to be able to understand, or to appreciate more fully, a given composition. Skilled listening, after all, is by no means simple, and depends largely on the development, however slowly, of a background of sympathetic understanding. One must try to hear what the composer has to say. Our attention must be led to direct itself toward definite goals,—toward the structural pattern of the music, its harmonic sequences, the instrumental tone colors involved, and so forth. Listening quite without any sense of challenge or attack is not likely to be very adequate musically or spiritually satisfying. Hence, we should plan listening experiences, in a way calculated to arouse musical ambitions,—ambitions to hear and understand better, and to hear more. Not always should we present easy and obvious music. It will quickly cloy. Pick out selections offering strik-

[1] MURSELL, J. L., and GLENN, MABELLE, *The Psychology of School Music Teaching*, pp. 213-216. Silver, Burdett and Company, 1931.

ing contrasts. A modernistic composition may produce an extremely interesting dynamic effect, particularly if we insist, in introducing it, that if one listens carefully and with discrimination, and is willing to hear the music again and again, what at first seems strange will be apprehended as logical and valid, and what at first seems cacophonic and hideous comes to take on a beauty not untouched by strangeness. There can be no doubt that one reason why many of us do not listen well is that we are not adventurous in our listening. We are conservative rather than eclectic in our tastes. To try out new types is an educative undertaking of high significance. The directed listening experience which is possible in the school should help us realize the challenge to broaden musical interests.

THE CONTINUATION OF MENTAL GROWTH: INCREASING PRECISION OF GRASP

Mental growth begins always with the sense of a challenging problem. But it does not end there. Through accepting and overcoming the challenge, one must move toward an increasing precision of grasp and fineness of insight. Herein lies one of the chief dangers of the project method in general. It provides significant, challenging situations. It initiates mental growth effectively enough. But often it does not allow for a proper follow-up from beginnings thus well made. The problem is dealt with only superficially. The learner makes no real advance toward solid mastery, fine discrimination, and expert grasp. On the other hand, the attempt to achieve precision of grasp and fine skill directly and immediately, and as an end in itself, is self-defeating. Very often it has the look of being the sensible, efficient, economical procedure. We want a pupil to gain a precise knowledge of history; and so we try to stock his memory with names, dates, treaty provisions, and definite facts generally. The trouble is that such things, at first, have little meaning to him. His mind cannot use them. If he continues with his studies, to become an advanced student in history, then a sequence of dates may be full of significance, and may prove a most important agent for organizing and ordering his ideas. But such precision is the end, not the beginning, of the process of historical education. We want to give a student exact notions about science and an exact grasp of its laws and principles. If we teach these laws and principles entirely out of a textbook, where they are abstractly stated with formal completeness, such knowledge does not function. The proper beginning is with gropings, explorings, experimentations, and contacts with situations which stimulate a desire to know and understand more completely. It can be real science without being complete science. Full scientific comprehension cannot be given all at once, at the beginning of things. It is the outcome of a lengthy course of mental development. Always the mind grows from a point where problems are genuinely felt but not yet adequately understood, and challenges recognized but only as comparatively vague intimations, towards increasing clarity, increasing insight, and increasing precision. The starting point of mental growth is the feeling that here is something worth mastering, though as yet one does not know exactly what it is or what mastering it means. And the movement towards effective mastery is a gradual, sequential movement towards clarity and exactitude.

In music properly taught, we can and should provide exactly the conditions which this process clearly indicates as necessary.

We can set up challenging situations, as I have already explained. In the course of meeting these challenges, precise insights and exact techniques can be acquired. Let us see how this takes place in connection with the development of four kinds of precision and skill which music demands.

(*a*) First consider growth in precision in the apprehension of tonal relationships. One of the great characteristics of the musically-trained mind is a firm and exact apprehension of the logic of tone. I mean by this, the tendential effects of the degrees of the scale. Lack of this is a very great musical deficiency. Many conservatory students certainly come to their freshman year without possessing it. Without it, music tends to be just notes. Performance is apt to be deprived of its valuable qualities of insight into and feeling for the tonal structure which is being uttered. And harmony and counterpoint become then studies of an almost entirely grammatical and formal type. How then may it be developed? On the one hand it certainly will not just come unsought and unaided by a sort of miracle. A person may take music lessons for years, and listen to innumerable compositions, without developing any effective feeling for the logic of tone. On the other hand it does not come by formal drill and the study of "theoretical music." Everyone knows perfectly well that students may and do take courses in theory without any increase in musical insight appearing in their performance, or any acquisition of a free ability to create valid musical patterns.

A fine and precise feeling for tonal relationships should be sought and found through the loving, attentive, painstaking analysis of music which one performs, or creates, or listens to. As we gain power, its progressive acquisition should express itself in a more musical performance, a fuller mastery of the resources of composition, and a more intelligent and appreciative listening. Earliest school experience is conducive to its acquisition, especially where the first ear training work deals with the tonic chord and its tendential neighboring tones. Such a device as the British "tonic *sol-fa*" is designed expressly to facilitate the acquisition of this sense of tonal relationship and tendency in connection with the actual making of music. Its originator, John Curwen, greatly emphasized what he rather awkwardly called the "mental effects" of the different tones, and insisted that the syllables be used in order to establish them in the mind of the learner. Many teachers have failed to sense fully the value of the use of syllables for lack of understanding the great importance of establishing the pupils' feeling for tonal direction. To Curwen, the syllables were a means by which the learner could be helped to think and feel tones in relationship, and thus grow in precision of musical grasp in this very important particular, in and through the singing of songs. As will be discussed later, some educators have advocated dropping the use of *sol-fa* syllables. If the practice becomes general, whatever new device is accepted must be reasonably easy of application by the average classroom teacher, and at least equal to syllables as an avenue of growth toward a precise and sensitive musicianship.

(*b*) Next, consider growth in feeling for musical structure. To a great many people whose attitude toward music is decidedly favorable and friendly, who attend many concerts and find genuine pleasure in doing so, the structure of music too often seems a very remote and esoteric affair. I recall being asked by a man far above the average in intelligence and background, in whose life musical experiences played a significant part, what one meant when one talked about phrasing. It was, to me, a revelation. How much more interesting, how much more significant music might be to such a person, if he were trained to listen to the elements of structural beauty which the composer has built into his tonal pattern. To wait for a course in musical form before one has any idea of how a sonata is put together, or of the texture of a fugue, or of what to listen for in the "continuous melody" of Wagner is both unwarrantable and absurd. The teacher with an understanding of the conception of music in the modern school expects to give this training from the very first song a child sings, as the first step on his way toward an ever better and more precise apprehension of musical shape. In performance, in listening, and in creation, the child should be learning to identify phrases and to indicate their beginnings and endings, to pick out the chief thematic material, to notice harmonic and melodic treatment. This is very far from requiring a series of abstract lessons. All it calls for is a proper direction of attention while one is actually making music and enjoying music. It should have the effect of enabling one to make music better and more satisfyingly, and to enjoy it more fully.

(*c*) Next, consider growth in power to use the musical score. Again we meet the two educational fallacies with which we have become acquainted elsewhere. An effective mastery of the score will not come of its own accord and without any guidance. Many music teachers behave as though this were so, and then excuse their failure to develop such a mastery in their pupils by saying that good readers are born and not made, which is about as preposterous a proposition as one can possibly advance. On the other hand, the proper approach is not by note pointing, memorizing rules for finding *"do,"* drilling on note symbols, and the rest of the familiar procedure of a technical approach. The score is the symbolic representation of the tonal pattern. The problem of mastering it is to connect what we see with what we hear or image. To be able to do this well is a genuine and important musical ability,—an altogether bigger and more significant thing than just being able to read at sight. Anyone who has really learned to use the score should be able to find more pleasure in music and to express himself musically with greater creative freedom and emotional zest because of this power. Once more, a precise mastery of the score should be sought by way of growth. Musical projects should never be turned into lessons on the notation. But the notation should be introduced to help the class along. The child should be led to feel that, as he masters the notation, he is better and better able to achieve his musical ambitions,—something which actually will happen if the score is taught properly. The thing to do is always to connect the score with actual, significant musical experience in the way of listening, performing, and creating, and to move on by progressive steps towards an organized, precise competence.

(d) The same considerations apply also to the acquisition of technical masteries, which constitutes the fourth type of musical precision to which I wish to refer. The characteristic process in developing the kind of control of the vocal mechanism, the fingers, and so forth, which we require for musical performance, is not formal drill. No technical problem is placed in its proper educational setting unless it is made a musical problem. That is to say, the problem always should be: How can I create such and such an effect? One does not build up a technique, line upon line, precept upon precept, by practising and rendering habitual each kind of movement which it is possible to conceive. One builds it up as a process of growth, which takes place in and through the attack upon concrete musical projects.

From all of this, certain general considerations arise which we should clearly understand.

First, it is the greatest possible mistake to think that music education can, or should, ignore development in precise grasp and definite expert insight. Without this, it can never bring to the learner the satisfying inner assurance of an advancing competence. A program which is all stimulation, all enthusiasm, all sentiment for beauty, but which involves no rigorous, ordered development, is profoundly defective. It may furnish the conditions for initiating mental growth, but it does not provide the conditions for its continuation. Never think that music education is going ahead satisfactorily, if all that it means is just the joy of singing songs, or the pleasure of listening, or the fun and interest of composing. In and through these things there must be a sequential growth towards a valid musicianship.

Second, the whole significance of increasing insight and precision of grasp lies in its setting. It exists for the sake of artistic achievement. It must be so taught and learned. That is to say, as the learner advances in skill from clumsiness to beautiful exactitude, and in insight from vagueness to definite clarity, what this must actually mean is not registering an improvement on some kind of scale, but a growth in ability to make music to his own satisfaction and to enjoy it adequately. Music, both as something to be performed and created, and as something to be listened to, must actually mean more and more to him as he gains a precise grasp upon the logic of tonal patterns, the general structure of compositions, the symbolism of the score, and the skills of motor technique.

Third, it is entirely possible to begin a valid course of musical development through and in music with young children. Unless we actually do this, both the individual and the social values of our work will in large measure be dissipated. Everyone who has to deal with freshmen students in a conservatory knows perfectly well that much of what masquerades as music education really does not deserve the name. Students reach the conservatory level practically destitute of the musical-mental precisions of which I have been speaking. For this there is simply no excuse. It is due to sheer bad, stupid teaching. If our music educators mean serious business, and if they wish to justify themselves and their work in the schools, then they had better see to it that their pupils are brought to advance towards musicianship in and through carrying out musical projects.

THE CONTINUATION OF MENTAL GROWTH: INCREASING BREADTH OF APPREHENSION AND OUTLOOK

Mental growth means not only increasing precision of grasp but also increasing breadth of apprehension and outlook. It means the development of a more and more adequate and organized intellectual background in terms of which experience may be interpreted, and which renders all the experiences of life more significant. Any subject becomes an agency for such growth when it leads the pupil towards a broader and broader outlook, when it widens the range of his interests, and enables him better and better to perceive the relationship of one life situation with another. History, mathematics, science, language, and all the rest of the curricular subjects are properly taught when they lead the learner into more and more extensive mental contacts and apprehensions and bring him more and more in touch with the infinitely varied aspects of human life and culture. Indeed, one may go so far as to say that the study of any subject becomes truly educative in so far as it leads the mind beyond the confines of that particular subject. When narrowly taught, merely as so much knowledge or skill, much of its human value is lost. Learning Latin, for instance, should indeed mean an increasing skill with the language itself. But it should mean a great deal more. It should, for instance, arouse the learner to an awareness of the Roman state and its vast significance, and perhaps of the whole great drama of the classical civilization. It may be a pathway towards an interest in and a study of the Middle Ages, or of ethnology, or, by the route of a comparison between the ancient and the modern world, of sociology. No one can tell where the learning of any particular subject may lead. *But the point is that it must lead somewhere;* it must result in a broadening of interests, a widening of horizons, a widening of mental backgrounds; or else we are bound to conclude that it does not really live in the learner's mind, and that it is not, in any full sense, a means for his education. This is precisely true of music. When it is narrowly apprehended, and narrowly taught, when the pupil's mind is limited to the horizons of the field itself, then some of its greatest and finest possibilities are being lost. So music education may and should be organized to provide and promote breadth of interest, apprehension, and outlook.

Just as fine precisions cannot be conveyed directly, but must come as a matter of growth, so also broad apprehensions and a comprehensive mental background cannot be given "ready made," as it were. When we try to do this we fail. Let us say that a pupil is studying English Literature, world history, Latin, chemistry, and art. Surely there is breadth enough and to spare. But it is so only potentially. There is only the opportunity for breadth. We know only too well that the pupil may fail to take actual advantage of it. All that may happen is that he learns a series of lessons in these five subjects. He may make no vital contacts with them. They may hardly enter into the texture of his thinking, or affect in any degree the way he lives. He is being brought into touch with five great realms of human culture. Yet there may be no awakening of the mind and no expanding trend in his real interests.

When this happens, quite definitely and undeniably, education has failed. What, then, is the reason for it? The material is presented to the learner and apprehended by him simply as knowledge for its own sake, rather than as an interpretation of significant and genuine experience. It lacks the essential quality of reality. It has no vital relationship with things he does and things he enjoys doing. Once again we are reminded that mere knowledge, no matter how rich and diversified, does not, in itself, illuminate and expand the horizons of the mind.

Now music provides one of the opportunities for rectifying this fatal defect. When one learns to sing a song, or to play a composition, a great deal more should happen than just the acquisition of certain motor facilities and the conquest of certain technical difficulties. One should be entering into an experience with natural, and very broad, cultural affiliations. One should do much more than *merely* learn to sing or play certain notes or phrases. One should grasp the composition in its broad cultural setting. This at once means two things. First, the musical enterprise, as such, is better performed; its direct artistic value is enhanced very greatly. Secondly, the cultural materials themselves are mastered, not in terms of a series of lessons, but as interpretations of a vital and enjoyable experience. The effect even of a seemingly small modicum of actual experience upon the educative value of subject-matter learning can be prodigious. It provides exactly what is needed,—the conditions of life—the conditions of mental growth.

Music, then, is an agency for mental growth, because it provides significant and appealing experience which relates itself naturally and readily to vast ranges of culture and knowledge. Consequently, music education should be definitely organized to take advantage of this. For instance, musical experience can be the means of rendering much of history meaningful and vital. When a class has learned some beautiful and appealing Hungarian folk song, a great educative opportunity has been missed unless they are brought to an understanding of the political trials and hopes of the Hungarian people, of their manners, customs, and arts, and of their geography and economic environment. Such understanding is not achieved by the formal route of textbook recitations and lesson learning, but by actual, moving projects which interrelate the learner's interests and make an understanding of Hungarian life indeed very real. Or again, the life and times of Beethoven can come to mean something very personal to a student who has learned one of the piano sonatas, or who has participated in an orchestral rendering of one of the symphonies or overtures.

As suggested above, musical experience can be the means of rendering much in geography far more meaningful and vital. To learn to sing or play or to listen to certain compositions is to come face to face, as it were, with the lives of peoples in distant lands, and to catch something of their spirit and outlook.

Music has natural and ready affiliations with science, though these are not very often capitalized. Consider the possibilities of the making of musical instruments, tuning, the tempering of the scale, and architectural acoustics. Very often, when musicians well advanced toward professional status come upon such matters in their training, they are found extremely illuminating. But there is not the least reason why such contacts with science cannot be mediated to the pupil at the junior high school level, or even below it; for, to speak with a frankness perhaps slightly brutal, much of the acoustics presented to advanced musicians in conservatory courses is not advanced beyond the capacity of the average high school student, and could have been mastered in secondary school, greatly to the advantage and educational enhancement, both of music and science. Once more, there are obvious and innumerable connections between music and literature, and also between music and the visual arts.

To teach music in a water-tight compartment is a flagrant absurdity. If we bring it into vital relationships with other spheres of culture, we greatly increase the significance of all musical projects. Remember once more, that our aim in our music programs must be, not professionalism, but general educative values. This applies all along the line, from the songs of the kindergarten to the work of the senior high school orchestra. A culture based upon significant musical experience can be, and should be, as broad as human life itself. In organizing our work to make it so, we fulfill one of the prime conditions of mental growth.

THE CONTINUATION OF MENTAL GROWTH: PERSONAL RELEASE

One of the most important factors in mental and personal growth is the overcoming of undue repressions and the progressive achievement of the power of free self-expression. Of course we cannot hold, as some extreme advocates seem to suggest, that any repression or inhibition is, in itself, a bad thing. The educated personality is certainly not the personality which has cast off all repressions and inhibitions entirely. This means mere chaos and certain ineffectiveness. Our aim must always be a disciplined freedom, a disciplined self-expression, which of course involves learning *not* to do certain things, because they are impediments to free action. But the great trouble with much school work is that it begins and ends with this negative aspect of freedom. A very large amount of what is done in school tends toward merely inhibiting the pupil, rather than toward setting up the controls essential for creative liberty. Insofar as this is true, its influence is in the direction of cramping, rather than expanding, the personality, and is contrary to the conditions of growth.

(*a*) In the first place, the school undoubtedly sets up, to a dangerous and needless degree, inhibitions upon free physical activity. Since the time of the Greeks it has been insisted again and again that there is, at this point, a most important correlation between the mind and the body, and that the mind cannot develop as it should so long as the body is "cabined, cribbed, and confined" in its reactions. We cannot here go into the traditional reasons why this correlation has been ignored through the ages, but the result has been that school work has been too greatly centered upon learning things out of books and dutifully reciting them to the teacher. (*b*) In the second place, the school tends to maintain a negative rather than a positive attitude toward the question of accuracy. The overwhelming preponderance of its emphasis is put upon the mere avoidance of mistakes. In mathematics, for instance, an interesting attack upon a problem may count for nothing, because of an error in computation which leads to "getting the wrong answer." In English, grammatical accuracy is often given much more weight than the sincere attempt to say something. In history, a slip in citing a date, or a failure to recall a proper name, may be heavily penalized. Notice that I am not arguing that accuracy is unimportant. I am merely saying that accuracy is not important as an end in itself, but only as a necessary factor in satisfying an adequate self-expression. An insensate worship of accuracy produces a negative attitude, and a fear of trying, which is the very reverse of what we desire, if education is to mean mental and personal growth. (*c*) In the third place, the school commonly offers far too little chance for free self-expression. The ordinary classroom recitation may seem to offer a situation which encourages this, but the appearance is superficial and deceptive. What is actually taking place is essentially an oral quiz administered to a group under competitive conditions. The aim of the whole procedure is for the pupil to demonstrate the adequacy of his preparation. But free social self-expression demands something entirely different. It requires organized opportunity for the individual to contribute towards a common undertaking. Evidently, as soon as he is under challenge merely to show what he knows and is aware that he will be marked on what he does, this opportunity is killed.

Music itself is often taught in the schools in such a way that some or all of these defective processes are set up. Possibilities for free integrated response are ignored and everything turns on the reading of notational symbols. Emphasis is placed upon the avoidance of note errors as an end in itself. Instead of the child being constantly stimulated to bring his own contribution towards a social purpose, seating arrangements and so forth are exploited to produce a competitive situation which is made the basis of marking. All such procedures are direct and palpable contraventions of the true genius of music. Properly handled, it should be a medium for creative and constructive release, and so for mental and personal growth.

1. We should teach musical action through free integrated response. The best teachers of drawing insist upon their pupils first of all looking closely and analytically at the object to be represented, and then blocking out its lines in single, unified sweeps of movement. To try to catch the visual essence of an object by fussy little sketchy movements, each made with undue care, defeats itself. One must try to see it as a whole, and then to express what one has seen by a single bold attack; and one must attend to detail, and make corrections later. The proper progression is from the whole to the parts, not from the parts to the whole. This is entirely true also of music. A musical rhythm is not properly apprehended by building up to it through getting each of its constituent parts just right, and then putting them together. Rather one should approach it by a single, unified, integral sweep of free movement. Mastery of the musical score does not depend on anxiously looking at each separate note, but on learning to sweep the eyes over the notation in such a way as to catch the tonal structure there indicated. The proper way to overcome a technical problem, whether in vocal or instrumental performance,

is first to set up a musical goal, and then push boldly and directly towards its attainment through an integrated response, leaving whatever analytic correction of detail may be necessary until later on. The importance of such motor freedom in all aspects of music education can hardly be exaggerated. When music teachers ignore it, they simply create gratuitous difficulties for their pupils. This is one reason why musical performance is often found so very difficult. Moreover, it nullifies one of the great educational values inherent in music,—the experience of positive attack and of the motor freedom and self-confidence which comes from it.

2. Music offers an avenue for disciplined release. This also should be capitalized in our work. Our great anxiety should always be, not to have pupils avoid mistakes, but to have them create effects. Errors are indeed serious and unfortunate. They are to be avoided because they tend to spoil satisfying and positive effects. This should be the emphasis in education everywhere. In the field of music, it is peculiarly natural and obviously desirable and feasible. One should never excuse slovenliness or allow pupils to suppose that beauty can be created without exacting effort and painstaking care. But the great purpose to be entertained is precisely the creation of beauty, and not the avoidance of wrong notes.

Notice how well and strikingly this combines two factors, often considered antipathetic—the factor of self-expression and the factor of discipline. Proper instrumental or vocal action, or the proper rendering of a musical effect by vocal or instrumental means, may be quite properly described as "natural." It looks right to the observer; it feels right to the performer; and its result sounds right to the listener. Every experienced musician knows very well what it means to have this sense of a natural musical delivery, this sense of everything going just as it should. He also knows only too well what it means to fail to achieve it. When we speak of the "natural" delivery of a musical passage, or of a "natural" vocal or instrumental action, we mean a response in accordance with the demands and requirements of the human body and the human mind. It signifies the efficiently coördinated activity of body and mind. It means a way of response which is, somehow, not foreign to us,—in the way that standing on a barrel is foreign to the nature of a circus elephant; but which is an expression of our nature, and which, therefore, we find satisfying and valid.

But how is such natural, self-expressive musical delivery to be achieved? Surely not without toil and effort. We cannot allow the child to hold his violin and bow just anyhow, or to adopt any unconsidered fingering of a piano passage, or to sing far back in his throat, or to make any kind of *crescendos* and *diminuendos* and retards and accelerations which he happens to choose. He will not, in such ways, achieve a naturally valid result. He will not be able to attain any significant self-expression. He must learn. Here the factor of discipline enters the picture. *Musical learning is a process of learning to be natural*. This is not easy. It takes time and effort. It demands constant self-criticism which grows sharper and sharper as our inner standards rise. But it is an utterly different thing from the kind of line upon line, precept upon precept, habit-building type of learning, which we too often find inculcated. It means having a musical purpose,—having something which we wish to express; and then seeking diligently for the means of expressing it.

3. Music offers an avenue for self-expression *in a social*

situation. This is also extremely significant. Just as self-expression must be disciplined rather than capricious, so it must be social rather than merely individualistic, if it is to have constructive educative and human values. Dr. Van de Wall has given us admirable examples of the possibilities of sanifying social self-expression offered by music in connection with his work with defectives. He tells of coming into the wards of a mental hospital, and how, when he started very informally to play the piano and sing songs in which the inmates could join, the icy calm of some dissolved, the excitement and impatient behavior of others was for the time overcome, and all these unfortunate beings participated in a normal activity. *"Social life* was born in the ward," is his striking phrase.[1] And what can be an agency for strength and growth for the deranged, can also serve the normal in similar ways. Every complete musical project involves precisely this. If we are performing, it is either to or with others. In both cases, our own individual contribution is essential. But also its integration with a social purpose and its conformity to a social situation is essential. In the best kind of listening, my own pleasure and insight supports and reinforces that of others. Whenever a group of children are composing a song, everyone is naturally encouraged to make his own suggestions and to express his own taste. Thus a musical group offers one of the most convenient and practicable of all media for an individual to find himself, and to be himself, in company with others. Its possibilities are dissipated when it is organized on competitive lines, or driven along ruthlessly in lockstep. In certain school subjects there may be an excuse for these

[1] VAN DE WALL, WILLEM, Musical Therapeutics in a Mental Hospital, *Long Island Medical Journal*, June, 1923.

things. But with music, it is so easy to avoid them and to substitute something radically different and enormously better that no teacher who clings to them can be free from blame. Along these lines music can be a most valuable agency for personal and mental growth. In it the shy, or socially inhibited child can find just the encouragement for personal expression which he needs. The opposite type, the "extrovert," is placed in a situation where stress is laid upon the coöperative, rather than the purely individual, expression of his tendencies.

Some Fallacies Regarding Mental Growth

In closing this discussion of music as an agency for mental growth, it will be well to consider certain fallacies which have grown up in regard to it, and which have influenced music education. Most of them have already become familiar to us in other connections; and the line which our reply to them must take has been implicitly indicated. However, there is a value in formulating them clearly, and in showing at what points they involve errors in theory and lead to undesirable practice.

1. The first of these is the disciplinary fallacy: the notion, that is to say, that music can train the powers and faculties of the mind. Here we have an absolutely false notion of the nature of mental growth. Mental growth does not depend upon any "strengthening" of the memory, or the reason, or the imagination, or the perceptions, or the will; or by any increase in accuracy, or quickness, or thoroughness, in general. Nor does any other subject become an agency for development by being used as a formal exercise, a sort of set of intellectual calisthenics, to bring about such ends. To anyone

familiar with the findings of modern psychology, this is such an old story that I recapitulate it here merely because it is still maintained by some teachers of music. A subject becomes an agency for mental growth only when it comes into contact with actual problems, and when it leads to the solution of those problems through increasing precision and insight, increasing breadth and outlook, and increasing freedom and sureness of self-expression. There is no doubt that music has what are often called "transfer values"; that is, the study of music may beneficially affect the study of other subjects in the curriculum. But this is not because it produces some magical mental strengthening which can be used anywhere we like. It is because music has natural and broad affiliations and can set up the sort of positive, self-confident attitudes upon which success in any undertaking often depends. If these transfer values are to be realized and not lost, this is possible only if we consciously organize our program for their attainment.

2. The second fallacy in regard to mental growth, and the value of music as an agency for producing it, is the idea that we ought to lay out our work in a logical order rather than a psychological order. The former means beginning with constituent detail and building up to integrated masteries by a systematic process of addition. For instance, it might mean any or all of the following: learning, first of all, the names of the notes and working towards the singing or playing of phrases; laying out the notational problems in terms of some nicely conceived scheme of increasing complexity; always being very careful to go from the known to the unknown; drilling on technique before attempting to make music; learning all the rules of harmony and counterpoint before daring

to try to compose. Here again we have a wrong conception of mental growth and a wrong principle for the organization of an educational program. Mental growth is anything but tidy. It persistently defies preconceived blueprints. It follows no elegant and logical order. What it demands is, first of all, a significant challenge,—a problem which appeals to the learner as real and important. It is brought about in and through the overcoming of this challenge,—the solution of this problem. As a general proposition, the elaborate nicety and care with which some music programs are worked out is simply love's labor lost, as far as producing a beneficial educational result is concerned. Just where shall we introduce the dotted-quarter note followed by an eighth note? What is the right moment to start part-singing? What is the proper grade placement for a certain song? The answer is: It does not much matter. What does matter is that genuine musical projects are going on, and that, through them, the children are making a definite advance in musical precision and in general broad outlook, and are finding opportunities for self-expression.

3. The third fallacy about mental growth, and educational agencies for producing it, is the doctrine that it depends upon the amount of ground covered. As I have already discussed this idea, I shall merely refer to it for the sake of completeness. What counts always is the quality, not the quantity, of effort. A very little genuine experience can revolutionize one's point of view. A very great deal of experience which has no intimate, inner appeal and meaning leaves us entirely unchanged.

4. The fourth fallacy is one against which the entire argument of these pages has been directed. It is the idea that we

can have a valid musical development which is not, at the same time, a human development. We find it in the worship of the "musical prodigy,"—that unfortunate type of child who is the miniature replica of that musical sport, the virtuoso. Translated into terms of educational practice it means narrowness. Finally, the effect of such narrowness is to cramp creative musical development and to deprive music of its educative worth.

SUGGESTED SUPPLEMENTARY READINGS

Creative Experience, ed. Hartman, G., and Schumaker, Ann. The John Day Company, 1932, pp. 67-139.

MURSELL, JAMES L. *Principles of Education,* W. W. Norton Company, 1934, ch. 3.

CHAPTER FIVE

Music as a Moral Force

MORALITY, EDUCATION, AND MUSIC

Education must have a moral outcome. If it fails here, it fails completely. This much is evident from our conception of education as the molding of life and the shaping of action. The essential thing about it is not the storing up of knowledge or the acquisition of skills. All these are indeed necessary. But they are means, not ends. More knowledge, wider understanding, higher expertness are desirable because they make possible a superior level of life and behavior. Education, in its ultimate aim, is the shaping of life and the molding of character. Hence, its purpose is morality in the widest and truest sense of the word.

The need for a moral emphasis in education is becoming more and more clearly recognized by all school people today. But the issue is so broad that it is often not well understood. There is much loose and general talk, but comparatively little clear and solid grasp of what is involved, and little helpful thought on how it may be achieved. We must avoid fine sounding but practically valueless conceptions. We must also avoid mysticism and educational practices based essentially on magic rather than on sense. This viewpoint is peculiarly important in connection with music. Many general educators have a belief that music somehow ought to exercise a moral force. In this they are perfectly right. But when it comes to seeing just how this can be done and what sort of procedures are requisite to its attainment, nothing helpful or clarifying is to be found. And the result is general disappointment and a feeling that music, after all, does not amount to so much as it should.

In the present chapter I shall try to explain, as definitely and concretely as I can, what seems to me the value and place of music in moral education. In this section, I wish first to raise the question as to what we really mean when we talk about morality, which, of course, is an essential point, if we are to define our aims; and then to point out the fallacies in thought and practice which our conception of morality enables us to avoid.

Morality has two sides, an outer and an inner. Outwardly, moral behavior is simply social behavior. The moral personality is the socially well-adjusted personality. Yet this by no means implies a mere conformity. Rather what is demanded is coöperativeness, the ability to create for one's self ways of propitious social action, and a flexibly accommodating yet individually significant and unique mode of adapting one's self to social requirements. We see all this most clearly, perhaps, when we come in contact with the ethically perverted personality; for instance, a boy in a reform school. We find such a person hard to deal with, secretive, sly, deceptive, cruel, dangerous, bad. If we have any insight at all, we quickly perceive that the trouble goes much deeper than any mere refusal to follow ordinary and accepted rules of conduct. Outwardly he may conform in many ways. But when he does violate accepted standards, what makes his case so extraordinarily troublesome and hard to deal with is that his action is obviously a symptom of a deep-lying complaint. The real disease is an imperfect and perverse social adjustment. There is no curing it by giving him lectures or laying down elaborate rules of conduct to be enforced by penalties. All this is merely an attack upon effects, not upon underlying causes. Betterment is possible only through the acquisition of a new social viewpoint. We must seek to integrate him, in new and better ways, with the social order, and to have him learn that greatest of all human lessons,—how to live constructively with others. Hence, one great aim of all moral education must be to produce a constructive and propitious social adjustment.

On the inner side, morality means personal happiness through self-fulfillment. Again consider our moral defective. He seeks self-fulfillment and self-expression, but in ways which, through the very nature of things, lead to conflict and frustration. A child who tells a falsehood to achieve an immediate purpose, or who steals money under the pressure of a sudden desire, is, of course, expressing his personality. But it is an unskillful, a stupid mode of self-expression. It involves him—or is apt to do so—in all manner of untoward circumstances which in the end lead to defeat. The fact that some people are able to "get away with" all kinds of outrageousness and crime does not alter or weaken our point. It merely means that they have extraordinary luck in the face of very adverse chances. The ancient Greek idea of nemesis involves a great and eternal truth. For wrong action nearly always has consequences unfortunate for the individual and leads to some kind of penalty. So we think of the immoral person as essentially selfish; as one who seeks to express and realize his inner impulse and purpose along lines which society has rendered, in the main, impossible; and so as one who, through an extreme of individualism, is on the road towards unhappiness. On the other hand, the ethically adjusted person is one who has learned the art of self-expression in a social medium and finds a way of living which leads to satisfaction, not frustration. It has been very truly said that the good life and the happy life have the same basic conditions.

Hence, our doctrine comes to this: self-fulfillment through social adjustment is the aim of moral education. This may seem vague. As a matter of fact it leads to a very definite program of constructive action. That this is so, we shall see realized particularly in connection with music. Moreover, it serves at once to show us the impossibility of certain educational plans and tenets, and exposes certain fundamental, often entertained, yet fatal fallacies.

1. First of all, there is the fallacy of supposing that moral conduct and personality can be produced only, or most characteristically, by precept. Putting the idea bluntly, it is that moral education means preaching. It is often exemplified in practice. Thus some school principal becomes agitated over the lack of ethical emphasis in his institution and seeks to meet the situation by having a series of talks given in the assembly period, dealing with ethical questions. Even in music education we find the notion represented. Some music educators think that the moral values of their work turn chiefly on having children sing songs about home and mother, or truthfulness, or loyalty, or elevated love, and so forth. One cannot help feeling that these worthy people lack not only adequate breadth of conception concerning what they are trying to do, but also, what is perhaps quite as important, a sense of humor.

I am not trying to argue that preachments or the singing of songs voicing elevating sentiments have no valuable effects, or that we ought to avoid them. But I most emphatically do insist that precepts, however eloquent and fine, are not the characteristic agency for building moral character. There are two reasons for this. (*a*) Moral conduct cannot be reduced to any scheme of rules. I may say to a child: "Always speak the truth. Always be loyal." I may, if I can keep a perfectly straight face, teach him songs about the beauties of truthfulness and loyalty. But his real problem is always to know just what truthful action or loyal behavior actually is in a given situation. This is exactly where the rules fail him. Many a college freshman flagrantly plagiarizes published work without the slightest sense of dishonesty. Many a person is torn between conflicting loyalties without any clearness as to the pathway of right action. Morality is no simple following of simple rules. It is an affair of choice, and often of extremely complex choice. Rules are broad generalizations, helpful only to those who have had much experience. They cannot possibly cover all the contingencies of behavior. It is in these contingencies that morality consists. (*b*) Moral conduct is the art of social living. Like any other art, it cannot be taught by precept. Ethical character and disposition are to be achieved only by dealing, under guidance, with moral situations. Its development depends upon actual and active moral experience. Words, precepts, generalizations have their proper place, but it is a secondary place. Always they must be commentaries upon, and expositions of, actual experiences of moral choice. Otherwise they cannot be effective. They cannot deeply influence conduct, no matter how noble and true. We shall find that a large part of the ethical value of music in education consists in the opportunities it offers to create for the pupils actual moral experiences of great significance.

The great practical weakness of regarding precept as the great medium of moral training is that it makes such training altogether too narrow. It limits it to a single subdivision of the educative process. It confines it within the boundaries of a single subject, as it were. But all education must be moral in its effect, since its great aim is the molding of personality and the shaping of conduct. Otherwise, it is not genuine education at all.

2. Closely connected with the foregoing is the fallacious idea that the standard subjects of the curriculum are destitute of moral significance; that reading, writing, arithmetic, history, mathematics, science, and of course music have no bearing at all upon human character. According to this idea, the essential content of education is intellectual and æsthetic, and morality is a "by-product"; the result, perhaps, of the extracurricular activities of the school. This is violently wrong. No subject is worth studying at all unless it contributes to our understanding and mastery of the art of living. To teach anything for its human values, which, you will recall, are also its educational values, is to teach it for moral ends. All the great subdivisions of the curriculum, including music, are moral influences simply because, rightly grasped, they enlarge and enlighten the social vision. Through them children learn what it means to live together and to live fully and richly. Music is a moral force because of its deep effect in modifying social and personal dispositions and in opening the way towards new patterns of conduct.

3. Yet a third fallacy lies in the notion that certain curricular subjects have a sort of inherent, magic, moral force. Math-

ematics is said to engender a respect for truth. Science is supposed to inculcate open-mindedness and toleration. The study
of history is indicated as a means for developing the spirit of
human brotherliness. And so on. Now the point of the error
lies in this, that the various subjects can be means to just such
ends, but only on the condition that we deliberately organize
them for such purposes. There is nothing in mathematics or
science as such which will teach anyone to be tolerant, or
open-minded, or respectful of truth. There is only mathematics, only science. But when the human values inherent
in these studies are brought out, then our ethical ends really
are achieved. No subject in the whole curriculum, no subject
we could conceivably place in the curriculum, has in itself
any talismanic virtue which makes it intrinsically either a
moral or an educative influence upon the learner.

There is probably no subject for which essentially magical
claims for moral virtue and value have been made more extensively than music. Again and again we find such ideas
recurring in the history of human culture. The Buddha pro-
hibited the use of music among his followers.[1] Plato called
the Ionian and Lydian modes "lax, effeminate and convivial." [2]
Certain compositions are said to be capable of inciting sexual
irregularities. Various worthy persons, nowadays, are quite
agitated about the alleged demoralizing effects of jazz. On
the other hand, some music is supposed to be inherently elevating in its influence and to promote all sorts of worthy and
admirable sentiments and tendencies. Apparently, if one learns
certain compositions, or even hears them, there is a grave

[1] PRATT, JAMES B., *The Pilgrimage of Buddhism,* The Macmillan Company, 1928, ch. 3.
[2] *The Republic,* translated by Davies and Vaughan, p. 93, The Macmillan
Company, 1914.

risk that he will rush forth and plunge into violent debaucheries, while if one chooses others, the temptation to lead a very saintly life will be almost impossible to resist.

I am not going to embark on a detailed examination of such claims. All that one need say is that they are essentially preposterous. Music is a potential moral influence of great value. Moreover, I believe that we can convincingly maintain, on a basis of solid reason and common sense, that good music is a potential moral influence superior to poor music; a point to which I shall revert later. But one thing is perfectly clear. No music, good, bad or indifferent, has in itself any direct intrinsic, magic, moral power. It is no spell, no abracadabra or fee-fi-fo-fum, the mere utterance of which makes leopards change their spots and turns saints into sinners and sinners into saints. *The human value of music does not lie in the music itself, but in our response to it and in what we do with it.* Its moral effect in education turns entirely on the way in which it is taught and learned. It is a moral force in education simply because it lends itself to the creation of morally and socially significant situations. In and of itself, it is like any other body of culture, educationally and morally indifferent, capable of serving worthy ends or base ones. Its moral and human values are determined wholly by our treatment of it.

Our discussion of these three fallacies makes the problem before us clear. How shall we organize music in education so that children learn the art of social living through it and attain more closely to the conditions of the good life? The doctrines we have already formulated will help us to answer this question, and by doing so, we shall cast a fresh light upon them.

MUSIC AS A MORAL FORCE THROUGH CREATIVE SOCIAL SELF-EXPRESSION

If we wish to make music a moral force, our first step must be to do what has so often been recommended in these pages, —organize it as an opportunity for creative social self-expression. A splendid, concrete example of success along these lines has been presented in a recent issue of the *Hibbert Journal*.[1] The writer tells us of her experiment with music in an English school of which she is the headmistress. The pupils involved were a group of working-class children with very barren home and play backgrounds. A definite attempt was made to enrich their lives through music. There was no deliberate, conscious musical instruction at all. A beginning was made with plastic movement, the effort being to free their bodily responses. Then they were led to make physical responses to simple melodies. Soon beautiful, creative, æsthetic expression was found possible. "Some show a spontaneous desire to work out in movement their personal emotional response to great music. Two children brought quite different but entirely characteristic designs in movement for the Bach Chorale 'Beside Thy Cradle Here I Stand,' which were moving in their sincerity. Some children readily design patterns in movement to show form in music. Others offer designs intended to show a special point, e.g., phrasing. Some love to set rhythmic patterns for their teacher to play and their fellows to step to, or double rhythms, bass to be stepped and treble clapped with the teacher to accompany. Some love to conduct. All love to improvise melodies, singing or playing them spontaneously,

[1] A HEADMISTRESS, Experiment in Educating the Mind Through the Body, *Hibbert Journal*, January, 1933, vol. 31, pp. 217-233.

or conforming to binary or ternary forms as suggested by their fellows, when desired introducing modulation to the dominant. They love to listen to and work out in music, the bass and treble, or bass, alto and treble of two- and three-part musical studies, and, having mastered the weaving of the parts, will step the rhythms of any as required. They have worked out, in this way, 'A Little Fugue' of Haendel, and a Two-Part Invention of Bach, as well as many simpler studies." At the time of the report, the group was working on a Nativity Play, with appropriate music. Some took up work at the piano, beginning with improvisation, and proceeding to the melodic and harmonic elaboration of their own musical ideas.

It should be evident to the reader, even from this very abbreviated report, that a situation of great educational and moral significance is here created. Let us try to examine and analyze some of the important points involved.

1. We have here both the internal and external conditions of moral conduct admirably exemplified. On the one hand, we have a remarkably integrated, active, purposeful group life, to which individual contributions can be made, and in which such contributions find their significance. That is, we have exemplified the condition of self-expression in a social medium, which we previously recognized as one of the characteristics of the moral life. The writer of the account particularly emphasizes the extent to which self-consciousness was banished. This evidently means that the individual children had an experience, all too rare in school, of complete personal absorption in a delightful social enterprise. It is significant also that this coöperative endeavor centered upon an enterprise which illustrates the possibilities of association with religious

teaching. On the other hand, internally, we find conditions which made possible a happy satisfaction of impulse. These children were learning far more than music. They were learning the art of expressing and realizing individual tendencies and desires in a social situation. The author writes of them: "They are busy, happy, balanced little people." In spite of a drab home life, meager recreational opportunities, and a school experience elsewhere none too dynamic, music was organized for them in such a way that it could mean a chance to live the good life, which is also the happy life.

2. Notice secondly, that valid musical experience is the indispensable core of the entire undertaking. True musical projects were going on,—listening and responding to music, creating it, and performing it. Also note particularly the quality of the music indicated,—far more austere, far more "classical" than would ordinarily be thought appropriate for young children, presumably of no great native endowment, and certainly of no considerable cultural background. I have already intimated that, in my opinion, music of the highest artistic value has greater possibilities as a moral and human force than music of poor quality. In this situation we come upon one of the reasons. Great music opens up far wider possibilities for subtle, many-sided, interesting expressive response than inferior music. Contrast what is offered to such a group as we have been considering by Handel's "A Little Fugue" on the one hand and by some trivial piece of musical nonsense on the other. I am no particular believer in the magic efficacy of even the very supremest music. But the case seems to me perfectly obvious. Indeed, the very difference between great and poor music lies largely in the opportunities they afford for expressive response,—that is to say, in their ex-

pressive significance. One corollary of this, however, is that we do not get the good out of fine music merely by exposing pupils to it, but only by leading them to respond dynamically and freely to its subtle, complex, yet potent appeal.

3. In the third place, notice the courage with which the technical aspects of music are kept in the background. There is no such thing as concentration on reading the score, on vocal placement, on hand position at the keyboard, on note names, and so forth. All emphasis is placed upon music as a social enterprise. Observe the rewards of this act of pedagogical faith in the progress of the pupils. For this underprivileged, poorly endowed group actually advanced far more rapidly than the normal rate, both in musical and in technical power.

Many teachers instinctively believe that, unless something is dull, it cannot be educationally or morally worth while. Value, to them, seems to lie in drudgery. When uninspired labor yields a very slow and meager return and an extremely gradual advance towards effective mastery, they do not in the least abandon their belief in the virtue and necessity of drudgery; they excuse its ineffectiveness by saying that, while the pupils may not be mastering the subject, they are at least training their minds. Now the educational, the human, and the moral values of music positively do not depend on making it an opportunity for an unenlightened round of dull hard work, which it most certainly can be. They lie precisely in its most stimulating and inspiring aspects, in its artistic and expressive values. Here I insist again, at the risk of seeming unduly to harp upon the point, that in emphasizing such matters is the secret of progress in music itself and of education through music.

4. Note, finally, the demands of a procedure, such as we have described, upon the teacher. To do the things which this headmistress accomplished may seem to you to be impractical. If by this you mean that they will not work if they are properly tried, you are certainly wrong. If, however, you mean that an inflexible, stupid, pedantic teacher, without imagination, creative impulse, and human insight cannot make them work, then indeed you are perfectly right.

Dr. Van de Wall has given us another illustration of the moral power of music as an instrumentality for creative social activity, though from a very different plane of life. He says: "I go to a penal institution where it would be absolute folly to bring the entire population together for any other group expression than community singing. One song of thirty-two bars of music lasting one minute and a half accomplishes more than all the keepers and matrons and disciplinarians and all the other 'arians' together. 'Old Black Joe,' 'A Perfect Day,' 'The Missouri Waltz,' the favorite of the detained for singing in harmony—they are all first rate disciplinarians, lifting and molding a horde of segregated individualists of the weaker sort up to a perfectly homogeneous social organization. Anti-social tendencies, such as ill-will, irrationality, emotional and mental over-activity, as well as laxity,—they are all conquered, even as the individual attempts of some of the irreconcilables are defeated, by the mighty appeal of orderly, good, and beautiful song." (Willem Van de Wall, Music in Correctional Institutions, 78th Annual Report of the Prison Association of New York, 1922.)

MUSIC AS A MORAL FORCE THROUGH MAKING POSSIBLE THE EXPERIENCE OF ACHIEVEMENT

Another respect in which music is a potential moral force in education is that it offers opportunities for the pupil to enjoy the experience of achievement. This aspect is exceedingly valuable. Failure is always apt to be demoralizing; or, if not that, at least it represents an absence of positive moral values. This assertion, undoubtedly, is a broad statement, subject to qualifications which will readily occur to the reader; for clearly, it is possible to convert disaster into triumph and to gain strength from weakness. Yet to undertake something and simply not to succeed with it means a limitation rather than an expansion of the possibilities of life and action. It represents, at best, an absence of any kind of moral advance, and at worst, a moral retrogression. It is exactly this kind of unrelieved and unmitigated failure which is only too often imposed upon the pupil by the ordinary organization of school work.

A great many school pupils study subjects they are required to undertake with little or no sense of "getting anything" out of them or getting anywhere with them; that is, without any experience of definitely increasing power. They may not put it to themselves in just this way or recognize explicitly what is happening to them. Yet the essence of their educative experience can only be described by the word failure. This inner, intimate, dangerous sense of failing is far more common than the distribution of marks would at all indicate. We know, beyond all doubt, that teachers constantly "pass" pupils in their courses who are really achieving practically nothing in the way of effective mastery. In part this is because it must be done. The teacher who insisted that he would only "pass" pupils who were able to show a real working mastery of science, or geometry, or Latin, or English composition, and who set up tests rigorous enough to make sure that this was being done, would quickly lose his job. The marks given by teachers are no indication at all of the prevalence of a disabling and demoralizing sense of essential failure among pupils in school. It is quite true that all curricular subjects, properly organized, must have a moral outcome if they are to be of any genuine human or educative value at all. But in order to have such an outcome, it is necessary that the pupils succeed in mastering them and become able to use them as controls and guides for thought and action.

Yet the pedagogical organization of very many school subjects actually favors failure rather than success, in spite of the fact that the majority of marks returned are of passing grade. Algebra, geometry, natural science, history, foreign language, English literature,—all these are commonly treated as abstract disciplines, to be learned for their own sake rather than as interpretations of experience and guides for effective living. Study perversely divorced from reality loses its chief dynamic; and many a pupil gets nothing from and nowhere with such subjects simply because they are carefully organized to seem to him not worth mastering. Moreover, when we have set up our subject-matter courses, we herd pupils into them irrespective of ability. Homogeneous grouping, as ordinarily managed, scarcely mitigates this obvious evil. We know that for effective mastery of many standard subjects as at present handled, a certain level of ability is imperative. We know that many pupils below that level enter such courses. Manifestly we are simply condemning them to a certain and unavoidable experience of failure, even though we credit them with passing marks, for charity reasons, and to avoid stalling our entire machinery.

Now all this is a very bad thing. It is one of the chief reasons why teachers are puzzled and amazed when they meet with the suggestion that there are definite ethical possibilities in every curricular subject. Such possibilities are assuredly present. If the pupil's preponderant experience in his school learning were one of success; if his algebra, and science, and Latin, and English were for him so many pathways into new modes of behavior and fuller and more creative living, those ethical possibilities would be evident to all beholders. But when we deliberately organize our work so that the pupil's preponderant experience is that of failing to learn algebra, or science, or Latin, or English—failing to see what these subjects are "all about"—it is not very astonishing that their moral values are completely obscured and their moral possibilities lost.

I do not believe that education must or should be organized in any such way. But I cannot here discuss what would be involved in a complete reconstruction of our pedagogy. I am concerned only with music. My point is that music offers a teaching situation where the preponderant experience may be one of success.

1. In the first place, as I have already pointed out, music naturally falls in with the project type of organization. This is a consideration of far-reaching significance. There is a world of difference between a logically organized sequence of lessons and a series of significant projects. The two situations create radically different conditions of individual success. If we have a series of lessons, no matter how skillfully

constructed and nicely graded, the problem for the individual is one of conforming, of meeting a fixed and for him an arbitrary requirement. The question inevitably becomes: Can he learn these lessons as well as, or better than, the average? Can he meet the standards which are set, and which must be set, with respect to average performance? Can he shape himself to the pattern required by an abstract educational blueprint? This is the real source of that sense of failure which broods, like a miasma, over so many school enterprises. If we set the standards of our lesson sequences high enough to be respectable in terms of subject-matter mastery, it is perfectly certain that a majority of our pupils will fall below the line, and that we shall have to resort to some kind of chicane in the marking system to smuggle them by. But if we cut our standards and make our courses excessively easy, they become educationally contemptible.

The project form of organization precisely avoids these difficulties. There is now no average standard, imposed in advance, to which it is the task of the individual to conform. There is only a joint undertaking, to which he is asked to make his own personal contribution. Of course, differences still exist. The child with beautiful vocal control, or a fine feeling for melodic line and appropriateness, offers more towards the performance or creation of music than the "monotone," or he whose musical sensitivity is of a low order. But the point is that the child of limited endowment is not condemned to any sort of failure. On the contrary, he makes his own personal success, and its inferiority to the success of someone else is not pushed into prominence. Why should it be? He is not incited to wrap his single talent in a napkin and bury it, but to use it for whatever it may be worth. We have created a situation which constantly favors genuine success for all, each according to his measure. We have made education individual, which it surely ought to be, without, however, ceasing to make it social. As a matter of fact, in a thoroughly reconstructed system of schooling, I think this would happen with every curricular subdivision. But it can be done here and now with music.

2. In the second place, if we wish to make music a moral force in education through giving the pupil the experience of successful achievement, *we must constantly emphasize process rather than product*. Elsewhere I have advocated the creation of audience situations for the sake of adding to the significance and reality of our musical projects. But here lurks a danger. For an audience may be ruthless in its demand for results and may simply ignore anything else whatsoever. This we must avoid. The ideal audience situation is not that of the concert hall, where a false note is a crime, and to forget, a major social tragedy. Rather it is a group of interested and sympathetic friends who wish to hear what one can do, who enter into one's difficulties, and who draw out the best in one. This is the audience spirit which we must constantly seek to evoke in our programs of music education.

Here, however, is but one aspect or special application of the principle of emphasizing process rather than product. It means that we must create musical situations to which the none-too-competent can happily contribute, while at the same time providing special opportunities for those of special excellence. A program flexibly organized in terms of multifarious and varied musical projects makes this entirely feasible. What the meagerly endowed child needs in education in general is a combination of his own enthusiasm and sustained self-confidence, with expert direction on the part of the teacher. In music we are in a position to give him just these things. His enthusiasm can be built up and his self-confidence maintained by the experience of contributing to group undertakings. He should be the object of our particularly solicitous efforts, as we seek to help him to overcome his special handicaps.

When we organize music along these lines, two very interesting and important things happen. First of all, we get a musical development so sure and rapid that it often seems almost incredible to the old-fashioned teacher. It is quite apparent that the conditions, even of musical achievement, are very seriously falsified in much traditional instruction in the art. There are few fields where enlightened procedures give a quicker and more positive return. Moreover, music so handled becomes a transforming power in education and in life. We have a report of its effect upon the bad boy and the dullard, which is full of meaning for the music teacher.[1] It is found that the chance to achieve and to experience a success personal to one's self can be the seed of a healthy moral growth and an improved attitude towards all the undertakings of life. While we see the influence of valid experience of achievement most dramatically in the case of the poorly adjusted, meagerly endowed individual, it has an equal or greater effect upon the able pupil. It is an experience of very great value. Both the private music teacher and the school music supervisor should see here a very great educational opportunity. In taking it, and in making music an avenue of positive achievement, they will not sacrifice musical values. They will

[1] FELLOWS, A., Creative Music and the Bad Boy, *Progressive Education,* April, 1931, vol. 8, pp. 348-349.

be organizing it to be what it should be,—a factor for moral strength and healthy personal adjustment to the demands of life.

Music as a Moral Force Through the Maintenance of Honest Educational Standards

The maintenance of proper and honest standards is one of the most important sources of moral influence at the disposal of the school. Music is a potential moral force of great value and effectiveness because it lends itself to defining and upholding standards as this ought to be done.

Let us see, first of all, why it is that standards improperly defined and maintained are demoralizing. To begin with, consider the effect of very low standards. Not infrequently we find them. Everything is made very easy. It is made possible to gain approval, both official and unofficial, without any particular effort. A great many very high marks are handed around. We all know schools, and teachers, and courses which exemplify all these practices. What then is wrong with them? In what way do they constitute a demoralizing influence? The answer is that they lead to self-deception on the part of the pupil. He is being taught to be satisfied with mediocrity and to regard it as excellence. He is being given something which has not been earned. He is lulled into contentment with less than the best that he can do. This deception manifestly tends towards a weak and morally undesirable attitude to the challenges and opportunities of life and towards the status and condition of the shirker. The "cinch course," the easy teacher, the school where contemptibly low standards are tolerated can obviously be criticized on intellectual grounds. In each case a false pretense of doing something is being maintained.

But also they can be criticized on moral grounds. They are working against integrity and strength of character. If education is to have desirable ethical outcomes, it must hold up adequate standards of achievement.

On the other hand, the proper procedure is not to rush to the opposite extreme and enforce very high standards by fiat. This is often done. Teachers sometimes pride themselves on giving very long and difficult assignments, on piling on the work, and on "marking hard." The best that one can say for this is that it is more desirable, and more honest, than to be easily satisfied with standards which are extremely low. However, we have a demoralizing influence powerfully at work. The pupils are still being led to direct their efforts towards undesirable and indeed false goals. Under such a system, the pupil is very apt to try to "beat" the teacher, rather than to master the subject. In various ways, flagrant or subtle, he endeavors to evade the full rigor of the law. The concrete result of this mode of dealing with standards, which is perhaps the most notably bad, is the tendency to cheat in examinations. There is reason to suppose that, in many institutions, this is quite widespread. To regard it with despair, as a manifestation of original sin, is highly unintelligent. What it actually means is the failure of certain most important educational influences. It should warn us that we are failing to convince the pupils that the standards of attainment set up must be *their* standards as well as *ours*. On the contrary, they evidently feel that such requirements are arbitrary and artificial; external to their life purposes; and to be evaded by any means whatsoever. Less flagrant, but still very striking attempts to dodge, rather than accept and meet, high educational standards are seen whenever pupils try to cadge good marks or to conciliate a teacher into passing them. All such things, and they are certainly common enough, are indications of a profoundly demoralizing influence. They are hostile to healthy social adjustment, to personal integrity, and to the development of desirable attitudes towards life and work.

What then is the solution? We must seek to create situations where the enterprise itself controls and sets the standards; where to succeed or to fail does not mean to gain, or fail to gain, a rating by a teacher, but actual achievement, or lack of it, in some undertaking. With most of the subjects taught in school this is not easily done. How shall we organize mathematics, or history, or English composition, in such a way that genuine success is just as evident to the pupil himself as to anyone else, and just as clearly differentiated from failure? We have a question hard to answer,—though not impossibly so. And this is exactly why, in most school work, we have imposed standards only; and success and failure defined by the teacher, rather than by the enterprise itself. We shall most readily find illustrations of self-imposed, intrinsic, automatic standards, if we look outside of school work. For instance, no one need tell me how well I play golf. My efforts speak for themselves, with indubitable clearness. I am so objectively certain about it, that, even if some professional were to follow the example of a very "easy" teacher and give me an "A" on my game, it would not for a moment delude me into thinking myself in the class of Bobby Jones. The mountaineer climbing a cliff, the man playing a certain position on a football team, the investigator carrying on a job of research, the executive organizing a sales campaign,—all of them are in positions where their own actual, immediate success and failure is just as manifest to them as to anyone else. Of course, there may be some optimistic self-deception. But essentially, standards are not imposed by anybody else, but by the task.

This is exactly how standards in school work would be organized and maintained under ideal conditions. Instead of being a policeman and a judge, enforcing an arbitrary law, the teacher becomes a helper and a guide. The pupil learns what it is to face an enterprise, and, after applying himself as best he may, to accept bravely the impersonal, inevitable outcome of his own endeavors. Standards so defined and so maintained become a moral agency of great significance. Music naturally offers opportunities for handling them so.

1. The evident pre-condition of intrinsic and direct, rather than imposed and artificial, standards is the presence of an undertaking which, in and of itself, appeals to the learner as worth while. Golf directly and naturally defines standards of achievement in this way, so that success and failure are entirely my own responsibility. Algebra, as ordinarily taught, does not; and success and failure are dispensed by the teacher. The difference is clear. Golf is a significant enterprise. Algebra is a series of lessons. When I start to learn golf, I have a clear and definite purpose. I want to go round the course in the least possible number of strokes. When I start to learn algebra, or any lesson in algebra, I have no such purpose. I want to live through the semester, to work through the book, and to "do" the examples. Under one set of conditions, standards are impersonal and direct. Under the other, such standards are impossible to maintain.

A soundly organized program of music education has a much closer similarity to golf than to algebra in this respect. It consists of a large number of varied, but perfectly definite, enterprises. When I set out to learn to play a piece of music, I can be just about as objectively aware of my success or failure as the golfer is of his own. My teacher may make some comment and criticism. He may disturb a too facile satisfaction. But he is not imposing his own standards upon me. He is showing me the standards implicit in the music. When I think that the job of learning has been well done, and he shows me that it is not yet complete, I go on working not because he tells me to do so and because I am forced to obey the arbitrary decree of a tyrant, but because his criticism has made evident to me the objective necessity for further practice. When I have been listening to a composition, in company with a number of others, and, in the discussion following, I make a very stupid comment and someone else makes a very bright one, it is quite apparent that a failure on my part has taken place. Musical projects set their own standards, just because they are significant and definite undertakings. Music can offer, under the present conditions of school work, an almost perfect example of how standards ought to be set, to achieve educational and ethical outcomes, for the reason that it naturally arranges itself in the form of significant undertakings.

2. Every musical undertaking must involve coöperative effort for the very best possible results. It is exceedingly important not to remain satisfied with slovenly and careless work, and always to seek the highest attainable degree of perfection. This may seem inconsistent with my former claim that we must emphasize the process rather than the result. But it is not. For we must consider the result always in relationship to the process, and, more specifically, in relationship to the abilities of the individual pupil. What, after all, is "the

highest attainable degree of perfection"? Is it the same for everybody? Is it a standard which would be acceptable on the concert platform in New York or Paris? Of course not. What we want is not to force the pupil up to any preconceived level at all, but just to have him do as well as he is able. And notice this: A pupil is almost always able to do better than he thinks he can. One of the greatest and most rewarding tasks of any teacher is to help the pupil discover his own powers. As a matter of fact, this is the teacher's true function in the business of setting and maintaining standards. If everyone is really working up to capacity, this is all we can possibly ask. The process of education is going just as well as it can ever go when the pupils are gaining self-confidence, moral fibre, and positive, overcoming attitudes by being led to attack significant undertakings, master difficulties, and achieve satisfying results.

3. Every musical undertaking should be regarded as a moral undertaking. Dr. John Erskine is reported to have said that, when he had to reconstruct his piano playing sufficiently to perform in public one of the Mozart concertos, it represented one of the most formidable moral tasks of his whole life. This very perfectly illustrates our whole present point. Music may be delightful. But it is not easy. On the contrary, the more we enter into its spirit and the more eager we are to reveal to others its beauty, the more exacting does it become. Consequently we emasculate our enterprise, educationally and morally, when we divest it of the element of hard work. Musical development must mean, amongst other things, rising standards, applicable both to one's self and to others. As one grows musically, one becomes more and more able to differentiate between degrees of excellence, more and more aware

of the gulf which separates the very best from what is just good enough. One achieves this insight through musical undertakings in which one is always led into a constructive self-criticism, always incited to do better, and to achieve more, so that the upper limit of both one's vision and one's accomplishment is continually rising. Here, once again, we see the identity of musical values, human values, and moral values. For when our instructional program is organized on this principle, it is organized for the best possible attainment of all three.

MUSIC AS A SOURCE OF STABILITY IN LIFE

Music is a moral force because, when a pupil learns it as he should, he gains something of permanent value, something which can be a source of strength and stability to him all through his life. *The beautiful belongs in the ranks of the eternal values.* To be able to enjoy it, to enter into it, and to create it, is to have gained something of permanent worth, something which cannot be taken away from one. Other things may fail us,—jobs, friends, domestic happiness. Music, of course, cannot compensate for such losses. But it has the quality of permanence. It remains as a source of solace and relief. It adds a definite and beneficent element to the resources of a man's life.

Can we say as much for most other subjects which children are brought to learn in school? We ought to be able to, but often we can not. The study of literature, for instance, surely ought to mean just this inheriting of a permanent possession. But frequently it does not. Very often the chief emphasis, and the most apparent purpose of the teaching, is to drill the children on archeological detail and historical reference, rather than to awaken them to the joys of reading and the strength for living which reading may supply. Again, when anyone learns mathematics, he should certainly be acquiring something which can be a source of strength and interest to him in his life. Pure mathematics is the greatest of all games, enormously superior to chess or contract bridge. Everybody knows that the majority of the pupils who take algebra and geometry will never use those studies for vocational ends. Why take them, then? The only good reason one can give is that mathematics is a most fascinating pursuit. But to teach it for such an end strikes us as positively grotesque. So one could go on calling the roll of the curricular subjects. To know history, or science, or civics, or anything else should be to have a new resource in one's life and for one's living. It should mean having an accomplishment which one enjoys using and is able to use, when, as, and if one needs it. Whenever learning a subject in school does not have such outcomes, it becomes entirely futile, both educationally and morally.

Teachers dimly recognize all this. They see that subject matter must function if it is to be educative and to supply a source of strength in life. They also see that, in any direct common sense manner, very little subject matter ever does function. They cannot accept the proposition that their work is futile. Hence, they excuse it by saying that it trains the mind. As I have already insisted many times, this is an appeal to magic to save the day which we have lost by our own stupidity and bungling. That such an appeal should ever have been made on behalf of music is nothing less than amazing. If any subject is worth mastering for its own uses and as an accomplishment which can be put to varied uses in one's life, that subject surely is music. Why in the world

should we think we have to excuse it by inventing the preposterous dogma of its disciplinary value? The only possible
reason is that it is often taught so very badly, and in a spirit
so narrow and formalistic, that its true and obvious human
genius is not recognized and released. Teach music in the
spirit, and with the techniques of the old-fashioned gram-
marian, and you will be unable to justify yourself. You will
be grasping at the delusive straw of the theory of formal discipline in the hopeless attempt to make out a case for the
indefensible. Teach music for use in life, and your work
will surely justify you. For music then becomes a permanent resource and source of strength for its possessor, and,
in the highest sense, a moral force.

Has Music Any Intrinsic Moral Effect?

Has music, in and of itself, any direct effect upon character
and morals? Is jazz essentially demoralizing? Is a symphony
by César Franck essentially elevating? Does a person who
takes part in or enjoys the one, run any risk thereby of becoming a worse man or of being led into wrongful action?
Does a person who enjoys or takes part in the other become
nobler and better because of the experience? We have already
considered these questions from time to time in the present
chapter. But they are so interesting, and also so important,
that it is well worth while to revert to them again in closing.
It seems impossible to answer them in the affirmative. Music
becomes a moral force in human life, not at all because of
some talismanic force which it contains in itself, but entirely
because of what we do with it. It is morally valuable simply
because it offers a type of experience so rich, so many-sided,
and full of such enduring values; and because, when we deal

with it properly, we create in ourselves attitudes which are so highly constructive and carry over so readily into other departments of life. We sometimes hear it said that jazz is dangerous because of its alleged sexual origins. Whether it really has such origins is a matter for the anthropologists to decide. But one thing is pretty clear. Jazz as jazz need have absolutely no sexual effect at all, either on performers or listeners. Indeed, it may be nothing more than boring. When it has a demoralizing effect, this is because of the total setting in which we indulge in it—because of what we do with it. In the same way, a César Franck symphony no doubt is a representation and crystallization of the mystical feeling of a profoundly religious temperament. But it preaches no sermon. It teaches no lesson. Hearing it, or participating in it, may have absolutely no effect in the way of making us wish to go out and serve our fellows or seek for communion with God. It is well established that even the minor mode is not intrinsically sad.[1] In view of the whole nature of music, as an art which can catch and convey emotion, but which cannot formulate ideas or doctrines, we are unable to resist the conclusion that, to attribute to it various kinds of intrinsic moral influence, is sheer superstition and mythology.

As soon as we take this position, two very important and illuminating considerations regarding the ethical and educational value of music clearly emerge.

In the first place, it is clear that we must not hope too much from music as a moral force. We cannot expect, for instance, that it will magically transform a bad man into a good one;

[1] HEINLEIN, C. P., The Affective Characters of the Major and Minor Modes in Music, *Journal of Comparative Psychology,* 1928, Vol. 8, pp. 101-142.

or that it is capable, alone, of preventing a child from sliding into a criminal career. Anyone who believes such things would be capable of crediting the stories about Orpheus, which may have a metaphorical, but certainly not a literal, truth. Music is like any other moral influence. It is a force for good which may or may not be effective; which may or may not be counteracted and overcome by other tendencies. Certain persons who doubt whether music has any ethical potentialities at all have pointed out that some very bad men are musical and are active in music, while some very good men are not; all of which is undeniable. But the reply is that when a very immoral person is actively interested in music, it means that he is not wholly bad. *This is one of his virtues.* It may be a favorable point of approach for the reorganization of his life. The essential argument of this chapter amounts simply to the claim that music properly organized and presented is a constructive factor in human life. Music favors the kind of attitudes leading to constructive and creative social adjustment and effective self-expression in a social medium.

Secondly, it may seem that if music has no intrinsic moral effect, so that a piece of jazz and a César Franck symphony are, in this respect, on a par, there is no good reason for insisting upon artistically superior music in our educational programs. If a person insists that he prefers music which we regard as cheap and trashy, have we any right to insist that he "ought" to learn to like something which we consider better? This is a very pertinent question, and we must face it squarely. Musicians all too easily assume that artistically great and worthy music must of necessity be the sort of music we insist upon conveying to everybody. They take it as a self-evident proposition. But it is not. Whenever some critic casts doubt upon it, they are at a loss. Now, if music in itself has no intrinsically humanizing and moralizing effects—and the whole argument of this book has involved the acceptance of this claim—then what case is there for artistically superior music as a superior educative agency?

Our reply begins with a repetition of the proposition that the educative and ethical value of music depends on what we do with it. *The superior educative value of superior music arises from the fact that one can do more things, and more important things with it, than with inferior music.* (*a*) Great music is a highly significant cultural product, while poor music is not. A masterpiece catches and enshrines the very spirit of an age. To learn it may be to enter into and sympathetically understand that spirit in a manner wholly new. Hence, the masterpiece opens up possibilities which the trivial or pedantic composition does not. (*b*) Great music possesses an emotional profundity which poor music lacks. It crystallizes and conveys the emotional experience of a great man. So it opens up depths of feeling and yields opportunities for entering into new and rich ranges of emotion in a way that the superficial composition never can. (*c*) Great music is likely to be subtler and finer in texture and structure than poor music, although the essential difference does not lie in technical construction. Thus, if we want to learn what rhythm can be, what melody and phrase can be, what harmonic progressions can be, the place to go is to the masterpiece. (*d*) Great music is more permanently enjoyable than poor music. This is fairly obvious for the simple reason that great music has survived a process of social selection, while poor music, on the whole, has not. The reason why the classics are still loved, and why Beethoven and Chopin retain a vast popularity and esteem, while

Clementi and Field do not, certainly is not due to the activities of the music critics. Moreover, while actual proof is not at hand, there is some real, experimental reason for holding that individuals continue to enjoy great music after many repetitions, while they become sick and tired of inferior music.[1] The great composition is something to which one can come back again and again, whether to listen to it, or to perform it; and it provides a wellspring of interest and pleasure which will not run dry in the course of a lifetime. But the same certainly cannot be said for poor music.

So we have every right to say that people *ought* to learn to enjoy the best music and that they *need* more of it. Also we may certainly believe that, while a person may be able to enjoy jazz and appreciate a Franck symphony too, a person who only likes jazz and fails to enjoy Franck, reveals a definite cultural and human limitation, and should be educated toward a better attitude. This is not in the least because of any snobbish or stupid preoccupation with high artistic standards or any belief in the magic virtues of even the finest works of tonal art. It is because the great composition has a wealth of meaning and opens up an amplitude of experience, and properly handled inculcates a range of propitious and constructive attitudes which are not possible when we confine ourselves to music of inferior quality and calibre.

Suggested Supplementary Readings

Fellows, A. Creative Music and the Bad Boy, *Progressive Education,* April, 1931, vol. 8, pp. 348-349.
Headmistress, A. Experiment in Educating the Mind Through

[1] Gilliland, A. R., and Moore, H. T., The Immediate and Long-Time Effects of Classical and Popular Phonograph Records, *Journal of Applied Psychology,* 1924, vol. 8, pp. 309-323.

the Body, *Hibbert Journal,* January, 1933, vol. 31, pp. 217-223.

HENLEY, H. Prison Music, *Atlantic Monthly,* July, 1929, vol. 144, pp. 69-76.

KILPATRICK, W. H. *The Foundations of Method.* The Macmillan Company, 1925, ch. 19.

MURSELL, JAMES L. *Principles of Education,* W. W. Norton Company, 1934, ch. 16.

CHAPTER SIX

Methods in Music Education

THE NATURE AND MEANING OF METHOD IN EDUCATION

The question of method is at once the great bugbear and the great challenge of all educational discussions. It is of supreme importance. Badly directed, clumsy teaching imposes enormous obstacles to the functional use of any subject because it makes the acquisition of that subject needlessly slow and difficult. This has certainly been the case with music. One chief reason why there are not many more competent amateur performers of music is that teachers have not known how to guide musical development economically and to bring it about swiftly. It has been made so hard that large numbers become discouraged and drop out of the race long before the end. Jaques-Dalcroze has made the startling claim that he can take a child and in a single year give him as much competence with the piano as is ordinarily achieved in three or four. A three or four hundred percent increase in the sheer efficiency of instruction is quite enough to revolutionize the entire social status of music. Hence, if we wish to organize music education for human values, we must assuredly pay attention to methods of teaching.

On the other hand, the study of method has led in the past to a fanatical worship of fads and tricks and an absurd deference to mechanical rules-of-thumb; and indeed, while there has been a marked change of attitude on the part of our best teachers, we are not yet wholly out of this particular wood. Everyone knows how often this has happened in recent educational history. First, the inductive development lesson was the only proper thing. Then everything was projects. Then supervised study dawned upon the horizon. So it has gone. All these procedures, and many others, have been recommended as cure-alls. Their proponents have insisted that, if one wishes to teach well, there is only one way to do so. Consequently, in the minds of many people, the study of education has been reduced to the mastery of a bag of tricks.

This dangerous narrowness of view, this mechanical interpretation of the educational problem, is peculiarly prevalent in the field of music education. When our schools began to develop comprehensive music programs, a new pedagogical situation was created. New teaching techniques became essential. It was very quickly seen that the old-fashioned procedures were hopeless and that they offered virtually no help at all. The conventional instrumental music lesson could not possibly be transferred to the school classroom. There was a great and humane tradition of vocal instruction; but this again was, on the whole, not applicable to the school situation. So it has been necessary to give much attention and to concentrate much creative thinking upon the elaboration of new teaching processes. One serious result has been a notable lack of balance. Music supervisors have gone method-crazy. Their special professional training has concentrated almost entirely upon the techniques and procedures of classroom teaching and has ignored those broader issues which so illuminate the classroom situation. Opposing schools of methodology have arisen, each advocating some pet procedure as the great solution. Shall we begin with the scale? Shall we begin with the "pattern" song? Shall we use or abandon the *sol-fa* syllables? Shall we follow, to the letter, the system of eurythmics? On such points formerly turned the great doctrinal subdivisions of the field.[1] Divisions and differences, pressed with an almost theological bitterness and cock-sureness, marked the generation which ended with the World War. Since then, the sectarian differences, based on essentially minor points, have given way to broader considerations of aims and objectives of the modern school.

Nevertheless, we cannot rid ourselves entirely of the problem of method. It is, as I have insisted, of the very highest urgency that the teacher shall be really expert in the direction of musical learning. Nor it is a complete solution to tell the prospective teacher about all the various methods which have been developed and used, and allow him to choose for himself, or to work out some sort of eclectic system of his own. Certainly any well-equipped teacher should know what is being attempted in his field of work and what results are being achieved by various procedures. Even this is more than is being done in many institutions where music supervisors are trained. But still more is necessary. It is essential to understand all methods on a broad educational and human background. For any method is not a mere bag of tricks, but an application and exemplification of certain educational principles. In these terms we must understand it, if we are to assess it at its true value, or indeed, properly use it ourselves. The real trouble with our ordinary viewpoint on method is not that we are making much of something essentially unimportant, but

[1] BIRGE, EDWARD BAILEY, *History of Public School Music,* Oliver Ditson, 1928, ch. 5.

that we are considering it in a manner altogether too narrow, too shallow, and absurdly partisan. We must reach an understanding of the nature and meaning of all method if we are rightly to comprehend and effectively to use any particular method.

What then is the ultimate nature and purpose of educational method? Method exists for one central purpose, *to make subject matter educative.* Perhaps a rather crude illustration may serve to make our meaning clear. In the manufacture of an automobile, a great mass of raw materials of many different kinds is brought together. In all manner of processes it is worked over and shaped up. Then there are various schemes and social mechanisms of distribution, advertising, selling, and finance. But everything is pointed towards one goal, to make the raw materials amenable to the needs and purposes of human life, to make them serviceable to man. In the same way, education begins with a great mass of cultural material—literature, science, the arts, history, and so forth. In its raw state it has no value to the individual. Like the metal and wood and rubber which goes into the automobile, it must be organized for the ends of human living. To bring this about is the great objective of all our educational processes. The choice of the curriculum, the administration of the school, and the procedures of the classroom,—all have this for their aim. Moreover, they are valid only in so far as they are well designed to achieve it. Classroom method represents the final stage of the affair, and it is, in some respects, the most intimate and essential.

This is a far broader, far more illuminating, and far more fruitful way of thinking about method than considering it in terms of procedures. Instead of concentrating upon procedure as such, we turn to its broad effect upon the learner. Are we succeeding in our endeavor to work over the mass of cultural raw material into such shapes that the learner can use it in his life? This is the great question. Instead of dealing chiefly with minutiæ, we grapple with wide essentials. As a matter of fact, no procedure or device—the *sol-fa* syllables, the use of the blank score, the employment of eurythmics—is in itself either good or bad. It is good or bad wholly in its total influence. Does it help us to enlighten the learner's mind. Does it bring music effectively into his life? When we put such matters in the fore-front of our thinking, we at once get away from that miserable sectarianism which is such a curse and weakness in music education. This is what method is for. It gives us our principle of evaluation.

The Characteristics of Good Method

Let us bring our general principle—that the purpose of all method is to make subject matter educative—somewhat closer to specific detail. It shows us what must be the ear-marks of good method and how it may be distinguished from bad method. It serves as a guiding criterion which one should apply to one's own teaching, and also to any teaching which one may see, or about which one may read. In order that subject matter may become educative, three conditions must be fulfilled. First, a conscious linkage must be established in the learner's mind between subject matter and life. Second, what have been called the "marginal" and "concomitant" learnings must be adequately provided for. Thirdly, what have been called the "direct" learnings must be expertly and economically accomplished. These are the three outstanding criteria of good method in general, and of good method in music education in particular. Let us see what they mean and how they apply to our work.

1. Unless an effective linkage is established between what a pupil learns in school and his life activities in general, his school learning will not be educative. He will learn things only to forget them, not to use them. Moreover, we cannot for a moment count on this linkage establishing itself by accident, or without conscious and carefully planned direction. All experience indicates that this will not happen, certainly as a regular matter. History, science, mathematics, and, of course, music are constantly taught in school without any directed relationship to life activities. Again and again it has been clearly shown that, under such circumstances, the subject-matter learning does not influence or transfer to the life activities. Lack of directed planning at this point is the secret of many an educational failure. A subject which obviously ought to function in life does not. The reason is that no conscious effort has been put forth to see that it does. Here is one of the great troubles with the conventional music lesson, one which simply teaches the musical techniques and leaves to the pupil the entire responsibility for applying them.

Then, too, when we ignore linkage with life, we ignore what is the great and central purpose of all education and of all method. Subject matter out of touch with life is divested of all its educative and human value, no matter how well it may have been learned for its own sake. Hence, to bring subject matter into touch with life should be the great endeavor of every teacher.

Here, then, is one most important criterion on which to judge all methods in music education. But what, exactly, does it mean? The doctrine of connecting school learning with so-called "life situations" is, of course, familiar enough. I have no doubt that most of those who read these words have heard about it many times. However, they may not have fully comprehended just what it indicates and requires. Certainly it is often misunderstood. Many teachers who undertake to put the doctrine into effect immediately begin to hunt about for all kinds of out-of-school applications of what their pupils are learning. This is good as far as it goes. But it is a partial and unsatisfactory interpretation and cannot lead to an adequate result. School, after all, is also part of life. Life situations must be created in the school, as well as sought outside it. Hence, what our criterion really means is this: Effective method must seek to have pupils learn music in school by actually making music and experiencing music, by actually *living* music.

This carries us still further into detail, and gives us still more specific implications to guide us. (*a*) Good method will turn on providing a sense of genuine and significant musical undertakings and experiences in the school. The music period must be made a real, human, musical experience. It is just as much a "life situation" as playing chamber music in one's home, or going to a concert, or performing jazz at a party, or anything else. It is not a time set apart when we prepare for genuine and appealing activities. It is a time set apart for the sake of engaging in such activities. Our pupils must live music in the music period, not just learn about it. Consequently, our procedures must be geared to this end. Contrast such a conception of method with one which is based entirely on an account of the proper devices to use in teaching and their expert and smooth application. (*b*) Another feature of good method which our criterion indicates as very necessary, is capitalizing opportunities for the actual use of music outside the music period and working deliberately and consciously for its use. We should not, however, suppose that the true educational dynamic works from the outside in, exclusively. We should not depend upon outside activities to render our music period vital. The impulsion must flow in both directions. Our music period must supply experiences and activities so significant and vital that they are constant incentives to the outside use of music. Its enjoyment in other life relationships, reciprocally, must illuminate our music period and help to give it the quality of something real. (*c*) We must break with the "music lesson complex." In effect, I have already asserted as much in this paragraph. But I make no apology for a repetition. Our business, if we are putting through a real job of teaching, is not chiefly to fit a child to do something in some other place, or at some other time. Our business is to have him do it here and now. (*d*) Notice in this whole connection the extreme importance of a proper choice of materials. This also is vitally related to method. If we are to treat the music period as an opportunity to live music, we cannot use feeble drill materials, worthless and unappetizing in themselves, whose only reason for existence is that they are supposed to inculcate reading habits to be used on other occasions. We must wish our children to live the very finest kind of music we can provide. It is well worth saying, with the utmost emphasis, that no teaching technique, however smooth and elegant, can render formal materials educative, or dead materials living.

2. An effective teaching method must favor proper marginal and concomitant learnings. This is a notion of great importance and wide fruitfulness that has been given wide

currency by Kilpatrick.[1] Perhaps it can most quickly be explained by an illustration. Let us suppose that two boys are assigned a lesson dealing with the French Revolution and that each of them is expected to cover the same set of facts regarding it. Further let us suppose that they are quite differently taught. One is forced to learn, simply because he knows that a test is coming; so he masters the material in his textbook and nothing more. The other is given interesting collateral readings, or engages in an appealing project of some kind, or is led to carry on some sort of independent research. At the end, both of them, perhaps, have learned the same body of history— the same facts, and names, and dates, and generalizations. Of course this will not quite happen, but let us assume it for the sake of our illustration. In both cases the *direct* learnings are the same. But a great deal more than direct learning is involved, and here the differences may be most striking. One of our boys may have acquired a distaste for the whole subject and a feeling that it is all pretty dull, dead stuff. The other may have acquired a living interest and a desire to go on and read more about the matter. In one case we have a mere lesson. In the other, we have a living, educative experience. Hence, we see that, if subject matter is to become educative, it cannot just be learned; it must be learned in the right setting. Its acquisition must go along hand in hand with the development of certain attitudes and interests. Therefore, in judging any method, we must ask what other things besides the direct assignment it leads the pupil to acquire. Is he gaining an increasing boredom or an increasing interest? Is he becoming more and more anxious to throw his book out of the

---

[1] KILPATRICK, WILLIAM H., *Foundations of Method,* The Macmillan Company, 1925.

window and be quit of the whole subject? Or is he growing more and more eager to find out more about it? To return to the terminology we have already used, our question must be: What is the effect of our method upon marginal and concomitant learnings—that is to say, upon learnings which go on beyond and yet together with the actual mastering of the assigned material itself?

Such marginal and concomitant learnings are peculiarly important in connection with music; for, unless they are propitious, music will not become educative. They are often ignored. The conventional private music lesson, for instance, usually aims at nothing else but an ability to go through a composition, or to play a scale or a study. Many teachers of school music have been satisfied to concentrate on a method by which their pupils will be able to read the score just as quickly as possible. In all such instances the educative value of music is lost. This kind of narrow outlook is one of the surest signs of bad method. But music offers extraordinarily favorable opportunities for the proper guidance of marginal and concomitant learnings. It should, indeed, offer little less than an object lesson of how this may be done. When method is applied to music, it may and should be seen at its very best.

Let us ask what are some of the marginal and concomitant learnings to be achieved in connection with musical projects which are the staple of a properly planned program of music education.

(*a*) First of all, the pupils should acquire a positive attitude towards the particular musical undertaking in hand. This is not gained by any gushing enthusiasm on the part of the teacher, or by assuring them that the music they are to sing, or play, or listen to is most delightful, or that to create a song will be extremely enjoyable. The whole setting of the undertaking must be planned to generate a firm belief that here is something well worth doing, something truly desirable. One must have this in mind in choosing compositions either for performance or for listening. One must, as it were, "sell" the new composition to the class. For instance, in a performance project, they may well be given a chance to hear it before trying it themselves. If it is really appealing, such an opportunity will make this evident enough without any flood of enthusiasm on our part. Such a positive attitude towards the immediate musical undertaking becomes cumulative as the pupil goes forward and as more and more musical undertakings are adopted. He learns, more and more, to like the music period and to look forward to it. We should point our teaching procedures to achieve just this result. It is a most potent force for musical development. When we find it, we are justified in hoping that our direction of the marginal and concomitant learnings, which go along with our musical projects, has not been too bad.

(*b*) Pupils should acquire a positive attitude towards music in general. We should never think of music education as just a matter of learning to sing this particular song, or play this particular piece, or listen discriminatingly to this particular composition. Always we should be aware of the general in the particular, and of the immediate purpose as contributory to the far-reaching end. The effect of our work upon our pupils should be to incite them to wish to hear more music, to seek opportunities for musical performance, to desire and attempt to write music. For this we must deliberately plan and directly endeavor. We should remember that the molding of musical desire, which is an obvious essential if music is to function in life and if learning it is to become educative, depends upon directed learning.

(*c*) Children should acquire the attitude of regarding and using music as an expressive art; that is, they should learn to attend to and endeavor to create musical effects by the use of dynamics, tempo, tone color, accentuation and subordination, and so forth, that shall be significant and pleasing to themselves and to others. All this will be lost if we emphasize the musical techniques and note by note accuracy to the exclusion of everything else. What we want the pupils to gain from their experience with musical projects is a sense of artistic effects in connection with listening, performance, and creation, and the attitude, when making music, of saying something to somebody in the tonal medium.

(*d*) Pupils should acquire the attitude of desiring the highest attainable degree of perfection and of being dissatisfied with musical results less excellent than they are able to achieve. This is to be gained chiefly by bringing each musical project to as high a standard as possible. One need not, of course, keep a class or an individual working continuously on a composition for an interminable time. Indeed it is often very valuable to lay it aside for a while and then return to it with a more competent grasp, after other things have been learned. But if we simply set ourselves to cover a great deal of ground, irrespective of the quality of the work done, the pupils will not learn the meaning of artistic standards. In the desire for perfection we find one of the mainsprings of musical progress. The proper attitude in approaching the acquisition of technique, for instance, is that one's technical limitations limit one's musical enjoyment, and thus must be overcome by concentrated effort if necessary. Such a general attitude may often be favored by allowing pupils to attempt music somewhat too difficult for them, but which they would very much like to be able to sing or play; for in this way they learn their own limitations and perceive the need for progress. Moreover, an exacting desire for excellence is one of the outcomes of music education which has the widest and most general human values.

3. An effective teaching method must expertly and economically direct the primary learnings. This is a most important point, and it is essential for us to understand it aright, because in connection with it we find two complementary fallacies. On the one hand, there are many teachers who regard the primary or direct learnings as the whole story. But then the trouble is that they cease to be educative. Everything depends upon their setting and the linkage which is established between them and the activities of life. On the other hand, we have some teachers who seem to regard the direct learnings as unessential, who deal entirely in inspiration and motivation, but never connect up the forces they evoke with any serious and definite progress or mastery. This dilemma reminds me of an old fellow who used to sell oranges on a railroad station platform in an Australian country town where the express trains stopped. He was something of a character. Sometimes he would shout: "Fine oranges! All juice and no skin!" Sometimes he would reverse himself, when it would be: "Fine oranges! All skin and no juice!" Some teachers seem to regard education as all juice and no skin, while others apparently think that it ought to be all skin and no juice. Oranges and the processes of education, however, require both skin and juice if they are to be worth anything. An educative result depends upon direct learnings, carried on in the right kind

of dynamic setting. But our point is that these direct learnings *must be carried on*. Moreover, they may require a certain amount of drill. But there is not the least objection to this, so long as it is closely integrated with a purpose apparent to the learner at the time, and so long as it leads him to an increasing mastery, in the steadily more effective use of which he can find enjoyment.

We must always understand that inexpertly guided and wastefully managed direct learnings can destroy educative values. The educative and human effect of a foreign language is greatly enhanced if we can find a way by which the pupil may quickly reach a level of competent use. A game is far more apt to figure prominently in the social picture, and have a place in the lives of many people, if we can make its acquisition reasonably speedy and certain. In the same way, the more efficiently we can guide direct learnings in connection with music, the more successful we are likely to be in promoting general musical activities in social life. Moreover, there is no doubt that most technical problems in music can be handled far more easily than we suppose. Many of the difficulties which center about the use of the score, or the acquisition of manipulative techniques, are fictitious at least in part, and arise simply from bad teaching. I do not mean to say that musical performance can ever be made easy, but I do most emphatically mean that teachers have made it gratuitously difficult. Hence, a direct and expert concentration upon such matters is most repaying. It effectively promotes the actual use of music, and therefore is an important factor in its organization for human and educative values.

AN EVALUATION OF SOME METHODS OF TEACHING MUSIC

Let us now bring our general principles regarding method into touch with some common procedures in music education. It will not be possible to offer an exhaustive presentation, or to consider all the methods now commonly in use, for they are too numerous and too divergent. But a discussion of some of them will be found repaying. It will serve to illustrate our general doctrine and to bring it into contact with practical issues.

1. First let us consider some of the methods which have grown up in this country for teaching the use of the musical score. Before coming down to detail, there is one important question to be raised. What is the proper place of the score in musical development and of the teaching of it in a program of music education? Some teachers make of the score what is nothing less than a fetish. They work on the assumption, which they do not usually even trouble to analyze, that teaching music, particularly in the elementary school, must mean teaching children to read the notation. This is entirely indefensible. The whole trend of the argument presented in these pages clearly indicates that here we have a false aim. The educational values of music depend upon music itself, not on the ability to read it.

Still, the score is very important. (*a*) It is a visual medium giving precision to the auditory impressions which are the essential stuff of music. It can reinforce and render more definite the mental processes, not only of performance but also of listening and creation. It can effectively direct the attention to such factors as pitch and interval relationships, tonality trends, and durational values. It has exactly the possibilities and also the limitations of a technical terminology or system of symbolism in any other field. Just as scientific names are very useful aids to scientific thinking—although knowing the names will not produce such thinking—so the musical symbolism is a valuable aid to musical thinking, feeling, and imagining, although its mastery will not, in and of itself, create in anyone the ability for such thinking, feeling, and imagining. (*b*) A mastery of the score liberates the child for an advance to more complex and exacting musical undertakings. For example, both part-singing and instrumental performance are quite possible without any grasp of the notation. One may sing or play "by ear" and do it extremely well. Indeed, even when one uses the score, one should still be singing or playing "by ear," for music makes its appeal and impression through the avenue of the auditory sense. However, such enterprises are made easier if one has a mastery of the notation.

The bearing of these two points is clear. The notation should always be regarded as an instrumentality through which one may grow in refined and precise musical power. But its mastery is very far from being the chief end of music education. Teaching the score for such purposes as I have suggested indicates that it should mean a great deal more than learning to read. This is but one of the possible uses of the notation. What we should desire is an ability to visualize the tonal pattern. And, as I have said, this is a valuable ability in connection with listening and creation, as well as performance. With this much clearing of the ground, let us come down to a consideration of specific procedures which are used in developing the notation.

(*a*) First of all, we have the proposal for the use of musical experiences preliminary to the introduction of the notation.

This is widely recommended. Indeed it cannot be avoided, because to try to teach the notation before the second grade is hopeless. So we find programs of music education which begin in the kindergarten and the first grade with rhythmic experience through bodily movement, with directed experience in pitch and tonal relations, and with experience in the pleasurable singing of rote songs. This is all entirely admirable. It is just what ought to be done in music education. There are no better ways of setting up the right kind of marginal and concomitant learnings and of securing a linkage between music and life. But one very serious question must be raised. Why should it all be regarded as essentially preparatory to the learning of the score? After having begun with rich and significant musical experiences, why should we hasten, as soon as the children are in the second grade and have begun to learn to read the vernacular, largely to reverse the order and narrow down their work to the business of acquiring the musical notation? This falsifies all our preliminary procedures. It makes them all unduly subordinate to a job of direct learning and of poorly selected direct learning at that. It is putting the cart before the horse. The score should be an aid in reaching competence with music. Music should not be an aid in reaching competence with the score. This plan of preliminary musical experience, so widely adopted, introduces a break in what should be a continuous scheme of advance. The types of projects so happily begun in the preceding years should be continued and amplified from the second grade on. No sharp division should be suddenly made between significant and educative musical activities, and learning to read. "Pleasurable musical experiences," as some supervisors like to call these preliminaries, instead of being regarded as the staple of the program, are treated as a kind of *hors d'œuvre*, to be gotten away with as quickly as possible, so that they may turn to really serious and worth-while things, such as technical drill. It seems incredible that teachers who are familiar with educational aims and objectives should persist in such practices in the face of the evidence against continuing them.

(*b*) Next let us consider the "scale method" of developing the notation. In essential outline, this calls first of all for the rote singing of the scale, using the *sol-fa* syllables; then the placing of the scale, in notation, on the board; then the writing of the scale in notation, on the board, by the pupils; and then the use of books. The central claim made on behalf of this method is, in effect, that it expertly and economically directs the primary learning process of mastering the score. This, however, is open to very serious doubt. As a matter of general theory it may be questioned whether music really depends on the scale, as the proponents of the scale method assert. And as a matter of concrete investigation, no one has ever succeeded in showing—or, so far as I know, attempted experimentally to show—that children learn to read more rapidly by this process than by any other. But the great and obvious criticism is that such a method completely sacrifices concomitant and marginal learnings and is in no way directed towards securing a linkage between music and life. Nor does one circumvent this criticism by accompanying such teaching processes with a certain amount of listening or "enjoyable" rote singing. All such things are regarded as so much "taffy," as lacking seriousness, and as devoid of educative values. They are not integrated with or supported by the increasing mastery of the score. Such a program splits into two parts, the nice but useless candy and the horrid but beneficial medicine.

What we must have is a unified scheme in which direct and concomitant learnings and linkage with life proceed hand in hand and mutually reinforce one another. Moreover, in actual school practice, a teacher who uses the scale method will almost certainly concentrate on ingenious scale drills and treat music as a secondary consideration.

(c) Next let us consider the development of the notation through the use of songs emphasizing diatonic progressions. The essential points of the procedure are as follows: A "pattern song," usually made to order, is taught by rote. Then the pupils follow it in their books. More advanced pupils serve as teachers to help the others, which produces a spurious appearance of a truly socialized classroom situation. The children are taught to point with their fingers at each note in the books, as they identify and sing it, a device which enables the teacher to see just where they are, and which is supposed to concentrate attention properly. Considerable drill with a blank staff placed on the board, or exhibited on a chart, is introduced. Then, as speedily as possible, new material is developed from the notation.

Here again the central claim is that all this expertly directs the primary learnings. But we can be reasonably sure that it is unfounded. There is an altogether undue emphasis upon the single note. Teachers who use such methods often talk a great deal about the vices of "note-wise" apprehension of the score. But they have the children point to the notes, one by one. Also, they have much to say regarding "phrase-wise" reading, but about as far as they actually go in such a direction is to teach the song phrase by phrase. The phrase serves as an obvious and convenient memory unit. It is not made the central functional unit of musical response and musical experience. The whole tendency is to lead the child to see the score as notes, rather than as an ordered assemblage of musico-tonal ideas in visual form. Once more, too, we have an almost complete sacrifice of advantageous concomitant learnings, and the factor of linkage with life is hardly considered. Made-to-order "drill" songs of the most arid type are freely used. The materials of the program are organized in terms of a sequence of notational problems. Usually there is very little experience in listening because so much time and attention is devoted to the score. Instead of creative music we have copy-book drills. Pupils are thrown absurdly on their own resources, for, of course, if one wants them to puzzle out problems in symbolism, it would be just as wrong for the teacher to help them through as it would be for him to solve their arithmetic problems for them. All in all, the procedure about as completely fails to meet the criteria of a good method as anything it would be possible to devise.

(*d*) Next let us consider the method which turns on the use of nothing but material of the type of the folk song. Its differentiating mark is not so much the employment of nothing but authentic folk music as the avoidance of material made to order to provide drill on notational factors. It is a complete contrast to the methods which have just been discussed. There is almost no systematic presentation of the score. The material is organized on an entirely different principle. And the notation is treated as wholly incidental to expressive æsthetic experience with music. Its unquestioned strength comes just at the point where other methods are weakest. It makes admirable provision for a linkage with life, because the song material usually has genuine vitality and appeal and represents the sort of thing that a reasonable human being might conceivably want to sing, either in school or outside it. It makes admirable provision for concomitant and marginal learnings of the kinds we have indicated as desirable. The most serious points of criticism against it seem to be that it offers little in the way of directed attack upon the primary learnings, thereby involving vagueness of method for the teacher and insecure competence in the pupil, and it lacks the variety of material necessary for giving students an all-round musical experience. Its proponents may well regard vagueness of method as a virtue, and may reply that the criticism holds only if we regard the method as essentially one for teaching the notation, which is, perhaps, not a proper interpretation. As a matter of fact, some conscious attack upon the direct learnings is made. The teacher will sing the first phrase of a song, and then the children may try to go on alone, following from their books. The teacher may start singing with the pupils and then drop out for a few notes. The pupils may partly learn a song, and next day try to sing it, using their books. Or a phrase from a song already familiar may be put on the board for study and recognition. Furthermore, there is no reasonable doubt that, providing generous time allowance is made for music, the method will work. To this extent it will be impractical for many schools. It also will lead somewhat slowly to a mastery of the score. However, the process of mastering it is carried on in the right setting, and the final result may well be satisfactory. In conclusion, to insist upon using absolutely nothing but folk song material involves an obvious and serious limitation. It means that we reject much admirable and entirely suitable music simply out of deference to a theory. After all, folk music is drawn from only one field of human experience. We may, indeed, heartily concur in the general educational principles maintained by those who insist upon the folk song approach. For their emphasis upon artistic sincerity and genuineness of feeling we have nothing but praise. However, we cannot avoid believing that to limit our program to folk music would constitute a serious weakness.

(*e*) Lastly, let us consider the method which turns on the use of tonic chord and neighboring tone material. A rote song, based on tonic chord figuration, is first taught aurally for future visual study. In learning it, *sol-fa* syllables and also neutral syllables are used to direct the pupils' attention to purely musical values. Identical phrases are discovered and sung and contrasting phrases noted. Some regard this method as a compromise between those which use either the scale or the diatonic progression and that which uses no pattern songs whatsoever. Its obvious excellence is its well-considered and practical attack upon the direct learning. The phrase structure is made the true functional center of the whole learning process, as it certainly should be. It is a great deal more than just a convenient memory unit. A second respect in which the approach through the tonic chord deals effectively with direct learning lies in the fact that the motives and figures based upon the tonic chord constitute the tonal vocabulary of music. The child who approaches music through material which has been selected because it contains this fundamental vocabulary is closer to the very stuff of great music than if he makes his approach through the scale method. Hence, the use of the tonic chord figure tends to simplify and rationalize the reading process in a way which is hardly possible otherwise.

A third important feature of the tonic chord approach is

that, if syllables are to be abandoned, the child must be brought to visualize, as well as recognize by ear, the tonic chord figures; for, unless he has absolute pitch, he will have to have some means of identifying and reproducing vocally interval relationships to which the tonic chord and the neighboring tones are the key.[1]

Although the classification of songs by phrase types may at first seem grammatical and remote from artistic values, the organization is admirable for effecting direct learnings. Moreover, it is only fair to say that this material is usually of genuine artistic and musical merit. Finally, the tonic chord structure is a linkage to the world of great music, and thus provides amply for marginal and concomitant learnings.

2. Next I wish to consider what may be described as a device, perhaps, rather than a method; namely, the use of syllable names for notes. This is a procedure very well established and widely used. It affords an interesting and instructive illustration of our general principles of method. And reciprocally, when we consider it in the light of those principles, we reach a better understanding of it and see more clearly how it ought to be used to further the ends of music education. Often it is quite unintelligently employed as a mere, accepted rule of thumb. But everyone concerned with music education may benefit by gaining clear and distinct ideas about its possibilities and limitations and also about the reasons which have led to its abandonment in certain quarters.

(*a*) The use of syllable names should be regarded as essentially a device for aiding tonal observation. It is a means of

[1] JACOBSEN, O. IRVING, More About Those Latin Syllables, *School Music* for January-February, 1934.

"putting across" an important piece of direct musical learning. This was certainly the conception held by its originator, John Curwen, as any acquaintance with his writings will demonstrate. He says that his "tonic *sol-fa*" can help musical development in two directions. First, it can bring sharply and clearly before the mind what he calls the "mental effects" of the degrees of the scale. By this he means their tendential or relational effects,—the tendency of the dominant to move to the tonic, of the leading tone to rise to the tonic, and so forth. In his own system this apprehension of the "mental" or tendential effects of the degrees of the scale, each with its own syllabic designation, is reinforced by a scheme of hand signs, which, however, are not much used in this country. Second, Curwen held that the scheme of syllable names and hand signs can bring sharply and clearly before the mind the values of the various intervals. These are both obviously important elements in musical development. Where the system is used intelligently (which happens all too rarely), it is used chiefly for these purposes. Putting it in our own terminology, it is a device for promoting certain significant direct or primary learnings.

(*b*) The movable *do* system, advocated by Curwen, and commonly adopted in this country, has the advantage of emphasizing general tonal relationships, but it also has certain serious defects. It emphasizes abstract tonal relationships rather than specific key. This means that it is extremely clumsy when applied to highly modulated music. To be sure, such a defect is not particularly serious in connection with ordinary school music materials, but it interposes a barrier to transfer from vocal to instrumental experience. Again, the use of the movable *do* creates a difficulty in passing from the syllables to the notational symbols, which, of course, are on a basis of absolute pitch. *Do* may stand for any one of the twelve tones; whereas each line or space of the staff represents one note and only one, save in so far as modified by sharps or flats. This again creates a barrier to transfer from the vocal to the instrumental medium; for, while the voice is essentially relative in regard to pitch, the instrument is essentially absolute. Moreover, the use of the movable *do* in no way points musical development towards the upbuilding of a sense of absolute pitch, which is something entirely possible to create, at least to some extent, by properly guided learning. Of course, the syllables do establish the fixed relationships of the major second, minor third, perfect fourth, and all the rest of the intervals irrespective of pitch. These seem to be its chief excellences and defects as an agency for the guidance of direct learnings.

(*c*) As a practical proposition, the fixed *do* system probably creates more difficulties than it solves. If one wishes an effective substitute for tonic *sol-fa* with movable *do,* perhaps one's best choice would be for the "Tone Name" system of Carl Eitz, extensively used in Germany.[1] The method is too complex to be described here, and unfortunately, so far as I am aware, there is no account of it in English. Essentially it is a scheme under which a separate syllable name is given to each of the twelve degrees of the chromatic scale, tonal relationships being indicated by the arrangement of consonants and vowels. It should not be too much to ex-

---

[1] EITZ, CARL: *Bausteine zum Schulgesangsunterrichte im Sinne der Tonwortmethode,* Leipzig, Breitkopf and Haertel, 1911; and BENNEDIK, FRANC: *Die psychologischen Grundlagen der musikalischen Gehörsbildung mit Beziehung auf die pädagogische Bedeuten der Tonwortmethode von Eitz,* Julius Belz, Langensalza, 1914.

pect that the professionally-minded supervisor ought to equip himself with an understanding of it, at least in connection with his graduate studies, even though he does not wish to use it.

(*d*) The great danger of the device of using syllable names is that it may be used as an end in itself, rather than as a means for promoting and assisting exact tonal observation. It lends itself to that grammatical approach to music so very tempting to many teachers. When so employed, it can obliterate all trace of effective linkage with life or of favorable concomitant learnings. Hence, there is, in America, a movement towards abandoning it, notable not so much for its extent, as for the distinction of those participating in it. No doubt we can teach music without using syllables, but to insist upon doing so may well be straining at a gnat while we swallow a camel. We are certainly not in the presence of one of the major issues of educational doctrine in our field. In addition, there is an obvious danger that, if we do give it up, we shall weaken our program by not caring adequately for a very important element in musical development, namely, directed tonal observation. Used intelligently for its true musical purposes, rather than mechanically as a mere step in the teaching of reading, the device seems defensible enough.

3. Next let us consider the system of eurythmics developed at Geneva by Jaques-Dalcroze and introduced both here and in other countries. This is not a method or device "on all four's" with others that we have considered. Rather it is a complete scheme of music education. It involves the use of rhythmic physical movement (the so-called "plastic rhythm," or rhythmic plastic, or moving plastic), listening, solfège, the approach to instrumental music largely by way of improvisa-

tion, and the general stimulation of artistic and musical sensibilities. It aims not merely at competence with music, but also at the development of the entire personality. Still, it provides some interesting illustrations of our principles. I shall here attempt no complete appreciation, but shall offer only a few scattering comments.

(*a*) In the first place, I want to suggest that the vital essence of the ideas of Jaques-Dalcroze does not lie in the exact sequence of procedural steps he has developed. When anyone invents a method or a system of education, there is always a temptation for him to say that it must be accepted whole and intact, and precisely followed, and that any deviation is sure to be fatal. The innovator also is apt to insist that only the specially-trained initiate can possibly handle the system safely and effectively. This has happened many times in educational history. For instance, it happened in connection with the kindergarten movement, which, for a while, positively worshipped every detail of the gospel according to Froebel. But it is never true. There is no reason to refuse to believe that the vital essence of the system of eurythmics can be accommodated to the situation and requirements of the American public school. The core of the doctrine, as I understand it, comes to something like this: Rhythm is the great essential, both for development in music and for the development of the personality through music. Rhythm can be properly apprehended only through the experience of free bodily movement, i.e., through the expressive "moving plastic." Rhythm must be regarded as part, but an essential, and indeed *the* essential, part of a very broad musical development.

(*b*) The idea that rhythmic grasp depends upon the experience of free expressive bodily movement is an admirable instance of the expert direction of a piece of primary learning. It is entirely and indubitably correct. To attempt to develop the sense of rhythm by essentially arithmetical means, such as counting and subdividing time values, is excessively clumsy.

(c) The general success of the system is very striking and instructive. Jaques-Dalcroze finds that it enormously facilitates mastery with musical instruments. This shows excellently how effective linkage with life and also the effective and propitious direction of concomitant learnings are made possible and easy when the primary learnings are expertly and economically guided.

4. Lastly, I wish to say something regarding the scheme of creative music, associated particularly with the name of Mrs. Satis M. Coleman and the Lincoln School of Teachers College, Columbia University. Here again is something far more than a limited and specific method or a particular device. The movement began with the making and playing of toy instruments as part of a program of music education. Many people think of it as no more than this. But it has broadened out into a complete, philosophically grounded system of music education, of which the toy instrument work is only a single element, though perhaps the most obviously striking and characteristic. The peculiar educational value of this differentiating idea seems to lie in its effect in securing a linkage between music and life. In the making and playing of toy instruments, music is integrated with many-sided activity on the part of the child. Moreover, it assuredly fosters admirable concomitant learnings, and particularly it engenders favorable attitudes towards music. Its weakness, so far, seems to be its relative neglect of important direct learn-

ings; that is to say, the actual mastery of worthy music and the increasingly firm grasp of tonal relationships. For this reason, one feels that its extension much above the primary grades is a mistake. The use of water glasses, where waters of different colors may indicate important scale degrees, and the problems involved in the tuning of instruments made by the pupils, may perhaps be taken as means of working towards tonal observation and the grasp of tonal relationships. However, they do not seem very economical modes of directing such primary learnings. As a mode of stimulating a will to be musical it seems full of value. Nevertheless, in its present stage of organization, it seems to exhibit rather definite limitations.

Some Common Fallacies Regarding Method

There are a number of fallacies in regard to method in education in general and in music education in particular which we should consider. By implication our discussion has already indicated the errors they involve. But it is well worth while to give them special and explicit attention, both because they are widely entertained, and also because they are not seldom put into practice by teachers, and even by teacher training institutions.

1. First of all there is the fallacy of holding that a method can properly and adequately be determined by a large number of minute and definite rules relating to classroom procedures. We very often encounter this naïve belief. Good teaching is supposed to mean doing certain things in a fixed and regular way. Just how shall we introduce a composition to which the pupils are to listen? Shall we ever sing with the pupils? What shall we do when a pupil makes a mistake? At what moment in the learning of a song shall we intro-

duce the use of the neutral syllable? These are but samples of endless similar questions. Proponents of a certain method often talk as though all will certainly be lost if some small point is not handled exactly according to instructions. The idea, however, is quite absurd, and reveals a very serious misconception. There are three considerations to be indicated in reply.

(*a*) The effectiveness of learning does not depend on the minutiæ of control but on its general spirit and aim. Hence, good teaching requires the arousal and direction of effective purpose far more than an anxious concern with small points of pedagogical technique and small ingenuities. (*b*) It has been proved that the detail of teaching procedures cannot be controlled by minute instructions. A method nominally the same always allows of innumerable inner variations. Two teachers may think that they are using the same method, whereas in reality they are doing very different things. This is what makes it so difficult to generalize about any given method and so futile to worry unduly about its detail. (*c*) Method should not be thought of in terms of procedure primarily, but rather in terms of the general end to be achieved and the broad effects which are being produced in the minds and dispositions of the pupils.

2. Another fallacious notion often entertained is that there must always be some "best" method for teaching anything. This, again, is entirely wrong. Anything can be taught effectively in a considerable number of ways. There is hardly ever any one, unique, "best" method. What we want is a teaching procedure which favors and makes possible linkage with life, which helps towards the right kind of concomitant learnings, and which guides the direct learnings economically and

efficiently. The detail of doing these things will vary with many circumstances, including the personality and aptitudes of the teacher, the ability and dispositions of the pupils, and the entire school situation. This latter includes such considerations as the amount of time allotted to our subject, its correlations with other subjects, and so forth.

3. Another fallacy is the idea that any method is just as good as any other. This is the complementary error to the one discussed above. It sometimes takes the form of insisting that the personality of the teacher is all that matters. Now the personality of the teacher is, no doubt, extremely important. However, it must have a medium through which to operate. Some methods—such as unmitigated and long-continued scale and technical drills, or note pointing—are educationally destructive to a high degree. A teacher of fine personality and enthusiastic musicianship may be able to mitigate their evil effects, but his work would be improved if he substituted some other procedures.

4. Another fallacy, and a very common one, is the idea that there can be such a thing as a general method which will be applicable equally to any subject, which can be used just as well with arithmetic as with music, or just as well with literature as with manual training. We have insisted that the whole meaning of method is to make content educative. Its aim is simply the working up of content for the sake of mental growth. Arithmetic, history, science, and music require quite different lines of educational treatment simply because their content and their place in the body of human culture is different. To be sure, there are certain *general principles of method,* but their concrete application will and ought to vary. We may be perfectly sure that any detailed method which can

be applied indifferently to any subject has something the matter with it. There is no such thing as a general method which, as the deacon said about the Doxology, is "suitable for all occasions."

5. Yet another fallacy exists in the idea that all one needs in order to teach well is a mastery of the material to be taught. This is a very lamentable error, because, unfortunately, we know too well that content may be grasped without any relevancy to the way in which it is assimilated by the human mind, or by the child mind in particular. Content mastery alone is not enough. Musicianship alone is not enough. Our expertness must have human quality if we are to use it for the promotion of human values.

6. Yet another fallacy, and the last I shall discuss, is the idea that one can teach well without a mastery of the material to be taught. This assumption, too, we often encounter. It usually takes the form of saying, or at least believing, that all a teacher really needs is a thorough knowledge of method. But if we deny that method consists essentially of procedure and insist, on the contrary, that its great aim is to render content educative, the absurdity of such a notion becomes very manifest. How can one shape up a body of material for educative ends unless one has a mastery of it? How can one approach a teaching situation with confidence, certain that one can cope, in an instant, with any problems which may arise; certain that one can freely and fruitfully follow up any winding by-ways that may allure; certain that one can stimulate and direct any creative effort which may reveal itself; except in so far as one knows the material he is teaching? Ignorance is a very great limitation to any teacher. It makes freedom, creative interest, and human quality almost impos-

sible to achieve, because one is constantly afraid that some point will be raised or some undertaking proposed which is beyond one's capacity to handle. No rules of procedure will enable us to teach as we should, because in a real teaching situation, the unexpected constantly happens and the unexpected is welcome. In order to present music for educative and human ends it is necessary that one be a musician.

SUGGESTED SUPPLEMENTARY READINGS

KILPATRICK, W. H. *The Foundations of Method,* The Macmillan Company, 1925, chs. 8 and 9.

MURSELL, JAMES L. *Principles of Education,* W. W. Norton Company, 1934, ch. 20.

MURSELL, JAMES L. *Psychology of Secondary School Teaching,* W. W. Norton Company, 1932, ch. 1.

MURSELL, JAMES L. *Principles of Musical Education,* The Macmillan Company, 1927, ch. 11.

MURSELL, JAMES L., and GLENN, MABELLE, *The Psychology of School Music Teaching,* Silver, Burdett and Company, 1931, ch. 4.

NORTON, ALMA M. *Teaching School Music,* C. C. Crawford, 1932.

CHAPTER SEVEN

Music and the Class

THE CLASS AS AN EDUCATIONAL OPPORTUNITY

Most teachers simply take the class for granted. They never ask to what extent and under what conditions of management it provides an ideal educational situation. They never inquire as to its possibilities and limitations. They seldom attempt to imagine any workable alternative. Teaching means for them simply the conventional direction of class groups. Yet practicable alternatives exist. Many of our universities and colleges have introduced systems of tutorial instruction. The Dalton Laboratory Plan, in which the class organization almost entirely disappears, has attracted wide attention in this country and has been even more extensively adopted elsewhere. Some of our largest school systems have developed various methods of individual teaching. There is a distinct tendency in modern education to give up class instruction, or at least to use it only for special purposes. Surely this ought to raise in our minds a very definite question. What unique and special educational opportunities are offered by the class? What is the reason for the various proposals for abandoning it? Would the best conceivable form of education be confined, entirely or largely, to individual contacts between pupils and teachers?

Such questions as these have a peculiar cogency in the field of music. Of course there has always been much group activity in connection with music education. It has always been found desirable to set up opportunities for vocal and instrumental ensemble performance and practice in school music work. Up to the present, however, private instruction has been predominantly of the individual type. Only very recently has there been an important development in the way of class teaching of music. In the instrumental field it is still regarded as a novelty. A great many persons seriously question the value of all such work, and, unfortunately, it is also true that those values are not well understood or adequately capitalized by many who carry on class instruction in music. Hence, a careful scrutiny of possibilities and limitations is peculiarly in order at this point. I shall try to show that, so far from individual instruction being the ideal towards which we ought to work, or for which we should hope, the music class can and should furnish an ideal example of the values of class teaching everywhere.

While the organization of education for class teaching is now generally accepted, or at least only rather sporadically criticized, this was not always so. Prior to the nineteenth century, most teaching followed an individual method. Although the teacher had before him, to be sure, a group of pupils, they were not all necessarily working at the same tasks. They did not "recite" as a group in the present day sense. They were called up, one by one, so that the teacher might "hear" them in their lessons. The social aspect of the situation was pretty well confined to the problem of preserving something which might resemble order. Class teaching was not introduced as an alternative to the old individual system for any philosophical reasons, or because it was regarded as educationally superior. It seemed to offer a decrease in school costs because it was a mechanism by which one teacher could handle a larger number of pupils. It made for better order and a more civilized discipline. It rendered possible a better administration of the entire school. While the development of class teaching proper thus came as an empirical reform, it brought about a very significant transformation, for, in setting up classes, an educational opportunity of an entirely new order was created, although this was far from the deliberate end in view. A perfectly sound educational principle, entirely obvious to common sense, was in effect recognized. This was the principle that the coöperative activity of a group of like-minded learners can exercise a very stimulating influence on each one of them. One need not look to the formal, organized processes of the school to recognize this as true. Everybody knows it. If I happen to be learning almost anything at all—Chinese history, mathematics, golf, French, contract bridge—I can do a great deal by simply studying and practising in isolation. But always I shall find it beneficial in many ways—and in different ways according to what it is that I am learning—if I can join with a group of others similarly interested. In this simple consideration lies the essence of class teaching. The special educational opportunity furnished by the class consists of this: It provides a social context for learning. Here is a notion which we should always keep in mind. It furnishes the key to the true effectiveness of class work.

We may put the matter somewhat differently. Learning may be said always to have two aspects,—one private, the other social. The acquisition of an ability is a private, an essential individual process, but its expressive use is social. I may ac-

quire historical knowledge from books and in complete se-
clusion. When I use my knowledge, I tell others about it,
or discuss matters with them in the light of it, or write about
it so that others may read, or shape my actions in some way
with regard to it. Always such use involves a relationship
with others, even though they may not be immediately present; as, for instance, when I write something which I hope
and expect that they may read. This analysis will apply to any
and every kind of learning. Always we may separate it into
an acquisitive and expressive side, the first being characteristically private, and the other, characteristically social. In some
of our best school systems this is expressly recognized. Individual situations are organized for the acquisition of knowledge; social situations are organized for its expressive use.
Hence, to apply our principle to an interpretation of the class,
we should think of it as existing primarily to provide opportunities for the social expression and significant use of acquired knowledge and power.

This enables us to avoid three great errors, which, put into
practice, translate themselves into three great abuses of the
class opportunity.

1. The first error is to use the class as a means of imposing
mass standards. This is done when the essence of class teaching is taken to mean putting through a given stint of work
in a given time. The task which we have blocked out, rather
than the individual learner, becomes the crux of our situation.
We speak of ourselves as teaching *the class*—which, of course,
cannot be done—rather than as providing social experience
and expressive opportunity for the individual. We fall into
one of the most besetting and also one of the most destructive
of all educational fallacies,—the fallacy of the average. In-

stead of trying to teach boys and girls, we try to teach that complete abstraction,—the average of the group.

The moment this is done, we run counter to educational needs and human values. The variable individual becomes a nuisance in exact proportion to the extent of his variation. Both the slow child and the fast child become "problems." They are not "problems" *per se,* any more than anyone else, but they become so the moment we make the average performance our ideal. Very often, perhaps usually, the class is used in just this way. It seems highly sensible and entirely practical. When we have everyone together in one place, the obvious thing to do seems to make everyone jump through exactly the same set of hoops, if possible, at the same time. The only trouble is that this is not really educating them. It is especially stupid with music, where the ideal of covering an average amount of ground in a given time is peculiarly untenable.

2. The second error is to use the class group for tutoring. This also is often done. For instance, the organization of board work combined with seat work in many mathematics classes is obviously for the purpose of making possible the distribution of at least a little individual instruction to everybody. Often, too, in a foreign language class, the attempt is made to give each pupil a little chance to show what he can do and to apply to him a little coaching. This instantly deprives our situation of its chief constructive meaning as an opportunity for the social expression of acquired masteries. The class simply becomes a poor substitute for tutoring. We do badly in the class what we could do far better if we took each pupil separately. The point is that we should do something quite different in the class from what we could do if

we took each pupil separately. Music classes, particularly in the instrumental field, are very frequently treated simply as opportunities for this kind of diluted individual coaching. Those who criticize such classes as cheap and poor alternatives to music lessons in the studio undoubtedly have such procedures in mind. Moreover, such criticisms are entirely justified. If we can find nothing to do with a group of learners that we would be unable to do if we dealt with them singly, and could not do much better so, then the only real justification for having a class at all is its cheapness.

3. The third error consists in making an arbitrary separation between the private and social aspects of learning. I have spoken of these two aspects as if they were entirely distinct, but they are not. Significant and effective acquisition of any mastery must be for the sake of its expressive use. Furthermore, it must be very closely associated with such expressive use. The desire to use a mastery must be the mainspring of motive for acquiring it. And in its expressive use, one's mastery of it is confirmed, consolidated, and, so to speak, rendered actual. It often happens in educational practice that these two aspects of learning are actually separated, even when the error of doing so is recognized. Thus one criticism which has been made of the celebrated school system of Winnetka, Illinois, is that it has set up, on the one hand, a scheme of individual study, and on the other, a scheme of group projects, but has not provided for any sufficient connection between them. S. A. Courtis, speaking of the plan of individual instruction in the schools of Detroit, admits it as a serious defect that this work is not closely geared with creative group undertakings.

The class, in short, must be a place where individually acquired masteries are exhibited and expressed, and where inspiration is found for the further establishment of such masteries. It is always found in practice that this is a difficult condition to fulfill, but with music it should be possible.

So, to repeat, in closing this section, class work must always be planned to furnish the social patterns for expressive activity. This is its peculiar genius. Here reside the special values which it has to offer.

GENERAL VALUES OF THE CLASS IN MUSIC EDUCATION

The class has a definite, constructive place in music education. Never should it be regarded as a regrettable and cheap substitute for private instruction in the studio. Let us make the not inconsiderable effort to imagine a school system in which all the teaching of music took the form of private lessons. Could we possibly regard this as ideal? Assuredly not. Certain very great values would be lost. The studio, though it has a very necessary place in a complete scheme, is yet a very imperfect and defective educational arena. A class, properly managed, can achieve many things which the studio can hardly accomplish. What, then, are some of these things?

1. In the first place, the class can arouse momentum and enthusiasm, and it should be definitely planned with this in mind. Of course a good private teacher will also have this aim, but we must find much significance in the fact that, in order to bring it about, he is very likely to organize his pupils into some sort of class group or groups. The tutorial situation in music does not favor the development of enthusiasm and momentum in at all the same way, or to the same degree, as does a social situation. These dynamic factors are of very great importance. Too often they are ignored in the ordinary music

lesson. Moreover, they are all too often ignored in the ordinary school music class. The emphasis is placed upon average progress rather than upon free contribution to group undertakings. Everything is dominated by the lesson-learning complex. However, a class furnishes us with a splendid chance to generate the potent stimulation of musical projects carried through with others. If we ignore this chance, the class loses much of its significance and constructive value. This arousal of enthusiasm, and of a positive attitude towards music in general and towards the particular musical undertaking in hand, is of peculiar importance with young children. Their whole progress in music may turn on the development in them of what has been well called "the will to be musical." This is one reason why, in an ideally organized program of music education, little children will be taught chiefly in class groups and to a much less extent by private lessons in the studio.

2. The class situation is admirably adapted to import into musical learning the essential sense of reality. The private lesson, by its very nature and limitations, tends to concentrate far too exclusively on the acquisition of masteries. But, as I have insisted again and again, no skill or mastery is of value for its own sake, and, what is very necessary for us to understand, if taught merely for its own sake, it will probably not seem valuable to the learner. Hence, the opportunity for an expressive use of mastery is just as essential an element in education as the acquisition of that mastery. Some private teachers, recognizing this more or less clearly, organize pupils' concerts as part of their work. Incidentally, they hope thus to kill two birds with one stone and to develop a little useful advertising, which, indeed, is all quite legitimate. But this is not enough. We must make the expressive opportunity a

proper and integral part of the teaching itself, not just an occasional chance to show off in public. Herein lies one of the great values of the music class. It is a place where musical interests and growing musical masteries can come to fruition through social self-expression. Of course, many music classes are conspicuously not built around any such purpose. Their paramount concern is with the acquisition rather than the expression of skill, and to this extent they are untrue to their own genius. This holds true in the case of the vocal class dealing chiefly with vocal technique and of the instrumental class, with instrumental technique. In any case it always means a sacrifice of those unique values potentially created by the very presence of a group. The true spirit of the music class should be a getting together to enjoy the hearing and making of music. It should be a social medium in which musical learning makes contact with the realities and delights of its use.

3. The class, properly directed, can foster a sense of cooperative responsibility. The great weakness of education organized in terms of lesson learning is that there is none of this feeling of a joint, shared responsibility. The children do things and learn things merely because they are so ordered. The lesson is assigned from above and imposed upon the pupils without any active acceptance on their part. They learn it just well enough to "get by," and the only effective standards are those created by the necessarily arbitrary, necessarily personal and fluctuating demands of the teacher. In the proper management of the class we find an opportunity for avoiding all this. An entirely different attitude of mind is instantly created when a pupil must learn something well enough to present it to his fellows, or well enough to be able to take

his share in a group enterprise. This should be our organized purpose in the music class. It is achieved simply enough in principle by managing the class as a group collaborating in musical undertakings. We may, for instance, encourage contributions to the class as a whole either by individuals or by sub-groups. Ways of doing this in connection with performance projects and creative projects will suggest themselves readily enough. But it is also possible in listening projects. For example, one may suggest that a pupil may bring to class, comment upon, and run off some phonograph record which he has greatly enjoyed. Again, the proper use of the class as an ensemble opportunity greatly favors a strong desire to do well for the sake of the general effect. This is a consideration of special importance in connection with the instrumental class where there should be a considerable amount of ensemble playing. Such influences are of great value for the so-called "monotone," who needs a strong musical stimulation, albeit sympathetically mediated. They are very strong, often, with pupils of high school age. Many supervisors well know that members of a high school orchestra, of their own accord, will often devote themselves most assiduously to individual practice, sacrificing vacations, and making all kinds of extra effort for the sake of doing their part with the organization. This should mean something to us in connection with our music classes.

THE CLASS AS AN AGENCY FOR MUSICAL DEVELOPMENT

We have seen that one of the most difficult practical problems in education is to bring about a vital connection in the mind of the pupil between the acquisition of an ability and its expressive use. This difficulty appears when we have, as at

Winnetka, a scheme of individual instruction on the one hand, whose aim is to build up fundamental masteries, and, on the other, social situations designed to afford opportunities to use them. The danger is that the connection will not be apparent to the learner, in which case expression will not reinforce and motivate acquisition and acquisition will not naturally and directly translate itself into use. In the music class, however, it becomes possible to avoid this dilemma. For many musical learnings are best carried on, or at least best initiated and reinforced, in and through those very social situations where they become functional.

The reason for this is that many musical learnings are peculiarly subject to the special influence of what is known as *social facilitation*. By social facilitation we mean an increase in efficiency produced in any function or performance when it is carried on in company with others who are also engaged in it, rather than alone. For instance, we find that such tasks as writing from dictation, doing mental and written arithmetic, learning nonsense syllables, and completing mutilated sentences go better and more effectively when the individual is working in conjunction with a group than when he is by himself.[1] A good many studies have called attention to this interesting phenomenon and have shown that the effect is produced in connection with many types of activity. In general, as we might expect, the influence of social facilitation is most marked with functions such that each individual is adequately aware of what everybody else is doing. It is one of the striking effects of the group upon its members. Happily, many musical learnings are of a type which renders them

[1] MURSELL, JAMES L., *The Psychology of Secondary School Teaching*, W. W. Norton Company, 1932, pp. 433-434.

peculiarly susceptible to social facilitations. We may even say that their best and most efficient acquisition requires the presence of a group situation. Thus to try to build up musical masteries and to promote the development of musical power entirely through the medium of individual effort is certainly a mistake. Hence, in the case of music, a very close linkage can be established between acquisition and use. Those very social situations which are so necessary for the expression of a musical ability also have a highly beneficial effect when our purpose is to help the pupil to gain such an ability. This enables us to see with still further clarity and completeness how natural and necessary a mechanism is the music class in an organized program of music education.

Let us then consider some of the most important types of musical learning which can naturally and effectively be carried on in the medium of the class.

1. A fine discrimination and a firm grasp of musical rhythm can best be engendered through group experience. Indeed, if we confine music study to private learning, we make the development of a sense of rhythm much more difficult, with the probable result that the pupil will never gain it in any fullness.

We know, beyond all reasonable doubt, that the great error in regard to rhythm is to approach it arithmetically. By this I mean attempting to teach it by concentrating upon the durational values of the notes, the time signatures, the bar lines, and counting. All this means making time rather than rhythm primary. In music, the power of precise timing depends upon rhythm, not rhythm upon timing. It may be that a pupil so taught will develop a strong sense of rhythm, but this will happen through the grace of Heaven and not by virtue of our teaching. Of course the study of the arithmetical time values involved in music should not, and cannot, be abandoned, but it should be used to render more precise a feeling for rhythm which has already been established. Such a study is an entirely false approach to the task of actually establishing the feeling for rhythm. Yet this is exactly what a purely private, individualistic type of music study inevitably tends to emphasize, and provides one of the chief reasons why so many private music pupils, both in the vocal and instrumental fields, never acquire an adequate grasp of and assurance with musical rhythm.

What, then, is the true foundation of our sense of rhythm? It is our feeling of bodily movement. We apprehend the rhythm of music through this medium. When we say that we feel the rhythmic demand of a piece of music, or of a musical phrase, what we mean is that we feel it as requiring a certain pattern of movement. This has led to the practice of teaching rhythm through physical movement, expressing the requirements of the music. Here is the root idea of Dalcroze Eurythmics, but it has been applied much more widely. It is an entirely sound and very important principle in music education. Every music pupil greatly needs the experience of free, large, flowing, coördinated movement in response to music. Lack of such experience is sure to compromise musical development. Moreover, it is also important that the movement patterns through which the musical rhythms are expressed and apprehended should be significant rather than merely calisthenic. They should have a mimetic quality. All this can be supplied far more naturally in a group than in solitude. The factor of social facilitation is here extremely powerful. The individual who undertakes to set up a free motor rhythmic response to music is likely to be somewhat inhibited. But when he is in the company of a properly directed group, his enthusiasm is aroused, his inventiveness stimulated, and his self-consciousness banished by the swing and sweep of the social activity. Moreover, the presence of a group makes true motor ensembles possible, so that each individual may take a different part, and yet all may collaborate in the creation of a moving plastic picture. To supply such motor rhythmic experience richly should be one of the chief aims of our class work.

Furthermore, the class offers opportunities for the ensemble performance of music, which is an exceedingly valuable agency for the development and refinement of the sense of rhythm. Solitary pianoforte practice, for instance, is certainly not an ideal situation in which to build up a strong feeling for rhythm. To collaborate with others in the performance of music, to fit into the corporate tonal picture, to follow the indications of the conductor, to take the lead and one's self direct the group as the conductor,—these are musical experiences of the greatest value. The pupil who lacks them lacks some of the most fruitful and vital of all opportunities for rhythmic and musical development. It should be the purpose of our teaching to supply them in and through the class situation.

2. Many of the factors involved in what we commonly, but none too happily, call "ear training" can best be engendered in a group situation. Ear training aims at a fine and precise grasp of those tonal relationships which are the basis of all musical effects. The development of such a grasp is peculiarly susceptible to social facilitation. Moreover, it should not be attempted chiefly by means of formal drills, such as the recognition of intervals, or of chords, or the analysis of chords,

or musical dictation of the ordinary kind where made-to-order tunes are played to and written down by the learners. It should be very closely associated with the expressive use of music. That is, it should turn on leading the pupils to *notice* the tonal relationships of music which they are performing, creating, or listening to. Let us see how group experience can facilitate the acquisition of some of these "ear training" abilities.

(*a*) Group experience can be used with great profit in developing the feeling for tonality. By this I mean the relationships of the tonal system, the tendential, or, as Curwen calls them, the "mental" effects of tones. It will be admitted that this is of great importance in musical development. It is one of the chief skills of the musical mind. Often it is regarded as something very esoteric and advanced, something which is the peculiar property of the professional musician, and to be taught only at the conservatory level. But this is due to a thoroughly wrong-headed notion about music education. What usually happens is that music education, below the conservatory level, as carried on in most private studios, amounts simply to a superficial and imperfect mastering of the notes of various pieces without the least attention being given to tonality, or indeed to any other ear-training factors. Then the student is introduced suddenly to the study of tonal relationships and tendencies by means of formal drills. But this method is merely making an essentially simple thing difficult and remote. All that is necessary is for the pupil, whenever he is engaged in any musical project, to be brought to notice the tonal trends upon which the musical effects depend. To treat tonality as a sort of grammar is entirely wrong. What we want is to establish in the learner's mind a system of tonal expectations which grow more and more refined with increasing directed experience. There is nothing particularly hard about this. It can be done in private teaching and individual study, but the presence of a group is a great help because such learning is subject to a marked degree to social facilitations. The class situation favors many procedures which can naturally assist in creating this system of tonal expectations. We can have pupils think the music before singing or playing it. We can have them suggest alternative tonal trends to the one given in the music; then experiment with the effects produced. We can place our whole emphasis upon phrases as functional musical units. Sometimes, in listening lessons, we can stop in the midst of a tonal sequence and ask them where they think it ought to go; and we can discuss the various answers given by different individuals. The coöperative creation of music, in which phrases are suggested by individuals and criticized and amended by the group, is of great value in developing this particular musical-mental skill.

(*b*) Again, group situations can profitably be used for developing a proper feeling for pitch. We know that the actual physical sense of pitch cannot be improved by training. The fineness with which any person can discriminate between small differences of pitch depends upon the structure of the ear, and this no amount of practice, however well directed, can better. But the feeling for pitch which is characteristic of the musician most certainly can be acquired and improved, and it requires training, even in the case of those with a very good "natural ear." When children sing out of tune, the difficulty may lie in the production and control of the voice, but also it may be due to an imperfect mental attitude towards tonality and pitch. The musician's feeling for pitch is essentially an ability to refer any tone he hears or imagines to its proper place in the tonal system. It shows itself in a number of ways; in the ability to sing back a tone which one has heard (which of course depends very largely on having heard it properly and adequately); in the ability to recognize a tone as accurate or inaccurate, "in tune" or not in tune; in the ability to name an isolated tone which one hears; and in the ability to produce any given tone on demand. All these are simply aspects of one and the same thing, which we may call "pitch mindedness."[1] Notice in passing that we make no sharp distinction between relative and absolute pitch, and that our statements imply, what is certainly true, that the latter capacity can be acquired, though to a different degree by different people. Now the essential factor needed to generate "pitch mindedness" is so very simple that one almost hesitates to state it. All that is required is experience in actually listening to and "taking in" the pitch of musical tones. Surely, one would think, any person who undertakes to teach music at all would make much of this, even with young children. As a matter of fact, such is far from being the case. The average private piano lesson deals almost entirely with manipulation and hardly at all with the careful and yet simple direction of listening to tone and pitch. Teachers of violin and voice are compelled to do a little more, but they tend to emphasize the mechanics of playing and singing reasonably in tune rather than the mental and auditory controls which are the true fundamentals. This ex-

[1] OGDEN, R. M., *Hearing,* Harcourt, Brace and Company, ch. 13; WATT, H. J., *The Foundations of Music,* Cambridge University Press, 1919, particularly chs. 2 and 6.

plains why much elementary violin practice is so excruciating. We certainly can do much to direct a pupil to listen to pitch in a private situation. But here again, social facilitation is very helpful We can have our pupils think a tone very carefully before singing or playing it; or we can have them make a tone and then stop and think about it; or we can have them listen attentively to the pitch of the group singing; or we can invite them to criticize the pitch control in the group effects. The monotone whose auditory sensitivity is normal (which often happens) is the extreme case of a person with a faulty mental attitude towards pitch. His training offers a type case of what may be done for all. He greatly benefits from such group procedures. What he needs is precisely not a large dose of formal drill, but an effective and enjoyable direction of the attention towards the pitch factors of music.

(*c*) Very similar considerations apply to the development of a feeling for tone quality, which is also a musical-mental ability of high importance. This too depends upon directed listening. Group situations may be very fruitfully used to make a child "quality conscious." A teacher who hopes to do this, however, must himself have a feeling for tone quality in music. I know of supervisors whose one idea is that good quality depends upon producing a hushed vocal tone. Consequently, the effect upon their classes is that, whenever the attention of the children is called to a defect in tone quality in their singing, they begin to whisper musically.

3. Group teaching can be made the means of an exceedingly helpful approach to the problems of motor technique. The weakness of most attempts to develop technical facility is that they turn on the exclusive, or at least preponderant, use of more or less unenlightened drill. The pupil is not made aware

of the exact nature of the difficulty he is attacking, or the exact means to be adopted in overcoming it. Moreover, technical practice is set off as a special subdivision or compartment of music education, and it is not intimately and continuously linked in the learner's mind with its expressive use in significant musical projects. This, I firmly believe, is responsible for enormous and outrageous waste of time and effort. The learning process, treated as a mere routine rather than as an acquisition of power for direct use, is thoroughly compromised, and the amount of effort needed to achieve a given result is increased beyond reason or necessity.

Now private individual teaching may, indeed, set up enlightened technical practice. The pupil may be made intelligently aware of the nature of the difficulty he is seeking to overcome, and he may be led to perceive its connection with a significant, and to him desirable, growth of musical power. Yet the group situation can add something further. The factor of social facilitation may be capitalized very effectively indeed. For, with the class, it becomes possible to institute a *coöperative social attack upon technical problems*.

(*a*) One may establish a good motor style *as a class fashion*. In vocal classes it should be the fashion to adopt a posture which favors good vocal action, avoiding both an unnatural rigidity and an awkward and lazy slumping. In violin classes, it should be made the fashion to hold the instrument and the bow in such a way that good tone and effective action become possible. In piano classes a workable position at the instrument should be the fashion. Of course we must always avoid the besetting danger of making some one fixed posture a fetish. What we want is a posture which is functionally good—which will free the action and render good tone possible. In many ways this can be conveyed better as a social reaction to a social situation than by individual instructions. Social facilitation—doing something as others do it and because they do it—may here be a far more effective influence than a great deal of nagging. It may build good motor style into the texture of the pupil's responses more efficiently than a great many words.

(b) The class provides the possibility of the social and cooperative discussion of individual difficulties. This may be very valuable, particularly in instrumental work. When a pupil encounters a difficulty, the proper procedure may well be not for the teacher to indicate the solution and advise some outside practice. The group may be encouraged to discuss the problem and to suggest ways and means of meeting it. In this way all may learn from the difficulties of each. Above all, an enlightened attitude towards technical problems is engendered, and the pupil is led towards dealing with such problems by the agency of intelligent analysis rather than brute repetition.

I have already insisted that the acquisition of technique should never be regarded as the chief end of the music class. We can go further and say that one-to-one pupil-teacher coaching in class is a waste of the opportunities provided by a social situation. But the use of the class for coöperative, enlightened attack upon technical problems arising out of significant musical enterprises is altogether proper, so long as it is not made the central factor.

4. The class situation lends itself much better than the individual situation to developing musical projects as culturally and musically significant undertakings. This is a most important element in musical development. Where the tendency

of the private teacher giving lessons to individual pupils is merely to set pieces to be learned, the class teacher may present compositions as expressive opportunities with rich and far-reaching meanings. (*a*) The class provides a natural audience for the performance and creation of music. (*b*) It favors the proper introduction of a composition which is to be listened to, or performed, or created. That is, every musical project may be projected upon a developed cultural background and apprehended as expressing a certain mood, or the spirit of a certain age, or the experience of some person. (*c*) It makes possible the discussion of music which has been heard, or performed, or created. To share the views and feelings of others and to express to others one's own view and feelings are among the best means of developing definite views and specific ways of feeling.

THE SOCIAL PATTERNS OF THE MUSIC CLASS

When we have before us a group of children brought together for musical activity, we have a challenge to social leadership. The task of the teacher is to create and maintain a social pattern of activity. Much of the educative and human value of his teaching will depend upon the social patterns he selects and seeks to promote. A great many teachers completely fail to perceive the true inwardness of the class situation. To them a class is merely a class and teaching it a routine performance. However, this attitude is just the spirit which we ought to avoid. The whole effectiveness of the class in music education depends on flexible and constructive group leadership for musical ends. The class which comes before us is the raw material of social enterprise. Just as the art of the sculptor consists in shaping the stone into significant and expressive form, so the art of the teacher consists in molding the raw material before him into propitious and effective patterns. Therefore, let us see what social patterns will be desirable and what will not.

1. The music class can fall naturally into the social pattern of the audience. Perhaps this is the most obvious of all considerations, and possibly for that very reason it is very often ignored. Moreover, the class makes attainable an audience situation more ideal than any usually achieved in the concert hall. The class should be used to fulfill the constructive functions of the audience, because those functions are extremely important in music. Do not, therefore, limit it to serving as audience for the performance of phonograph records or radio selections. Performance by the teacher, or by some visiting artist or amateur, may be of great value. So may the performance by individual pupils, or by groups of pupils. Bear in mind that much of the beauty of a music class as an audience is that it renders possible much informality. The group can discuss together, and with the performer or performers, the music to which it has listened. Or it can ask for repetition of what has been enjoyed or of what has not been adequately understood. The inventive teacher will find a great many charming and valuable ways in which such a situation can be manipulated. Audience opportunities of such a type bless both those who give and those who take; they favor musical development in both performers and listeners; and they help to make music a truly educative force, full of rich human values.

2. It is equally evident that the class can fall into the social pattern of ensemble performance. This should be done, even with the piano class. We have already discussed the values of

such experience for musical development. To overlook them is exceedingly foolish.

3. The class may fall into the social pattern of the collaborating group. We see this when a creative project is undertaken, for the proper direction of this activity requires that everybody work together in elaborating the new composition. In the same way the class may work together in building up expressive interpretations of music they are learning to perform. It is far better to have the pupils suggest interpretative effects, rather than merely imposing them, even though some time is lost in arriving at a given point.

4. The class may, and should, fall into the social pattern of the physically active group. This takes place in all activities in the way of rhythmics. Such opportunities should be regularly provided. They should be linked with musical projects, and never made into the semblance of formal drills, carried on for their own sake.

5. The class may be divided into sub-groups for appropriate musical projects. For instance, they may split up into small groups, each of which undertakes to learn a quartet to present to the entire group. Or a number of them may be hived off to work up and compose a piece of music, first to be presented to, then to be learned by, the entire class.

6. The class may fall into the social pattern of the study group. This happens when we develop group concentration upon tonal trends, pitch values, tone quality, or technical problems.

7. The class may fall into the social pattern of a discussion group. This may happen after listening to a piece of music. To discuss the experience will tend strongly to add to its educative value. But we should not limit discussion to the listen-

ing project. Much the same thing can be done after they have learned a new song or returned to an old one. After they have worked out and composed a piece of music, and have heard its effect, talking it over together may yield fresh insights and lead the mind towards new things.

8. Lastly, let us mention some undesirable social patterns for the music class. (*a*) It will not be desirable to set up the social pattern of a number of isolated individuals, each to be coached by the teacher, and so immobile and unresponsive save to such coaching. This evidently means the very poorest possible capitalizing of a social opportunity. Indeed we have a situation which is social only in the very limited sense of everyone being together in the same room. (*b*) It will not be desirable to set up the social pattern of a group advancing in lockstep and having, as its ideal, the covering, all exactly abreast, of an educational, measured mile. For all purposes of musical development, and, indeed, for all the ends of a genuine education, this is little better than pernicious. (*c*) It will not be desirable to set up the social pattern of a competitive group. To emphasize the relative excellences of the pupils is to make prominent something which is of secondary importance, and which is yet so interesting and arresting that it can obscure all other considerations. If we seat the good singers in the back rows, let us do it for musical rather than for competitive purposes. We should not allow a front seat to be a place of humiliation and an implication of failure, nor a back seat to become something which is the goal of a frantic rivalry. By all means let us make a genuinely excellent performance on the part of any pupils an example and incentive to the rest. Moreover, this should be done in a positive and constructive spirit, as showing them what they may do and

enjoy, rather than as revealing what they have not done. (*d*) It is undesirable to set up the social pattern of a group dominated and directed by the teacher, rather than that of a socially interacting group. The function of the teacher is to lead, and to create conditions where a group will and intelligence may develop and may express itself without blunders and inhibitions. (*e*) We should not always maintain the same social pattern in all our music classes. We need not always maintain one social pattern throughout an entire music period. Indeed, much of the art of teaching consists in the kaleidoscopic shifting of emphasis and social design, according as the teacher perceives the needs and dynamic trends of the situation.

SOME GENERAL CONSIDERATIONS

Let us now gather together some of the general considerations arising from the discussions of this chapter.

1. The class offers a situation definitely superior to the studio for the elementary musical instruction of young children, both in the vocal and instrumental field. We have seen that it brings the acquisition of masteries and their expressive use into very close conjunction. This relationship is urgently needed by the little child. For him, musical enthusiasm and musical feeling are much more essential than a very early technical development. This is true even of the very talented child who is destined from the first for a professional career.

2. Class teaching should have a place in music education, even up to very advanced levels. Only when it is regarded as a substitute for individual instruction, doing poorly and cheaply those things which the studio can do better, does it

seem inappropriate. We should consider it as a complementary agency of essential value.

3. As we advance from elementary to higher levels, our class procedures should presuppose more and more in the way of individual preparation and individual practice. But always it is most important that the class be not used as a means of policing individual practice and of ascertaining whether assignments have been done. This constantly happens in education in other fields, but it is manifestly wrong in music. Our endeavor should be to make the projects of our music classes so appealing and to build up the sense of corporate responsibility for the joint effect to so high a pitch, that we inspire our pupils with a desire to work with and practise at music by themselves.

4. As we advance from elementary to higher levels, class work should be more and more supplemented with studio teaching. Just as the class is superior to the studio for some purposes, so for others the studio is better. When our pupil reaches the point where he urgently needs extensive, expert direction in the acquisition of masteries, then he needs the services of the studio teacher. But he is best brought to that point by participation in group musical projects of varied kinds, with the emphasis upon expressive use rather than acquisition. To what extent any school system is justified in setting up individual instruction in music, I shall not here discuss, for it will differ with many circumstances, but there is no doubt that our social teaching of music must gear into individual instruction, as the musical development of the pupil progresses.

5. Class teaching may help to break down the poisonous distinction between "applied" and "theoretical" music. This

distinction is largely an outcome of unenlightened studio teaching, with its concentration on manipulation and its obsession with merely learning "pieces." The very foundation of all group teaching is the possibility it offers for a wide variety of musical experiences and undertakings. On the one hand, this should make it possible to avoid the grievous error of teaching pieces on a purely manipulative plane, with no emphasis upon their tonal constitution or cultural significance. As we have seen, the class situation definitely favors the right sort of concentration upon the tonal and rhythmic elements of music. On the other hand, it avoids the equally grievous error of teaching a sort of abstract and dry musical grammar called theory, entirely divorced from effective musical experience or enterprises. The outcome of a well-planned program of music education should be a continuous, many-sided musical development, both mental and physical. Pupils so educated should be just the kind of people any conservatory in its senses ought to welcome.

6. All that I have said implies that class teaching is an educational device which should not be confined to musical instruction in the schools. The private teacher should be ambitious to develop class work, both for elementary and for more advanced pupils, not just to be abreast of the times, or to increase the numbers of his clients, but because of the genuine constructive values of such work. There is something here far more significant than a commercial opportunity. It is a great educational and musical opportunity. The private teacher who is content to work wholly in terms of individual studio lessons is certainly blind to his own best interests and to the full possibilities of his calling.

SUGGESTED SUPPLEMENTARY READINGS

ALLPORT, FLOYD, *Social Psychology,* Houghton Mifflin Company, 1924.

HOWES, F., *The Borderland of Music and Psychology,* Paul, Trench, Trubner and Company, 1926.

Twenty-fourth Yearbook of the National Society for the Study of Education, Pt. II, 1925, sections II and VI.

CHAPTER EIGHT

Music and the School

THE NATURE AND PURPOSE OF THE SCHOOL

It is the argument of this chapter that music to an extraordinary degree is compatible with the essential purposes of school education, properly understood. Music, properly organized and taught, affords a most excellent object lesson of just the kind of thing the school should do everywhere in order to educate. That education is not confined to the school is manifest as soon as we regard it as the sum total of those influences which adjust us to life, and which enable us to deal constructively with life problems. All experience, all social contacts, shape personality and mold our living. All of them are educative. Society itself has often been called the great school, and every one of its institutions in a genuine sense is an educational institution. The school is merely an institution set apart to do consciously and planfully what the rest do incidentally and without deliberate intent. And the music program should be a standing revelation of the meaning of school life, and of how the school may best set about its task of molding personality and shaping life.

John Dewey has given us a classic characterization of the school as a simplified, purified, and balanced environment. This statement has proved seminal for many discussions. The idea which it contains has been caught and expressed in many ways by many men. It represents the true doctrine as the purpose and nature of the school. Let us try to see what it means and how music fits into the picture of the school so understood.

1. First and foremost, Dewey's statement means that the school must be regarded as *an environment for living*. It must never be considered, or treated, merely as a place where one prepares for a life carried on outside its walls, either now or in the future. This at once involves a break, but an extremely fruitful one, with many of our traditional prepossessions. Ask most people how the school educates and they will be inclined at once to reply: By teaching lessons, of course. They think of its mission as the storing of the mind with knowledge and the endowment of the individual with skills, which somewhere and some time will turn out to be useful. But this is an error. The school molds personality and shapes life, not at all by setting up some form of preparation,—of no present significance but justified by a future usefulness—but by providing the conditions for better and more ideal living here and now than would be possible otherwise. Going to school should mean, for the child, the opportunity to do things which would not be open to him elsewhere,—the opportunity for a better way of life than he could otherwise achieve. Hence, the great aim of the whole institution must be to provide for the conditions of this better way of life. The very derived meaning of the word "school" signifies "leisure." Therefore, being a pupil should mean freedom from the pressing and encroaching cares of earning a living, opportunity for wide and fruitful contacts and appealing and enlightening activities, and a chance to broaden the horizons of the mind, to expand his interests, and to grow mentally.

A wise and humane educational administration seeks to provide for every pupil just such chances. It seeks to organize for him a full and significant life.

If we so conceive the educational meaning and mission of the school, we shall find the music program entirely and indeed strikingly compatible with our purposes, and we shall think of it as being just as serious and valid a part of our enterprise as anything else. This will not be the case if we regard the great purpose of the school as preparation for life by storing the mind with material to be used later, and if we take its characteristic mechanism to be lesson learning. One reason why so many educators treat the music program with less respect than arithmetic or foreign language study is precisely that they take this latter point of view. It leads them to think of music as pertaining to the extra-curriculum rather than the curriculum, as a sort of educational addendum to be tolerated and as not belonging within the sacred circle of serious school activities. It leads them to deal with it in this spirit whenever questions of allotment of credit and of time allowance arise. Children in the elementary school, let us say, sing a great many songs and listen to a great many compositions. Students in high school become members of the band or the orchestra. But is all this really serious business? Is it the kind of thing the schools are for? No lesson is being learned. One cannot argue, as an arithmetic teacher plausibly can, and a foreign language teacher less plausibly, that their minds are being stored with content some day to be turned to good account. We seem to be dealing with an entirely different and altogether less serious process. Hence, music is relegated to a place on a level with minor athletics, or the general social life of the place.

But, as I have said, if we think that the great business of
the school is to provide an environment for living, then our
attitude towards such activities as singing good songs under
competent direction, listening intelligently to fine music, and
playing in the high school orchestra will be entirely different.
These will be type cases of just the sort of activities which we
wish to organize into the texture of our institution. They are
obviously and undeniably elements in an attractive and effective way of life. This is their manifest nature, and as such we
will welcome them. Notice carefully that as yet I am not
raising the issue of the ultimate value of music as an element
in the curriculum. With this I shall deal in the following
chapter. My point here is that a properly conceived music
program is entirely compatible with the purposes of a school
considered as an environment for living, and that one reason
why educators relegate that program to a secondary position
is merely that they implicitly regard the school as a place for
preparation and lesson learning, and this quite apart from
any theory of curricular values which they may entertain.

2. But it is not enough to say that the school is essentially
a place where life is lived, and that an educative result is produced by the experiences which such a life affords. Dewey's
point is that the school must provide a certain kind or quality
of life and must choose certain types of experience to mediate
to the pupils. Society as a whole may be the great school, but
we cannot turn a child adrift in it and expect him to be
adequately educated. This might be possible in a very primitive, simple social order, but never in a civilized one. A
civilized social order is too complex and baffling and has
too many ends irrelevant to the conscious guidance of the
young. In such an order a special institution must be set up

for deliberate, planned education. It must never be isolated from the social order as a whole. It must reflect the major meanings of society. It must select those elements most suitable for the guidance of the young and must bring them to the child in such form that they can be assimilated. This again is exactly the purpose of the school.

The school must provide an environment for living which is *simplified*, for general social life is too complex to serve educative ends. The learner subjected to it is merely bewildered. Very urgently does he need guidance in the choice of interests and activities. The school must provide an environment for living which is *purified*, for a great many casual social contacts and experiences are detrimental and lead towards frustration. And the school must provide an environment for living which is *balanced*, so that the individual may have a reasonably complete round of contacts. It is evidently undesirable to specialize in one direction to such a degree that one misses important types of experience and fails to enter into important aspects of our common life.

This conception of the school as providing for a simplified, purified, and balanced way of life makes the claims of music still more plausible. At least it is clear that music may very properly be given a place of importance in such a way of life. It provides a type of emotional experience which is certainly of high significance, and which can hardly be supplied by any other available agency. It furnishes a powerful means for personal and mental growth and release. It offers many valuable moral situations. And it carries with it a wealth of cultural background. When we seek to plan the ideal life for the child, it is often extremely difficult to know what to include and what to reject. However, such reasons at least make it appear that the inclusion of music is anything but unreasonable. Evidently the music program will be thoroughly compatible with the basic aims of any school organized on such a principle.

MUSIC AND PRACTICAL SCHOOL REORGANIZATION

Many superintendents, principals, teachers, and working educational leaders entirely concur in the conception of the school as a purified, simplified, balanced environment for living. They are aware of the fallacy that education is primarily preparatory and that its characteristic mechanism is lesson learning. They desire to make the school a place of significant living, and they believe that its educative efficiency depends upon the quality of the life which it sets up and of the experience which it mediates to its pupils. The attempt to put this doctrine into practice, as a matter of fact, has been one of the chief motives for progressive school reform in modern times. All along the line, from the most elementary to the highest levels, we see endeavors to realize it. Such practical school reorganization in terms of a basic principle may be found in the kindergarten movement, in various changes which have been made in the grade schools, in the junior high school movement, in senior high school reforms, and in far-reaching alterations at the university level, as well as in the so-called "progressive school" movement itself.

But such changes always encounter very serious obstacles, particularly in the public school field. The public, who must furnish the ultimate support of any advance, are not clearly aware of the nature of the ideal aimed at, nor fully convinced of its validity. Without having thought the matter out explicitly, their natural prejudices are in favor of the school as a place for lesson learning, because this has been the nature of their own school experience. A great many teachers object in practice to the numerous changes which must be made in any fundamental transformation of the schools on more vital lines, even when they agree to the guiding principles of such a transformation as a matter of theory. They tend to grudge the necessary effort, and they are not always well equipped to readjust themselves to any great change in the conditions of their work. A matter of less consequence, though far from unimportant, is that, in spite of the ambitious building programs of the last ten or twelve years, our schools more or less lack the physical facilities for the most vital type of educative activities. We are certainly moving in the direction of a schooling organized in terms of life, but the movement is slow, and clogged by the prepossessions of the past. School people are not magicians. They cannot shatter the existing system to bits and then re-mold it nearer to the heart's desire. They cannot achieve the new at a single bound, however desirable it may seem. They must proceed step by step, carrying with them the body of their constituency.

All those who seek a practical reorganization of our schools along progressive lines may find in music and the music program an agency by which they may advance towards that for which they hope. This is so because music and the music program so perfectly harmonize with the nature and functions of the ideal school. In that program it is possible to realize just what is wanted everywhere, and this is so for three reasons, which I shall discuss in detail in the next three sections of the present chapter. (*a*) Music presents a picture of an ideal school activity. (*b*) The music program, properly handled, embodies and represents the principle on which the whole internal organization of the school should be governed. (*c*) The music program affords essential contacts between the school on the one hand and general society on the other, between school life and life in general,—a relationship which is recognized as one of the great needs of modern education.

Today a very special need exists for demonstrating the significance and appeal of school work organized along progressive lines. The schools are under heavy fire, and they are being denuded of many most valuable elements. The trend in many quarters is backwards,—towards the curriculum of the "three R's" and towards lesson learning as the predominant educational mechanism. There is no small degree of suspicion abroad, directed at progressive principles and practices, as needless, ill-founded, and extravagant. However, a scheme of education progressively organized is its own best defense. We can do far more and get much further by actually showing people how the thing will work out, and what it can mean to their children, than by all kinds of talk and propaganda. Hence, we should seek ways and means of actually showing what education organized in terms of life can be and what an influence it can exercise upon its pupils and constituents. We may not be able to set up such a school in its entirety, but school education as living at a high level can be revealed in all its essentials in the music program, which may be a microcosm of the ideal institution. That program can serve as a testimony to what a school may and should be, even at a time when many things are under challenge, or have been discontinued.

MUSIC AS AN IDEAL SCHOOL ACTIVITY

Music offers a type of activity ideally suited to the demands of the school situation. More than almost any other subject in the curriculum, it falls into just those patterns which are at once practicable and desirable in a progressively managed school.

1. Music calls for and supplies significant group activities. As I have pointed out in the preceding chapter, it cannot be taught adequately in the absence of such group experiences. In this respect it contrasts very sharply with many other subjects which do not naturally arrange themselves in group-activity patterns. In science, history, and mathematics, for instance, social projects are certainly possible, but they do not present themselves so inescapably, nor in such varied profusion, as in the case of music. Moreover, in this respect, our subject stands in contrast with those social activities within the school which have no very extensive educational significance, and which, accordingly, are regarded traditionally as belonging to the extra-curriculum.

2. Music calls for expressive activities; that is, it demands situations where it can actually be used, as well as learned. Such situations can very readily be provided within the school.

3. Music calls for, and renders possible, creative activities. This is true in a much more comprehensive sense than that involved merely in what I have called the creative musical project. It constantly provides situations in which the individual may feel himself as making his own personal, unique contribution to a group undertaking. As I say, this is by no means limited to the creative project itself. In performance,

the individual's consciousness of doing his own part in his own way, and yet of accommodating himself to social purposes, can be, and should be, very prominent. The same thing is true in the listening project, more particularly in the discussions turning on the æsthetic evaluation of the music heard, with which such a project may well close. Musical situations lend themselves very readily to this feeling of individual creative contribution, as opposed to mere conformity with class requirements, and the assimilation of assigned content planned for the class average.

4. Musical activities tend to create their own standards. This is sharply in contrast with most other subjects, where standards must be set by the teacher and imposed from without upon the pupil. A musical project is almost unique in the extent to which it lends itself to the setting of intrinsic rather than extrinsic standards. In such a project, and particularly a project along the lines either of performance or creation, one is constantly aware of actually making something. Good work becomes its own best witness. Bad work stands condemned by its own immediate effects. This is one great reason for the suitability of musical activities for school purposes.

5. Musical activities can be organized in a comprehensive program, pointed towards a sequential advance, which is yet based upon a psychology of mental growth, rather than upon an abstract classificatory logic. Through musical projects it is possible to secure a steady increase in sophistication and insight, and in capacity for controlled and complex response. This again renders musical activities admirably suited to school purposes and to the school situation which must provide for the needs of maturing individuals.

6. The music program can and should offer a scheme of

highly diversified and various activities. It should include listening, rhythmics, singing, instrumental music of various kinds, ensemble and solo experiences, creative music of various kinds, and so forth. Thus it is capable of accommodation to a great range of individual differences in aptitude, interest, and ultimate purpose. It can be many-sided to a degree very difficult with any other single subject. It can go a surprising distance in being all things to all men, without losing its own meaning and integrity.

Because music is capable of affording an activity program with these very valuable characteristics, it fits admirably into the scheme of the progressively managed school. It can furnish concrete testimony as to what a progressive educational process can mean. But all these values are destroyed when the music program is conceived in terms of lesson learning, rather than in terms of living and doing.

MUSIC AND THE INTERNAL ORGANIZATION OF THE SCHOOL

It has been pointed out many times that the great danger which has always beset the school, and which besets it today, is a divorce from life. This is a nemesis which always threatens any institution set apart to discharge a special purpose. It is one of the universal characteristics of all social evolution, and the price we pay for increasing complexity and efficiency. We find it in great business and financial houses, in highly organized professions like medicine and the law, and in the church. All such institutions tend to develop a special and limited point of view, and a set of traditions and procedures peculiar to themselves. In their specialized preoccupations, they easily forget the mission for which they live and the fulfillment of which gives them vitality. They build up walls between themselves and society. Within the confines of those walls they are tremendously busy, but their activities are apt, more and more, to lack genuine significance. It was said of a great, organized, religious movement which was set up in this country a few years ago that it developed a sort of movement within the movement,—a movement of filing systems, and accounting, and promotion, and routing which increasingly lost touch with surrounding social realities. Obviously the ultimate end of such a tendency is bound to be disaster. The business or financial house, the professional organization, the ecclesiastical group, no longer serves the public need. The harder it works, the worse it grows. At last there comes a collapse.

This is exactly the danger which continually confronts our educational institutions. They develop certain procedures, certain traditions, certain routines. Their personnel builds up an increasingly specialized and limited point of view. They exist more and more for their own sake, and less and less in the interest of a broad social service. At last the tension between the school and society reaches the breaking point. The gap becomes intolerably great, and we have a forced educational reform.

Everyone can recognize the signs and symptoms of this divorce of the schools from life. The contrast, in respect of quality and whole-heartedness of effort between what pupils do in school and outside it, is matter for common remark. Many a commencement orator implicitly acquiesces in, and accepts this most serious evil, when he informs the graduating class that up to this point they have been preparing, but are now about to begin to live.

For it is a very great and serious evil. If we admit that the

educative value of study is its human value, and that nothing is worth learning save for the sake of living, then to
cut the schools off from contact with society is to deprive
their work of its characteristic significance. They become places
where traditional lessons are learned, rather than arenas for
significant experience and for living at a high level. Their
procedures are aimed at teaching subject matter for its own
sake. They become afflicted with an increasing educational
impotence and come to represent a mere convention in society,
rather than a vital force.

How, then, may this fatal divorce of the school from life,
which is always threatening and must always be resisted, be
cured? Partly by setting up the right kind of internal organization. Partly by maintaining effective external relationships. In both cases the music program may point the way and
exemplify within its limits the true constructive solution.

The true constructive principle on which we must build
the internal organization and work of the school is already
familiar to those who have read these pages and who have
grasped the educational philosophy which they seek to present. The school must be organized, through and through, as
a place where life can be lived at a high level. Subject-matter
learning must be made part of living and must be apprehended by the pupil as contributing to life interests and life
needs. A great many admirable efforts are being made along
these lines today. For instance, we have the wide development of the project method. Much textbook reform, too, is
pointed towards this end. The modern textbook is no longer
a dry-as-dust compendium of facts, put together to be memorized and recited upon rather than read as a reasonable being
might be expected to desire to read. It tends to be an interest-

ing, more or less discursive account, with much literary quality and human appeal. And our music program, as I have insisted, can perfectly exemplify this leading principle of organizing the school as a place for worthy living. For here we have a whole segment of school work which can and should be set up as a life activity complete and self-fulfilling in itself. It would be difficult to point to any other segment of school work of which as much could be said.

Inasmuch as the idea has already been discussed in other connections, I do not wish to dwell upon it here, but it seems well worth while to contrast the educational pattern into which the music program naturally falls with those other patterns, only too familiar to all of us, which are characteristic of the school divorced from life. This should serve to teach us two lessons which cannot be too clearly understood and firmly grasped. First, we shall see that many of the procedures which we take to be the accepted conventions of education are really not educative at all; rather they are the conventions of a school-keeping which has become unduly preoccupied with its own internal tradition. Second, we shall see that a real job of education may mean doing certain things which may seem strange, and different from custom, and yet which are entirely sound.

1. The music program represents an educational pattern in terms other than those of book-swallowing. The major elements in the organization of the traditional school are based upon the notion that education must mean, and can only mean, "learning one's book." The course of study is planned as a statement of what books must be "covered." Textbooks are assigned, bit by bit, for the sake of piecemeal sequential cramming into the heads of the pupils. Examinations are

built to find out how well pupils retain what they have read, and the entire credit structure is constructed upon this foundation. Herein lies one of the tell-tale symptoms of a divorce from reality. Books, of course, are essential tools; and the ideal school envisages a wider and more diverse range of reading than is even considered in the conventional system. But when we make books ends in themselves, then the whole influence of our work is in the direction of limiting the processes of our pupils to learning and reciting upon their contents, rather than in the direction of guiding those processes towards a better adjustment to the demands and problems of life. Now the music program stands as a startling and effective witness to the fact that we may have in school, activities which are educative in the most valuable and serious sense, and yet which have nothing at all to do with memorizing the contents of a book. It amounts to a breach with a very firmly established and widely held educational convention, and it reminds us that much in the accepted pattern is educationally nonessential and even destructive.

2. Again, and closely following from the foregoing, the music program should represent an educational pattern in terms quite other than those of memorizing. The memory is one of the great fetishes of the pedagogic mind, and conventional school organization points straight towards the memory as the seat of education. Facts, formulæ, theories, scientific principles, rules, and so forth are laid out to be learned by heart, and an intricate mechanism is set up, first to get them so learned, and then to find out whether they have been retained for a standard length of time. The thing reaches its acme of absurdity when the proofs of geometrical theorems are memorized as though they were a kind of poem

which it would be well to be able to recite from time to time. However, the trail of the same doctrine is everywhere to be seen in school work. If mental reorganization and personal growth were really brought about by storing things in the mind, all would be well. We know it is not so. It is just another symptom of divorce from life. The schools then turn themselves into cloistered institutions, where children are shut away from vital contacts and activities and made to spend their time committing all sorts of material to memory —and then forgetting it again. So strongly entrenched is all this in the traditions of school-keeping that many otherwise intelligent persons never even question it. Now once again, the music program stands for a breach with a deadening convention. It is a program of activities which have high educative value, and yet which have nothing whatever to do with the storing up of facts and no essential relationship to the memory processes. Music reminds us that the true requirements of a vital education may mean an abandonment of a traditional way of doing things in school.

3. The music program represents an educational pattern in terms other than those of the setting of tasks. Again we have here a school tradition symptomatic of a divorce from reality. It is necessary to have an authoritative machinery for the setting and policing of tasks, largely because those tasks seem entirely unreal to the learner. In effect, the situation amounts to this: The child complains that he sees no point whatever in learning something we want him to learn. We tell him that we don't care in the least whether he sees the point or not; he must learn what we tell him to learn, simply because we say so. Yet we must remain sane in our criticism. We shall never get away from the need of requiring obedience

on the part of the child to a wisdom greater than his own. But there is all the difference in the world between imposing an essentially non-significant task by fiat and using the means of an urgent persuasion—which may also include imperatives—to get the child to learn something or to do something, the value of which will quickly and surely become evident to him. Yet it is surprising how many administrators and teachers will regard this fault as a virtue and assume that, unless tasks are set and policed, serious education is impossible. The whole witness of the music program is against this point of view. The essence of that program consists of significant experience and undertakings possessing the unmistakable hallmark of genuineness. And it shows us, and reminds us, that where such things are going on, there we have effective education which may be known by its fruits.

4. The music program represents an educational pattern in terms other than those of the passing of courses. Much of the unreality in the internal organized life of the school come from working everything over into water-tight subject-matter courses, which must be "passed" if one is to have the stamp of the educated man placed upon one. This stereotype has an exceedingly firm hold upon our minds. Yet it is generally admitted to be bad, even by those teachers who stick to it most rigorously and who yet advise their pupils not to work for marks, though, paradoxically, they continue to give them. Now music is thoroughly unsympathetic to this regimentation into subdivided courses. It calls for diverse experience, diverse activity. It tends to lead the mind across the conventional boundary fences of culture, rather than between them. Its whole essence consists of the effective living of music in all its varied aspects, and the program would still have its

full human and educative value, if not a mark were given, nor a single course organized.

The reader will notice that, in these points, we have summed up and stated the claims of music upon the school. The fact that it is antagonistic to conventional patterns and procedures should not lead anyone to suppose that it does not deserve serious consideration or a serious place. Indeed, that fact should have an exactly contrary meaning. The music program should be taken as pointing towards a new and better way of education. At this point two very practical concrete points are involved. (*a*) As regards time allowance, and placement upon the schedule, music should have the most generous treatment that can possibly be given. It should most certainly not be treated as a sort of appendix, to be shoved off into any odd corner we happen to be able to find. (*b*) It also deserves a generous credit allowance. The question of just how much credit to allow for music is essentially artificial and arbitrary. There is no principle which will give us a valid answer, because the credit system itself is invalid. All we can say is that the educative values of music are such that it deserves a thoroughly serious treatment and an ample recognition in terms of school credits.

MUSIC AND THE EXTERNAL RELATIONSHIPS OF THE SCHOOL

To overcome that divorce from life which is the besetting danger of all schools, we need, besides an effective internal organization, the institution of effective external relationships. We must seek to integrate the school, wherever possible, with general social and community undertakings. This helps to develop in the pupils a sense that what they learn in school is actually being used in life. School activities become regarded as aspects or parts of general social activities, and they become educative thereby. Here again the music program furnishes a concrete example of what may be done, for it is an admirable avenue of contact between the school and society.

There are so many examples of the fine work being done in this connection that space alone prohibits an extensive discussion. One of the most remarkable instances of school music functioning in after life is the Alumni Chorus of the Ithaca, New York, High School, under the direction of Miss Laura Bryant. The annual concert is an event in the community, and singers return year after year to take part in the programs. Many *a cappella* choirs, taking the lead from the Flint organization which was the first, have reached equally high standards of accomplishment. The choir from the Omaha High School, directed by Mrs. Carol Pitts, is notable for its artistic performances. The Madrigal Singers from the State Teachers College at Emporia, Kansas, approach the perfection of the English Singers themselves. These examples could be multiplied many times, but the principle remains the same,— that the music of the school becomes an integral part of the life of the community and provides an opportunity for singers in school and afterwards to continue their cultural interests.

1. The school music program should definitely operate to motivate musical activity and music study outside the school,— a relationship which is one of its most natural contacts with life in general. Contrast this with the type of life contact established through the medium of most other subjects. Too often it amounts to little more than assigning "home work," to be done under duress; whereas the music program offers the opportunity of carrying a school activity far beyond the

school, through inspiration and the arousal of inner purpose and desire.

2. The school music program may and should reach out and mold a large number of institutional contacts. This is a matter which I have already discussed and I return to mention it here simply for the sake of completeness. Perhaps the most notable of these institutional contacts is that with the home. A program of music in the public schools should mean a change in the cultural status and the richness of life of many of the community homes. Through influences such as these, pupils gain the sense that what they study in school is used elsewhere. In this way school study becomes truly educative.

3. The school does not fulfill its total function until it assumes a community leadership in culture. Here again is an enterprise in which the music program is well fitted to collaborate. In many an American small town or rural center, the school can become the community agency for music, putting on programs of its own talent, bringing in visiting attractions, calling attention to notable radio broadcasts, organizing visits to outstanding concerts given at a distance, and generally promoting an effective and enjoyable musical life. It may seem strange to think of this as in any sense a part of a program of teaching music in a school. It seems less strange if we think of our program as one of *living* music. If we can have music function in the community, many of our knottiest educational problems in school will solve themselves, because our work will be invested with that prestige which comes from a sense of its reality as part of human living.

In some respects the rural school offers a field where all

these ideas can be worked out and applied more directly than is often possible in the city school. Music can be set up as a highly diversified project activity. Choral organizations can be developed with much value and effect, and similar undertakings can be integrated with an orderly, well-planned sequence of musical instruction. When we take such measures and manage to render music vital in the rural school, it tends to carry over into the community life very naturally and simply. The projects can be correlated with the cycle of the seasons, and with special occasions, such as Hallowe'en, Christmas, and Thanksgiving. If one has a children's choir, what more natural than that they should sing from time to time at community gatherings? Under such conditions we have a flow of cultural interest both into and out of the school, which becomes what it ought to be, a radiating center for the promotion of a higher level of community life.[1]

SUGGESTED SUPPLEMENTARY READINGS

DEWEY, JOHN. *The School and Society,* University of Chicago Press, 1899.

DEWEY, JOHN. *Democracy and Education,* The Macmillan Company, 1916.

HUGHES, C. C. "Music Instruction in Junior and Senior High Schools in Forty Representative Cities," *School Review,* 1927, vol. 35, pp. 452-457.

HUGHES, C. L. "Secondary-School Music Instruction: Past and Present," *Education,* 1928, vol. 48, pp. 581-584.

[1] MCCONATHY, O.; MIESSNER, W. O.; BIRGE, E. B.; BRAY, M. E., *Music in Rural Education,* Silver, Burdett and Company, 1933. This book deserves to be read by all music teachers, whether specially engaged in rural school work or not. *Note:* The authors' description of what they call the "Project Plan" is not quite the same as what we have here called a program of musical projects.

HUGHES, C. L. "A Study of Credit Allowed for High School Music Instruction," *School and Society,* 1928, vol. 37, pp. 306-308.

McCONATHY, O. "Music Education," Chap. 9 of *Biennial Survey of Education in the United States,* U. S. Department of Interior, Bureau of Education, Bulletin, 1931, no. 20.

Yearbooks no. 5 and 6, Department of Superintendence, National Education Association, 1927, 1928, chs. 14 and 19 respectively.

CHAPTER NINE

Music and the Curriculum

THE PROBLEM OF THE CURRICULUM

The problem of the curriculum is the most important single issue with which educational discussions have to deal. It is a problem of the utmost urgency for music education. In general that problem takes the form of asking what studies should be taught in school. As applied to our own field, it takes the form of asking why music should be taught in the schools, and in order to answer it, we must bring to a focus the entire argument of this book.

In the past, the curriculum has simply been taken on trust. It has been assumed that pupils in school should study certain things, and no particular effort has been made to ascertain why. Thus the content of education has been determined largely by tradition, rather than by careful and critical analysis. Elementary education meant, very simply, learning "to read, write and 'figger,'" while secondary education dealt with Latin, Greek, and certain portions of mathematics. New subjects were introduced gradually, not in accordance with any general plan or well-considered theory, but largely under the pressure of specially interested groups who resorted to various forms of propaganda and pressure. This, for instance, was the case with the natural sciences, which came in during the latter half of the nineteenth century, and whose claims were very eloquently defended by Herbert Spencer and Thomas Henry Huxley. The same is more or less true of music. It has reached its present enormous, and indeed astonishing proportions in the schools, not in response to an intelligible educational philosophy which clearly demanded its introduction and extension, but as a result of extremely effective and plausible promotion.

This kind of curricular evolution has brought many evils in its train, under the effects of which we all labor today. (*a*) In the first place, we still find a large amount of non-functioning material retained in the curriculum. Counts, in his study of the senior high school program, has shown that many of the subjects are certainly not calculated to yield maximal values to the students.[1] While great advances have been made in revising the offerings of the elementary school, yet in many instances we find an unwarrantable emphasis upon formal English grammar and advanced arithmetic in spite of many demonstrations that they do not have their supposed effects. Many such things still remain with us, not because it has been shown that we need them, but because they have always been there. (*b*) In the second place, the curriculum becomes more and more crowded, because it is always easier to get something in than to throw something out. Every subject establishes a vested interest and enlists a group of supporters who will fight for its retention and extension. The result is that there are so many things to be done that nothing can be well achieved. A constant competition goes on among subjects for an ampler allowance of time, for inclusion in preferred categories like that established by the college en-

[1] Counts, G. S., *The Senior High School Curriculum*, The University of Chicago, 1926.

trance requirements, or for the status of a general curricular requirement. The outcome can only be an outrageous hodge-podge, rather than a clear, simple, effective, and intelligible scheme. (*c*) The newer subjects, whether more or less valuable than the old, are nearly always placed in a position of inferiority, and are not given freedom to work out their manifest destiny or to express their peculiar and individual genius. Music has suffered a great deal from this effect of our curricular evolution. In order to make itself regarded as "respectable" in the family of subjects, it has been unduly influenced towards assimilation with the great and dominant linguistic tradition. This is why so much has been made of note reading as the real source of its educative value, which is, quite clearly and undeniably, a belief in sheer myth. All in all, our curricular evolution has made it impossible to put first things first and to relegate everything to its proper place in a rational hierarchy of educational values.

Naturally, I am not prepared to say whether a time will ever come when a group of philosopher kings, endued with a supernal wisdom, will reveal to the world a new curriculum in all its symmetry and completeness, like a new decalog; and when we shall all fall down and cast our crowns at their feet, accepting their edicts with cries of hallelujah. I have a notion that educational propaganda will continue to be a considerable force for quite some time to come. Yet it is perfectly clear that the present situation is one which cannot be tolerated. What we must work towards is some kind of feasible scheme of relative educational values based on reason. In order to be retained in the curriculum, every subject must be able to demonstrate a utility in terms of life. We must be able to show that a part of the none too enormous span of time which the pupil has to spend in school will really be well invested in learning any such subject. We must not allow ourselves to be put off with vague excuses to the effect that it may, perhaps, train his mind. What we have a right to know is whether, and how, it will affect his living. There is no point at which our conception of all educative values as human values becomes a sharper weapon of critical analysis than when we use it as a criterion to separate what is worth while from what is not in the proposed content of the curriculum. Music, too, must be subjected to this winnowing process. If it cannot withstand such an analysis, this means that it has no proper place in the school curriculum, or certainly not a very considerable one. Hence, in the discussions which follow, I shall try to bring to bear the entire purport of this book in answer to the question: What reason is there for including music among the subjects taught in the public schools?

A Critical Evaluation of the Claims of Music for a Place in the Curriculum

I think the best way, perhaps, to get hold of the issues before us as definitely and sharply as possible will be to imagine ourselves confronted with a critic thoroughly hostile to the whole idea of including music in the school curriculum, or at least thoroughly skeptical of the value of doing so; a critic who regards the entire proposal for a music program in the schools as a waste of the taxpayers' money and the pupils' time. We will imagine further that our critic asks a number of questions which strike at the very roots of what we are trying to do, and urges against it the strongest objections which can be found. We shall see to what extent it is possible to develop convincing replies on the basis of the ideas which have been discussed in these pages.

1. Let us suppose our critic to begin his attack by saying: "I see no particularly good reason why music should be made a part of any serious plan of school education. It may be a nice enough accomplishment for those who happen to like it. So is stamp collecting, and needlework, and the study of Sanskrit. This is a free country, and I see no objection to anyone following any harmless pursuit in which he cares to engage. But why teach music in the schools?" This, of course, is the most fundamental question he can possibly raise. How shall we answer it?

(*a*) First of all, we shall point out, as a matter of historical and sociological fact, that music is a very important element in our common culture. It is a pursuit to which a considerable number of men of the highest genius, and multitudes of others less supremely endowed, have devoted their most serious efforts. From the earliest times it has played a notable and imposing part in the common life of western civilization. Now clearly this is a very strong argument for its inclusion, to some degree at any rate, in a school curriculum which undertakes to reflect our common cultural heritage. If it had the status of a mere hobby, like numismatics or philately, for example, then it would have no claim on a public school curriculum, however admirable we might think it, or however much we might respect its devotees. But this is not so. If we ask why men have devoted so much effort and genius to the development of music, and to expressing themselves in it, and, more particularly, why this has happened in connection with our own civilization—the civilization historically based upon Christianity—we may be unable to answer. At least this is a point which I shall not discuss in these pages. Moreover, if we should try to discuss it, all we would get would be a theory, and we want to answer our critic with facts. It is enough to point out that, undeniably, music has played, and still plays, a very great part in our common culture, and that it is the right of every child to be brought into touch with the significant elements of his cultural heritage.

(*b*) Second, we shall point out that most people derive much pleasure from musical experiences and activities. There is no need to argue that people also derive some intrinsic benefit, some intrinsic strengthening of mind and improvement of morals, from such experiences and activities. Enjoyment which does no harm is a recommendation in and of itself. Whenever a person learns something about music, it may be very plausibly argued that this opens up to him certain avenues for permanent enjoyment which clearly can make his whole life seem more worth living. Moreover it is also clear, and can hardly be denied even by the most cynical, that a person who has no æsthetic interests suffers a very great limitation. He is shut off from a whole vast range of human experience. Man does not live by bread alone, and a scheme of education which aims at nothing but enabling him to earn it cannot but be considered defective.

(*c*) Third, we shall point out that music, properly taught, can provide an admirable means for mental growth and personal development. If a person can play, or sing, or compose, it is clear that he has a valuable avenue of self-expression. Moreover, while it may seem paradoxical to say that, when we study music intelligently, we readily become aware of and interested in all sorts of things outside its range, this is perfectly true.

(*d*) Fourth, we shall point out that the great increase in leisure time imposes a responsibility which education must recognize, and which must affect the curriculum. Some part of every child's school activities may reasonably and profitably be invested in acquiring resources for recreation, and music is an admirable leisure time pursuit.

All this makes a strong *prima facie* case for some degree of curricular recognition for music.

2. But our critic is by no means satisfied. So far he has given us an easy problem. Now he raises a much more difficult one. "I admit," he says, "the force of your points, so far as they go, but I do not think they adequately establish the claims of music to a place, or at any rate to a very important place, in the school curriculum. I admit that music appears to be a very valuable factor in human life. But just how valuable? This is the crux of the matter. Human culture contains a great many valuable things; a great many things which it would be splendid to teach to children—if we had the time, but our time is very limited. Therefore, we must try to choose only those things which are *most* valuable, and you have not made out a clear case for music as being among them. Obviously some things are more essential than music. It is more essential for a person to be able to express himself adequately in speech and writing, and to be able to read the vernacular, and to have a mastery of numbers adequate for the needs of everyday life, than to be able to play, or sing, or compose, or to listen intelligently to fine compositions. To throw out reading, or oral speech, or writing, or elementary arithmetic and substitute music would be downright grotesque. I think the argument can be pressed further. Any school subject, properly taught, can become an agency for mental growth;

this is no special prerogative of music, although it does indicate that music has a value not always recognized. As for the importance of æsthetic experiences and interests, I freely admit the force of the point, but does this uniquely call for music? Why not derive such values, for instance, from the visual arts? As for the argument about recreation, surely there are all kinds of profitable ways of using leisure time besides listening to and engaging in music! Music may, indeed, be a valuable factor in a happy and well-lived life, but one can carry on such a life without it. Why then should we pick out music for an important place in the curriculum in preference to many other possible studies?"

Such questions are entirely legitimate. To what extent can we answer them?

(*a*) Anyone in his senses will admit that written and oral speech, reading, and elementary arithmetic are more essential than anything else, including music. They are the absolutely indispensable elements in our common culture, the elements which everyone must possess, even though he has nothing else. But three very striking changes have deeply affected the status of these subjects. First, they are now taught far more efficiently than heretofore, so that children master them with far less time and effort, and thus have more time for other matters. Second, certain portions of those subjects which used to consume a great deal of time are being deleted,—more particularly formal grammar and the more advanced parts of arithmetic. Third, children are staying much longer in school than used to be the case. So the competitive pressure of the "three R's" is not what it was. We are getting better results with less time, and we have more time at our disposal.

(*b*) Beyond the so-called "fundamental masteries," it is ex-

tremely difficult to indicate any subject, or any group of subjects, which stands out above all the rest as possessing definitely and indisputably superior values in terms of life use. It
is very true that various educational authorities have tried to
make out a case for certain subjects and groups of subjects as
possessing superior values of this kind, but whether they
have proved their point is certainly open to question. That
their contentions have been universally accepted by all reasonable and competent persons is simply untrue. There is good
reason to contend that we face a situation in which a certain
small group of studies has an absolutely paramount importance, so great that we must teach them if we are to teach
anything; and that, beyond this, there is a great mass of subject matter which exhibits but small degrees of difference in
educative value, and that even such small differences are open
to argument. Perhaps the most plausible claim for definitely
superior value in any subject beyond the fundamental masteries can be made on behalf of the social sciences; not the
social sciences as conventionally taught, but as an enlightening interpretation of our common life. These are often called
the "new humanities." We may, perhaps, not unreasonably
allow that, once the child has learned to express himself orally
and in writing, to read, and to do elementary arithmetic, these
"new humanities" should be the core of his curriculum. Beyond this, however, authoritative claims for outstanding preferential value become extremely nebulous. This, of course,
is a negative argument. It does not carry a great deal of com-
fort to those who wish to establish the place of music in the
curriculum, though it is better than nothing, but it does not
entirely exhaust the case, and does not bring us to the end
of our reply to the questions raised by our critic.

(*c*) Music opens avenues for emotional experience. I have already pointed out that this must be a guiding principle in our teaching of it. Here again the point becomes highly important. It indicates that when we have built our curriculum, beginning with the fundamental masteries and going on to organize a core of social science, the next subject to introduce will be music. To continue onwards, constructing our curriculum out of materials whose appeal is primarily intellectual will obviously throw our scheme of education seriously out of balance. Of course it is possible to make an excellent case for the life values of literature and science, and perhaps for those of language work. There is still plenty of room for all of them, or at least for the first two, especially as the greatest general values of science do not seem to demand a large amount of advanced work engaged in by everybody, and as the greatest general values of foreign language study can be achieved by an efficient two year program, leading to a reading mastery. We have not yet entered the region of cut-throat curricular competition. Music has this distinct and seemingly quite solid claim for priority.

The undertaking of provision for worthy emotional experiences in school life is one to be regarded with the utmost seriousness.[1] Emotional maladjustment is a major cause of unhappiness and ineffectiveness. Education should assuredly set up a constructive program to guard against it. A purely, or very predominantly, intellectualistic curriculum cannot provide our pupils with all that they need in coping with their present and future problems. We must seek to bring them

[1] FORMAN, H. J., *Our Movie-made Children*, The Macmillan Company, 1933.

something entirely different, and we may hope to do so by bringing to them the gift of music.

Moreover, the other arts, admirable and desirable though they may be, cannot be considered adequate substitutes. Our critic has asked why we should not substitute the visual arts for music. Here is part of the reply: There is ample and adequate psychological evidence that music is the most profoundly emotional of all the arts.[1] Distinguished æstheticians have said that "all the arts tend towards the condition of music." This is not to cast any aspersions, or to deny that drawing, painting, sculpture, and so forth may have claims of their own. If, however, we wish to bring to our pupils the opportunity for an emotional type of experience rarely to be found in school our natural and logical first choice will be music.

(*d*) Then again, music is a naturally social art which expresses itself most characteristically in social situations. The bearing of this notion upon our teaching I have already considered. Again we have a point relevant to our present discussion. It makes music extraordinarily amenable to the school situation and extraordinarily usable in all kinds of life relationships. When we teach a person music, we give him something which he can use in a very great many different ways. When we teach him to paint, or to draw, or to model, or to plan buildings, or to act, we give him something which he can use only in a few ways. This distinction is no slight consideration if we are building a curriculum whose values are determined by life use.

---

[1] DISERENS, CHARLES, *The Influence of Music on Behavior*, Princeton University Press, 1926.

(*e*) As to the point which our critic makes about music in recreation, this is perhaps the easiest of all to answer. Obviously one can use leisure time in many ways besides listening to or engaging in music. One can design a costume, or collect stamps, or do crossword puzzles, or play jackstraws. One may find such pursuits a source of happiness and strength. No one will want to deny this, but the point is that music is an extremely significant pursuit in the cultural sense; that it brings us into all kinds of new relationships, and awakens in us all kinds of new interests. No leisure time pursuit is, in this sense, more worth-while, and most of them are very much less so. Surely one need not construct an elaborate argument to show that musical activities have a potential cultural and general value far in excess of contract bridge or the reading of detective stories. May we not then legitimately construct a curriculum which, in effect, recommends music as an admirable and practicable leisure time pursuit?

(*f*) Lastly our critic has said that it is possible to live a good and effective life entirely without music. No doubt this is also true, but if we made up our curriculum on the principle of omitting everything without which such a life was impossible, we would have exceedingly little left. It has been managed by people who could not count and by illiterates. What we want to know is how best to enrich life; not to what extent we dare impoverish it without complete disaster.

Such, as I see it, are the arguments for the preferential place of music. Perhaps they are not conclusive, but they have very considerable force. I know of no reasons which decisively invalidate them.

3. Our critic now raises still another point. "Your proposal

is," he says, "to carry on a program of musical instruction which includes both listening, performance, and 'creation,' or composition. I question the value and appropriateness of the last two undertakings. For one thing, it is very difficult to learn to play or sing, and also to compose, in at all a satisfactory manner. A great many people have taken music lessons at some time in their lives, but few of them are amateur musicians sufficiently good for their efforts to be appreciated by others. For another thing, the strong tendency is for performance and composition to become more and more specialized and professionalized. This was initiated, perhaps, by the rise of the virtuoso, due primarily to the influence of Liszt and Paganini, and the development of mechanical music through the phonograph and the radio has hastened the change. It seems as though more and more people were listening to music, and fewer and fewer of them actually making it. Should we not, therefore, confine our music program chiefly, or perhaps entirely, to listening, or, as it is sometimes called, appreciation?"

(*a*) Our first comment, in reply, must deal with the claim that musical performance and composition are exceedingly difficult. There is no doubt that they have been *made* exceedingly difficult. The assumption has been that, in order to be able to begin to do anything worth while with any of the major instruments, it is necessary to go through years of patient and grinding study. The idea that anyone could even consider composing without an elaborate conservatory training has hardly crossed most peoples' minds. However, as I have argued elsewhere, many of the difficulties relating to musical performance are almost certainly fictitious. They are due quite largely to badly directed learning. Jaques-Dalcroze, as we have seen, reports the possibility of an increase amounting to from three to four hundred percent in the efficiency of instrumental instruction. There are a good many commercial music schools which claim to give one some working competence in a very short time. To be sure, we cannot regard the results as in any sense ideal, but, considering all such things, we are bound to believe that most instrumental instruction has been inexcusably round-about and wasteful. As to composition, we may be quite sure that a great deal of the difficulty attributed to this has been due to its being regarded as a sort of holy-of-holies, which one must not even dream of entering without long and laborious preparation. But we have reason to believe that one of the chief reasons why an ordinary person cannot rather readily learn to create fairly effective music is simply that he has been taught self-distrust and never given any incentive to try, nor shown how to set about it. Rimsky-Korsakoff composed some of his most distinguished orchestral works before he even knew what a six-four chord was or had even heard of a dominant seventh. Musical utterance is natural enough and is no more confined to the person with the endowment of the potentially great composer than English composition is confined to those destined to be Shakespeares.

I am not arguing in the least that great artistic achievement and fine perfection are possible without labor. To achieve such things is, indeed, supremely difficult. My contention is that our ordinary notions about the location of the difficulties in performance and composition are entirely wrong. Under competent direction, a pupil can quite quickly begin to have the experience of really "getting somewhere," and can put up socially acceptable results. How far beyond this he may go towards full artistic competence is quite another matter, but the difficulties connected with performance and composition are certainly not such that they make it hopeless for us to try to teach these things to most people.

(*b*) Apart from making performance and composition direct ends in our work, we may hope that, through performing and creating, better standards of appreciation and a capacity for more intelligent and enjoyable listening will be developed. Our critic may again challenge us. This, he may tell us, is a very familiar doctrine but a doubtful one. He insists that a great many people find great enjoyment in symphonic music, although they cannot carry a tune with the voice or play the simplest piece on any instrument. Moreover, he asks, and very pertinently, how the sort of bungling elementary performance too often heard can be expected to do anything towards refining musical taste or improving musical understanding. This last point strikes at the root of the issue. It all depends on how performance is taught. If the teacher concentrates everlastingly on notes and still more notes, and turns music lessons into reading drills, then there will be no beneficial effect produced in the way of improved appreciation. But this is exactly what should not be done, even for the sake of teaching performance economically and effectively. If, on the contrary, the child is led to concentrate on musical effects and musical expression from the very start, then the case is altogether different. We have an exact analogy in the visual arts. The ordinary drawing lesson, which is a copying of a conventional design, with a breathless and niggling care for detail, probably has no effect in the way of making a child better able to appreciate a great picture. But a drawing lesson which aims to have the child grasp, above everything, the total visual feeling and value, the mass and the line, of what he is trying to represent, most assuredly does have such an effect. In such a lesson the child, in his own small way, does the same *kind* of thing which the great artist does; the difference is not in essence but in developed technique. Such an experience teaches the child, more effectively than anything else can, what it actually means to look at things with the eye of the artist. In exactly the same way, lessons in musical performance and composition may bring to the child experiences which, though vastly different in degree, are yet the same in kind as those of the great creative tonal artist.

(*c*) As to the claim that performance is tending to become more and more specialized, while listening grows more and more universalized, we have a perfect right to ask for a bill of particulars and to challenge our critic to produce his statistics. This he will certainly not be able to do, for the point has never been subjected to any adequate statistical survey. There are some impressive figures which make it seem quite doubtful. Thus we have in this country in excess of 59,000 high school bands and orchestras, enrolling some 1,500,000 pupils. Furthermore, as Zanzig has pointed out in his book,[1] amateur music is most certainly on the increase in many places.

Even admitting that we were in the presence of such a tendency, what of it? Must education simply accommodate itself to every social trend which happens to appear, even though it may be a minor one? It is said that recently there has been a great increase in crime, but so far as I know this has never been used as an argument for setting up high school

[1] ZANZIG, AUGUSTUS D., *Music in American Life*, Oxford University Press, 1932.

courses in safe-blowing and forgery. What if we think this tendency unfortunate? Why not try to combat it? If it exists, it has been instituted by human means, and we may hope that human agencies may suffice to reverse it. Education must aim, not at what is, but at what it ought to be. This is a far-reaching curricular principle, and it has an application here.

4. Our critic still has a formidable thunderbolt up his sleeve. "It is manifest," he says, "that the American people desire to listen to a great deal of music, and they are willing to pay large sums of money for the privilege. Nevertheless, they seem very well satisfied with much music of an inferior variety. Music which is superficial, flashy, striking, and novel seems to give them as much, or even more, pleasure than great and serious compositions. To enjoy such music takes no particular education. If music exists for enjoyment and recreation, why is not experience of this kind just as valid as any other? Does not this undercut the whole proposal for setting up a program of music education in the schools?"

(*a*) In reply we must raise, first of all, a very fundamental point. What is education for? A familiar statement of its purpose is that it exists *to enable people to do better what they would do anyhow*. This applies most appositely to the present issue. We have, let us admit, a great range of musical activities which owe little or nothing to any kind of formal education. This condition, however, most certainly does not prove music education to be supererogatory. We have a great range of civic activities, and yet the average city politician or the average indifferent voter is certainly not much influenced by anything the schools have been doing. Is this, then, an argument for not teaching civics and social science? The truth is the precise contrary. It is an excellent argument for hastening to teach these subjects more effectively. Exactly the same thing holds with music. The very extent of musical interests and activities is a paramount argument for seeking to improve them by educational means.

"But," our critic insists, "of exactly what does such an improvement consist? How does the principle of helping people to do better what they will do anyhow apply to tuning in on the radio, to selecting victrola records, or to singing at a luncheon club? If people are already satisfied, why not let them alone?" Well, many a political grafter is perfectly satisfied, but few educators would think it ideal just to let him alone. To be even more specific, let us come down to cases. In effect, I have already answered the point in giving reasons why "good" music is preferable to "poor" music. Good music offers possibilities of experience and carries implications which are lacking in poor music. There are excellent reasons why people *ought* to prefer it, and why we do them a kindness when we teach them to prefer it. Moreover, they need to be taught and can be taught. As to the luncheon club, a group which can sing together really well can derive a thrill which cannot come from the most bacchanalian of barber-shop chording, as everyone who has been in the two situations knows beyond all doubting.

(*b*) It is said that a great many people prefer "poor" to "good" music. Is this really true? May not such a preference often be due to having the mental set that good music is "highbrow"? Do people maintain such a preference constantly and consistently? A very accomplished and sophisticated musician may sometimes get a great deal of fun out of a marimba solo, or from listening to a vaudeville performance on the ocarina, or even from the static whine of R. F. C. Theramin.[1] The point is that he gets more and richer enjoyment out of other things. Our ideal must not be a kind of kid-gloved musical snobbishness. On the contrary, our music program must aim at catholicity of taste, sympathy, and understanding. But to deny the validity of musical standards because a great many people get some kind of thrill out of artistically inferior music seems to me recreant to our whole philosophy of education in life.

To repeat, are we so sure about this alleged preference for "poor" or "superficial" music? A recent *Literary Digest* poll on radio preferences has shown an enormous majority vote in favor of symphonic music. It may be replied that those who took part in the poll were of superior intelligence and cultivation, and that their standards of taste were unusually high. Let it be so. If one says that they are "superior," and attaches any particular meaning to one's words, one surely implies that the standards they accept are also "superior," and that is, more desirable. From whose opinions shall we derive our standards, the upper tenth or the submerged tenth? May we not consider it reasonable to endeavor to improve alleged low standards of taste, than merely to capitulate to them?

FURTHER CONSIDERATIONS ARISING FROM THE FOREGOING ANALYSIS

What I have presented in the foregoing section is, so far as I can now see, the only effective line of reasoned defense which can be offered on behalf of the music program in the face of the criticisms that can be urged against it. Those

---

[1] Note: the name of the inventor of an instrument by which high frequency electrical waves can be translated into sound waves.

criticisms are serious and weighty. Music educators will be well advised to give them most careful heed. They are certain to be advanced; indeed, they are even now being advanced in influential quarters. If they should come to be generally accepted, it will be a dark day for school music. That they are not well founded and that music deserves a place of great importance in a curriculum which seeks to select not only things that are good but also the very best available materials, I firmly believe. I have also tried to explain why, but our music program requires a great deal more than a defense in words. Words must be translated into deeds. We must justify the claims we make for our subject by organizing it in such a manner that it will actually achieve the aims which alone make those claims valid. At this point I am particularly concerned to show that the defense I have suggested for the place of music in the curriculum, and the interpretation of that place which I have offered, has certain highly practical implications. It requires that we construct our music program on certain very definite lines.

1. Clearly, the great aim of our work must be to promote musical activities of various kinds. We want to induct our pupils into the amateur practice of music as vocalists, as instrumentalists, and as composers. We want to promote the higher, more intelligent, more discriminating, and more deeply enjoyable types of listening. Unless we do this, the entire structure of the defense collapses; our program lies at the mercy of its critics; and it stands condemned as educationally valueless. It seems strange to have to insist upon such a point. If these are not the aims of a program of music education, what else can it possibly be for? One would suppose this to be a consideration of the merest and most obvious com-

mon sense, and yet, unfortunately, we find it most urgently
necessary to insist upon it. For a great many music programs
in the schools manifestly have for their central aim the teaching of music reading. Their protagonists may talk a great deal
about other things, but their actions speak louder than their
words. This is what they do. One can only call it a most
astonishing and disastrous perversion. It seems to depend
upon a particularly stupid argument from analogy. To read
the vernacular, as everybody admits, is an extremely important ability. Therefore, the contention appears to be that reading music is similarly important. In reality there is no comparison at all. Reading, at best, is one of the secondary tool
skills of the musician, certainly for the amateur, probably for
the professional. It is a means, not an end; instrumental rather
than ultimate; secondary rather than primary. By no possibility can an intelligible argument be made to show that the
reading of the musical score is a necessary element in school
education or that it has any effective claim upon our crowded
and competitive curriculum. A music program which centers
upon reading cannot benefit by the defense elaborated in the
preceding section. As a matter of fact, those who insist that
reading is the main thing never embark upon any reasoned,
analytical defense. They merely insist stupidly that they are
in the right and shower sarcastic abuse upon those music educators who in their view are so fantastic and soft-minded as
actually to hold that the chief end of musical instruction
ought to be—music. When they find themselves in a corner,
they resort to the many-times-exploded disciplinary fallacy and
say that work on the notation develops quickness of perception and strength of concentration. Whether they expect any
enlightened student of education to be impressed by such

arguments does not appear. Slaves of one of the narrowest pedagogical routines ever devised, they are too uninstructed to be aware of the force, and the sinister implications, of the criticisms which are gathering against them. It would, as a matter of fact, be far more sensible to use school singing to teach the minutiæ of vocal technique than to use it to teach reading; for then at least we might expect some sort of musical result. If we insist on making reading the focus of our work, we are putting music out of court with all modern educators and depriving it of all valid claim to a significant place in the school curriculum.

2. The curriculum, envisaged as a whole in modern educational thought, falls into two great functional subdivisions, the general and the special. The general division of the curriculum has for its aim to provide those experiences and promote those activities which provide the foundation for a *common way of enlightened living*. It seeks to select those materials in which all must share if they are to be effective members of a civilized society. Notice that this is quite different from the older conception of a general or "cultural" education, which was supposed to be an education that had no particular application, and which consisted of language studies, pure mathematics, pure science, and so forth. That is to say, it was general in the sense of being made up of generalized or universalized studies; and it regarded the application of what the pupil learned as a minor and irrelevant consideration, and sometimes even seemed to take pride in being useless. Today general education, as we understand it, however, is so in the sense of seeking to promote a general or basic social adjustment, rather than an adjustment to specific interests and pursuits, vocational or otherwise. This segment of the

curriculum is the more important, simply because adjustment to common social living is the most important achievement for any human being. Far from being useless, it is exceedingly practical; and in its human practicality lies its importance. Many educational authorities hold that the pupil should be dealing chiefly in terms of this general curriculum, at least to the end of high school, and probably up to the end of sophomore year in college. Specifically this would mean that all pupils in school should be taking substantially the same studies up to that point.

The special studies in the curriculum, on the other hand, seek to serve special interests, needs, aptitudes, and life adjustments. Our best illustrations are drawn from the vocational and pre-vocational subjects, which are very important and valuable for some, but not for all. These are apt to seem more practical than the general studies because their applications are more obvious, immediate, and tangible. If our general curriculum is properly organized, however, this will be largely illusory. It is always a serious question how far a public school system ought to go in the direction of specialized education. Certainly it makes a great mistake if it sacrifices its program of general social adjustment for any kind of special or limited interests.

Now the trend of our whole argument in the preceding section was to the effect that music has its proper place in the general curriculum. I ventured to suggest a certain ranking of subjects in that curriculum, in terms of relative life values. I am well aware that this is a serious over-simplification, because we are not dealing with strictly commensurable values which can be placed in an ordered sequence of greater and less. Particularly obvious is this in the case of music,

which offers something unique; namely, an emotional type
of experience, and so cannot be compared with other subjects
precisely in just this way. I would not wish to press this suggested ranking very far or to insist upon it unduly, but it does
serve to clarify our thinking and to give it point. The most
essential elements in the general curriculum beyond much
question are the fundamental masteries,—oral and written
speech, reading, and elementary arithmetic. Without these a
common way of life at the civilized level becomes impossible.
Next in importance may come the social sciences, the "new
humanities," which constitute an enlightened interpretation of
that common civilized life, and next to these, on the argument I have presented, comes music. If we were so hard hit
by another business depression that we had to discontinue
a whole range of subjects, music would be the third last we
would drop. This, exactly, is the position here taken. Of
course I do not mean that the fundamental masteries, the
social sciences, and music would alone constitute a complete
or adequate general curriculum. I am talking about what
would have to be done in the way of orderly and sequential
educational retreat, if the unhappy necessity for it were forced
upon us, and if we were free to act upon a reasoned theory
of educational and human values.

When we propose to assign to music such a place in the
general curriculum, we say an exceedingly significant thing,
but its full significance may be obscured by the rather technical language I have used. What we mean is that the great
business of the music program is to promote a very widespread amateurism. We are saying that one of the best ways
in which the schools can go about the business of raising the
level of our common life is to seek to build up in everybody

a better and more intelligent type of listening, and abilities to perform either vocally or instrumentally or both, and abilities to compose music. I have put the matter thus bluntly and nakedly so that the reader may appreciate the formidable magnitude, as well as the precise nature, of the claims which are being advanced; and also so that he may see the seriousness of the responsibility which such claims imply.

Will our music program, then, have no relationship to professional training? Certainly it will. But its main, direct aim will never be to build up professional skills or professional habits of mind. Special interests must derive from general education. The program of general music education should be the seminary of professional careers. It can function in this respect in the following ways. (*a*) The child may discover an interest in music through the general program. He will, of course, not be apt to do so unless that program is built about musical projects, or if its main concentration is upon reading. (*b*) The child may reveal, both to others and to himself, his musical abilities through the general program. By far the most certain way to find out whether a child is likely to succeed notably with music is to have him engage in musical projects. Music tests may have their uses, but the idea that, by applying them in the first grade, or the sixth grade, or somewhere in high school, we can instantly discover talent of professional promise is most certainly false. (*c*) A program of general music education offers a far healthier start for a professional career than a specialization unduly early and narrow. It is better to postpone the attack upon the higher ranges of technique for the sake of breadth and balance. (*d*) How much specific pre-professional training should be offered in the public schools is always doubtful. In music it is especially so, because appropriate pre-professional study, either in performance or composition, is also study well suited to the needs of the interested amateur. On the whole, the school music program must be considered as aiming at amateurism, and as serving only as a starting point and an orientation for a professional career.

3. Another respect in which music properly taught exemplifies the principles of the curriculum which modern educational thought has envisaged lies in the fact that it offers striking opportunities for the integration of the pupil's learning. It is generally recognized that the subdivision of our work into rather narrow, mutually exclusive courses, is a most serious weakness. No subject learned in isolation can be properly learned. History, language, science, literature, art, mathematics must be fused together in the pupil's mind, if they are to yield their true educative effects and human values. On all sides attempts are being made to reorganize our school programs to bring this about. What has to be done is clear. Instead of building our curriculum out of subject-matter courses of the conventional kind, we must build it out of units of activity or "centers of interest." Music offers very excellent opportunities for so doing because, as I have already pointed out, it has a very rich cultural significance. When children come in contact with important music, whether in the way of listening or performance, all sorts of avenues are open for far-reaching and richly repaying exploration. A composition is a geographical, historical, and ethnological phenomenon, full of human meanings. It is the work of a certain personality, impinged upon by certain circumstances; or, in the case of folk music, the creation of a way of social living. When the pupil is made aware of such background factors, his feeling for the music itself is enhanced, and he learns many

things as he should learn them,—that is, informally, and in close connection with living, concrete experience. Moreover, a musical composition has important scientific aspects which can readily be capitalized. The point need not be labored, for once one's attention is drawn to it, many practical possibilities present themselves. Musical projects should be treated as educational nuclei, and should serve as opportunities for the correlation and integration of the learner's mental possessions.

4. In an effective music program we see the collapse of the distinction between curricular and extra-curricular pursuits as a significant functional classification. That distinction is essentially one of book-keeping rather than of values. The curriculum carries a credit rating; the extra-curriculum does not. It is highly artificial and arbitrary, and also highly destructive. So, on the one hand, we must guard our program against a regimented credit system and on the other against contempt as a mere extra or unessential; and we must build it upon its functional human values.

SUGGESTED SUPPLEMENTARY READINGS

BOBBITT, FRANKLIN, *The Curriculum,* Houghton Mifflin Company, 1918, ch. 6.

MURSELL, JAMES L., *Principles of Education,* W. W. Norton Company, 1934, ch. 17.

MURSELL, JAMES L., and GLENN, MABELLE, *The Psychology of School Music Teaching,* Silver, Burdett and Company, 1931, ch. 15.

O'SHEA, M. V. (ed.), *The Child: His Nature and His Needs,* The Children's Foundation, 1924, ch. 17.

Fourth Yearbook of the Department of Superintendence, National Education Association, 1926, ch. 11.

Twenty-sixth Yearbook of the National Society for the Study of Education, Pt. II, 1926, chs. 3, 6, 11.

CHAPTER TEN

Music and the Teacher

THE TEACHING CONTACT AND ITS CHARACTERISTICS

To carry on a program of music education in such a way that its possible human values may be achieved makes no small demands upon the teacher. Without effectiveness here, it cannot be done, and yet the enterprise is an inspiring one, for no other subject offers better opportunities for an ideal type of teaching contact. That contact is far from being exemplified as it should be when the chief thing done is to assign tasks and to hear lessons. Its essential characteristics are *participation, sincerity, and leadership*. Music education offers an admirable medium in which these characteristics may display themselves.

1. The ideal teaching contact requires a mutuality of participation as between teacher and pupil. It should not be considered by the teacher as a setting of something to be learned by the pupil. Rather it is the creation of a situation in which both pupil and teacher may share in a significant enterprise. Partnership, not domination and submission, is what is wanted. This explains why it sometimes happens that a teacher whose preparation is somewhat meager may teach extraordinarily well, if he is eager to learn. Henry Adams has told us of his conduct of a course at Harvard about which he

knew very little.[1] His class was a small one, and he worked side by side with his students, sharing their efforts, and building up a knowledge of the material along with them. I would not wish to recommend this as an example to be widely copied, but it shows us quite clearly that good teaching does not call for an autocrat who issues ukases and takes stern measures to see that they are obeyed. The teacher must not think it necessary to have the point of view of a dictator, external to, and far above, the tasks he imposes upon his inferiors, and tasks in which he himself is only mildly interested. Certainly this seems no good way to favor learning processes which involve a group spirit and a mutual enthusiasm.

Music offers admirable opportunities for this sort of mutual participation as between teacher and pupils. The teacher himself should not merely direct the musical undertakings through which his pupils learn. He should also share in those undertakings with real enthusiasm, even down to the humble level of kindergarten songs. In a listening project the teacher should be one of the listeners, entering into the experience with enjoyment and not just as a sort of presiding officer. In performance, whether or no he actually takes a part, his pupils should feel that he is really inside the undertaking. In creative work, also, the teacher must be more than an external director. The true status of the teacher is not that of an austere external spectator and judge. Any kind of musical project should be an artistic activity in which both teacher and pupils join, and in which they find new sources of mutual pleasure—new to the teacher as well as to the pupils.

[1] ADAMS, HENRY, *The Education of Henry Adams,* Houghton Mifflin Company, 1918.

Such an attitude brings into the whole situation a reality which is highly stimulating and has great educative value.

2. The second outstanding characteristic of the effective teaching contact is sincerity. By this I mean the earnest desire to convey something, to help the pupils possess something worth having and worth enjoying. Nothing can contribute more to the effectiveness of teaching than a real feeling for the power and value of the enterprise which is being launched. The sense of a message should under-run and affect everything which the teacher does. He needs to come to his pupils each day armed with the belief that the group has met together to attempt an undertaking worth carrying through, to gain a skill worth having, to recognize a beauty worth appreciating. Very often class teaching notably lacks this sense of urgency and importance. It is marked by a dry and listless formalism. Frequently it amounts to no more than "going through" a lesson or to "covering" part of a book. Always this is an offense against the spirit of an education whose values are human values. Perhaps this is more evident in the case of music than elsewhere. A musical undertaking is a great and genuine opportunity for enjoyment, accomplishment, and growth. The teacher needs to retain and keep fresh and living, in spite of the endless repetitions of the school year, this consciousness of coming to the pupils charged with a revelation and prepared to enlist them in a project which may be a means of living value to them all.

3. The third characteristic of the teaching contact is leadership. Very often we think of this before anything else, but we need to understand it in the perspective of participation and sincerity. For leadership must not mean domination. Every teacher needs constantly to remember that all educa-

tion, in the very nature of the case, must be self-education. Every pupil must do his own learning, and that learning depends upon his own personal will and not upon the will of another. This tends to be forgotten when the teacher deliberately plans his work in such a way as to dominate the situation. Lessons are set. Rewards and penalties are assigned. This is the familiar pattern. What ought to be done is to create and sustain situations where educative results become possible and desirable. For this result we must have a participant and coöperative leadership, not a dictatorial domination. Of course we must have effective leadership none the less. It is quite true that the situation, rather than the teacher, does the work of educating, but we cannot go to the lengths of some so-called progressive schools and allow things to proceed exactly as they will, without any firm and wise guidance. What happens then is that chaos supervenes, the situation falls in ruins, and the educative process is stultified. The great business of the teacher as a leader is to carry on and guard against interruption and perversion significant group situations in which significant projects become possible.

Notice that in this analysis I have said nothing about the teaching contact requiring specialized skill. No mechanical criteria have been set up. The teacher, for instance, has not been represented as a person who is, *par excellence,* a virtuoso in method. The suggestion is that one cannot casually visit a classroom and, by noticing the procedures in use, instantly decide on the quality of the instructional process going on. For the thing to remember always is that the teaching contact is a human relationship; that it must always be considered in human rather than mechanical terms; and that its essential values are human values. Socrates long ago put the essential thought of this section with a brilliant and enlightening simplicity. "How," he asked, "can I teach anyone but my friends?" The rest of this chapter will consider what sort of a person a teacher must be in order to be able to sustain what we regard as a desirable teaching relationship.

THE TEACHER AS EXPERT

In order to maintain anything like an ideal teaching contact, the teacher must be an expert. Studies have been made which have investigated the causes of success and failure among very large numbers of teachers. It is found that the most frequent reason, either for success or for failure, is *competence* or the lack of it, by which is chiefly meant mastery of the material to be taught and knowledge of how to handle it. Thus the prestige of the teacher depends upon his competence or expertness, and prestige is very necessary for the ideal teaching contact. Without it no effective and genuine leadership is possible. The teacher who lacks that solid status which comes from a thorough knowledge of his business must work by issuing orders backed by threats. His whole position with reference to his pupils is hollow and precarious, and his control of the teaching situation is apt constantly to be disrupted. Let us see in what particular directions the music teacher must be expert and must function as an expert in the teaching contact.

1. The teacher must function as an expert in the exceedingly important matter of determining standards of achievement. It is very true that, under ideal conditions, the teacher himself does not directly "set" the standards. These should arise from the music. That is, what is desirable is not for the teacher always to be saying "do this" or "do that," or

"that is not good enough." The pupils must be brought progressively to recognize what the music demands, and to be aware of the extent to which they are falling short of, or measuring up to, its requirements. At the same time, all this will most certainly not be achieved without very skillful guidance on the part of the teacher. Hence, the teacher must be expert enough musically to be able to reveal musical possibilities. This has little or nothing to do with the possession of high technical skill. It is equipment in the way of musical mindedness and musical feeling, and it is absolutely indispensable for effective teaching. No skill with methods, no understanding of children—nothing—can substitute for it. For instance, one expression of such expertness on the part of the teacher consists in being able to get good vocal tone from a group. We know that some leaders can do this and that others conspicuously fail. We usually find that the successful leader of group vocal projects has a refined and precise musicianship and is able to concentrate it upon the particular matter desired. In the same way, a teacher ought to be able to develop group singing which sounds musically intelligible because of the refinement of its phrasing; and this requires that he himself possess a keen feeling for tonal structure. Again, to be able to lead a group, or an individual, to sing or play with proper nuance and expression is possible only to the musicianly personality. Some teachers exhibit a positive genius for developing in their pupils the capacity for creative musical self-expression. They do so because they themselves have a musicianship at once so secure and so human that they can enter as guides and sympathetic friends into a joint musical enterprise, instead of merely dominating the situation and giving orders. The genuine musical expertness of the teacher reveals itself most convincingly in the refinement and the musical quality of the work of his pupils.

2. Again, the teacher must function as an expert in the matter of dealing with and overcoming difficulties, both mental and motor, which his pupils encounter. This, too, is an absolutely necessary element of that prestige on which the effectiveness of the teaching contact depends. Compare, for instance, the work of a band leader who merely waves a stick and issues a few orders and an occasional generalized scolding with that of a man who knows every instrument in the ensemble so well that he can not only indicate with precision each fine shade of effect he desires, but also show each player how to get it, and why he has failed to do so. In grade school singing, expertness of this kind is not quite so obviously necessary as when one is dealing with pupils of high school age in an instrumental ensemble, but the only reason for this difference is that with younger children the possibilities of bluff are more extensive and the difficulties, in making music, seemingly less dramatic and formidable. But everywhere this power to get at the heart of difficulties and clear them up is a mark of the real teacher. Nothing so powerfully recommends a teacher to his pupils than their own recognition of his ability to help them to "get results." When he succeeds in this respect,—and most of us have known music teachers who have so succeeded, his work constantly testifies for him, and his pupils have the most compelling of all reasons to accept his leadership and defer to his prestige.

Consequently every music teacher should constantly seek to improve himself in this kind of expertness. It is truly a musical expertness. It comes, not from a knowledge of method as such, but from an increasing insight into those situations in which music is made and an increasing appreciation of the problems which they involve. It is gained by careful observation of one's own learning processes and the learning processes of others, constant experimentation and discovery, the disposition to capitalize on all the musical experience which comes to one, and the pondering about the problems of executant musicianship in all its phases. Notice particularly that such expertness is peculiarly essential, if we are to have a progressively organized music program, for the very good reason that grading material by difficulty is less thoroughgoing than in a more mechanically planned scheme, so that we must often be able to help our pupils through taxing compositions. Notice, too, that such expertness cannot be achieved by trusting to any general rules of teaching procedure, for essentially it is a matter of individual diagnosis and direction. One must be secure and flexible enough in one's approach to be able to deal freshly with fresh problems as they arise.

3. In the third place, the music teacher must function as an expert in bringing wide musical knowledge and understanding to a focus on the teaching situation. No one can hope to capitalize the human and educative values of music along the lines suggested in these pages unless he has a broad and sure background of musical knowledge and insight. Some teachers are extremely limited in this regard. They are familiar with only a small amount of musical literature and know but little concerning the traditions, personalities, history, and social settings of the art. In this case they are condemned to rely exclusively on some organized series and to a slavish following of its sequences and instructions. Their teaching is not uniquely their own, and is not directed uniquely to the par-

ticular group of learners with whom they are dealing. Limitation in mental range on the part of the teacher reflects itself inevitably in rigidity and narrowness in his teaching contacts. If a teacher is deficient in this respect, obviously it is indispensably that the material used should open up the widest possible musical horizons. Such a situation offers an additional reason why the musical content should be drawn from many sources rather than the eclectic few.

THE TEACHER AS GROUP LEADER

We have seen, in general, that leadership is one of the most important functions of any teacher. Elsewhere in these pages we have also seen that musical instruction requires group situations, and the evident conclusion is that the effective music teacher must function as a group leader. This is a consideration of the utmost importance. In our preoccupation with the lesson as the characteristic educative pattern, however, it is too often overlooked.

1. His group leadership should express itself in the class. Indeed, if it fails here, it is apt to fail everywhere. We have seen that the class, in essence, is a social opportunity, and a most important element in all good class teaching is simply effective social leadership. The aim of the teacher becomes the creation of group patterns of behavior through which educative musical experience may become possible.

2. The leadership of the music teacher should express itself in the school. He should be one of the most important social nuclei of the school as a whole. This, of course, is not for the sake of popularity, but because music demands the widest social expression and the most varied social contacts, if its educative values are to be fully achieved. We are bound to be-

lieve that a program of music education which does not express itself in terms of social activity in the school has failed educationally in a most important respect.

3. The leadership of the music teacher should express itself in the community. Community service along cultural lines is becoming an increasingly important function of the music program. Hence, the director of school music increasingly takes on the aspect of a leader of community musical undertakings. Such a status makes his work in the class and the school far more vital than it could otherwise be, and the program justifies its existence, in part, in such an act of community cultural leadership.

The Preparation of the Music Teacher: General Considerations

The training of teachers is a point of the highest strategic importance in any educational system. It should exemplify with unique force and clarity the educational philosophy which we hope to build into our system. It should inculcate that philosophy not only by precept but also by example. A certain thread of doctrine should be apparent in all its subdivisions and special courses. The general outcome should be that our beginning teachers grow familiar with this central core of doctrine, not only as a form of words, but as a personal possession in which they strongly believe, which they eagerly desire to apply, and whose practical bearings they understand.

Unfortunately this has not been the case with the training of teachers in general or with the training of supervisors of music in particular. It has been evident that the preparation of the music teacher must consist of three major elements,—

general culture, music, and pedagogy, but the precise function of these three divisions has not been clearly understood. The result is that they have been taught for their own sake, and the student has been left to discover their applications for himself, if he can. This is precisely contrary to the educational principles which we have been developing, and according to which the value of any study lies in its applications to life and practice; the clear inference being that such applications should be evident, not only to those who plan the curriculum and teach the courses, but also to the student as he learns. A direct result of presenting the three major divisions of the preparation of the music teacher for their own sake is that they have been handled in water-tight compartments. They have been three different, relatively unrelated processes, rather than three necessary aspects of a single process. From this many faults have come. In many teacher training institutions there is a desperate competition for the student's time as between those responsible for the cultural studies, the musical studies, and the pedagogical studies. The programs have become so crowded as to impede any kind of effectiveness. The tendency has been towards producing a cluttered mentality, rather than an integrated vision of what it means to be a music teacher. The work has been organized to achieve minimal rather than maximal educational values. Remembering these things, can we wonder that our teachers often regard progressive ideas as visionary? They may have read about them or heard them proclaimed, but in their own proper persons, and as part of their training, they have felt the force of quite other conceptions. This certainly should be remedied. So let us see what the place and function of these three elements in the training of the teacher ought to be, if they are to conspire in generating an understanding of, and a belief in, a sound philosophy of music education.

THE PREPARATION OF THE MUSIC TEACHER: CULTURAL BACKGROUND

While it is generally recognized that a certain proportion of the preparation of the music teacher should be devoted to general culture, this often amounts to nothing more than a vague prejudice, accepted on faith. What courses of this kind he ought to take, how many of them, and why, are questions seldom answered, or, indeed, even approached very intelligently.

1. The essential reason why the preparation of the music teacher cannot dispense with general culture beyond the realm of music is that music must be regarded as a significant cultural phenomenon. It cannot be rightly apprehended or presented if it is taught as an isolated accomplishment,—as a trick, or a skill, or an ornament. Its educative value largely depends upon the ability of the teacher to project it upon a broad background. Hence, the more universal the mind of the music teacher, the better, potentially, will his teaching become. This will be so, even if he achieves such breadth of understanding and interest at some sacrifice of musical facility. As we shall see, he will not be called upon to make *essential* sacrifices in this direction. What he very likely will have to give up is the chance to go very far towards the status of the virtuoso.

2. Our principle then is that the cultural elements in the preparation of the music teacher are for the sake of giving him a broad basis for understanding, interpreting, and presenting music as a human achievement. They are not for

general "broadening," or the inculcation of knowledge merely for the sake of knowing things. This may seem to suggest that we should exercise extreme critical care in their selection; that we should spend much effort in getting an answer to the question as to what fields or aspects of culture will serve the prospective music teacher best. Now it is quite true that we should take all possible pains to organize his cultural studies in terms of function. They are a proper part of his professional preparation. In and of themselves they have no value. Their worth lies in the use to which he will put them, and yet we must not plan those studies too rigidly or definitely. The elective principle should certainly enter in. We must always remember that what may be relevant to music for one person may not have the highest relevance for another. Relevance is dynamic, not static. It depends upon will and interest rather than obvious logical relationships. Hence it is desirable to offer the student a considerable latitude of choice.

3. Immediately following from this we should remember that the mode of contact which the mind of the student makes with the cultural materials is also of great importance, as well as the choice of those materials. For instance, I know of one teacher training institution in which students preparing to work in music are virtually required to take a highly factual course in European history during freshman or sophomore year. So far as I can see, the educational advantages are practically zero. The work is in no way contributory to their major interests or to their adjustment to life problems and needs, even if it obviously could have been made so. From this we may generalize to the effect that the cultural courses for prospective music teachers should not be built on the ordinary

academic pattern, which makes them essentially preparatory
to more advanced studies in the same field. What the student
needs in his contacts with science, or history, or literature, or
foreign language, or economics is not a chance to store up
knowledge, or to lay a foundation for further work in the
same subjects, but rather the arousal and broadening of his
interests. Such courses should be directly planned to stimulate
in him a tendency to think and to grow, and to develop an
awareness of the content with which they deal and of its relationships to music. They should be introductory courses, not
in the sense of constituting beginnings for advanced courses,
but in the sense of awakening appetite and interest. They
should be of the type of the orientation courses now being
developed at many of our leading universities.

4. In an ideal situation—which of course we can only approximate—these general cultural studies will be very intimately integrated with the student's musical interests and
development. In any case we should approximate to this as
closely as we can. Two reasons make this manifestly wise.
(*a*) We are dealing with students whose vocational choice has
already been made, and musical interest should be treated as
the integrating center of his education, simply because it is
the integrating center of his life. This is far from implying
what is often called a "narrow vocationalism," which I take
to mean a training wholly devoted to the specialized tricks of
the trade. In our present connection such an educational emphasis would be a travesty, for there is nothing narrow about
the vocation of teaching music. But it does mean a *functional
vocationalism,* which is a building of all education about effective life interests and tendencies. (*b*) Quite apart from any
vocational leading, a strong and definite musical interest is

an admirable integrating force in education. Very often, in teacher training, the student's musical interest is simply ignored, although his teachers know perfectly well that it exists. This intentional blindness is downright perversity and comes from the worship of blueprints instead of the respect for human values. Such an interest is a legitimate, valuable, and powerful force. Why treat it as though it did not exist? History, literature, science, mathematics, sociology, language,— all may be made more real and educative when thus brought into touch with a fundamental and altogether legitimate interest.

5. When we are confronted with the question as to how much cultural study we should require of the prospective music teacher, we must answer quite frankly that no reply can be given in terms of credit hours. Such requirements are ordinarily stated in the most mechanical, externalistic manner possible. Here, of course, is one of the major defects in our whole scheme of educational administration,—one which great efforts are being made now to rectify. When state boards of education or national bodies like the Music Supervisors National Conference make recommendations as to the right amount of culture for the prospective music supervisor, it is quite apparent that they are only guessing when they use the credit-hour yardstick. Such recommendations come from the pulling and hauling of committee debates and compromises, rather than from the logical application of basic principles, for basic principles yield no such precise, arithmetical recommendations. All we can say is that the student should have a chance to grow mentally and to develop a general background through his cultural contacts. Incidentally, we should bear in mind that much more is involved than

planning for a certain number of credit hours. The sane and constructive budgeting of the student's time is the heart of the issue, because an excessive crowding of the schedules can go far to wreck all educational values. It is far better to do a few things well than many badly. We must organize for our student time for growth and time for thought, or his cultural studies become a mere farce.

The Preparation of the Music Teacher: Musical Training

Trained musical power is absolutely essential for the music teacher. Without it he cannot function as an expert musical leader. Lacking a full measure of it his teaching is sure to be limited. He cannot help, inspire, and direct as he should. He must rely unduly upon fixed rules-of-thumb from which he dare not depart. The more free and creative teaching is to be, the more it demands an expert grasp of the material to be taught, for the teacher must be free to shape up musical situations in any way that may be needed. He must be able to extemporize. Even very elementary teaching requires musical quality for its proper discharge. To lead young children to sing with good tone quality, to help them to achieve intelligible musical utterance through phrasing and nuance, to guide a creative project, to carry on work in rhythmics with spirit and spontaneity,—all these things call for a musically-minded person.

Musicianship means a number of different things, and what we must have is a musicianship expert in the right way and sufficiently understanding and humane to apply to educational situations. The training offered by the average conservatory is none too well suited to develop this. There is an altogether undue worship of the virtuoso, who is held up before the students as the ideal musical type. The work in "theoretical music" is unduly severed from the work in "applied music." It is made a study of the dry grammar of harmony and counterpoint, and has no functional contact with either musical or educational activities. Content courses, such as that in the history of music, are treated as mere addenda; they are often exceedingly factual, and do not serve to interpret the musical processes and enlarge the musical understanding. There is a gulf fixed between the study of music and the study of education, thereby involving disastrous results on both sides. Our great criticism of much conservatory training of this kind is its narrowness of aim and emphasis. The products of such an environment often become good teachers, not at all by applying and developing what they have been taught in school, but by progressively recognizing its faults and limitations. What then do we want in the way of musical training for the prospective teacher?

Above all we want a musicianship which shall be of the mind and the heart rather than of the fingers and the larynx.

1. It is entirely legitimate to require that the prospective teacher shall be able to perform in several musical mediums, vocal and instrumental. This ability should be considered as something more than a useful accomplishment, though it is that also. For a person who knows what it means to make music with more than one medium, knows and understands music better and feels it more adequately than he who can perform in one only. Hence our chief emphasis should always be upon fineness of musical discrimination, clarity of musical utterance, and effectiveness of motor style, rather than upon highly developed brilliancy. We shall not despise such brilliancy if a student shows it, but it will never be our chief

end. Often we have the requirement that students preparing to teach must be able to play the piano up to a certain level of difficulty. This is extremely artificial and mechanical, however, and is not a legitimate and direct way of setting our standards. The important thing always is the musical quality of the performance, and competent instructors at the conservatory level can determine this very well, if they are brought to concentrate on it as the root of the matter. Does the student's performance show capacity to recognize the demands of tone quality, phrasing, harmonic sequence, rhythmic structure, expressive nuance, and so forth? These should be our crucial questions. Does he play and sing like a musician?

2. The student preparing to teach needs a mastery of the tonal structure and relationships of music which actually functions in his musical activities. Expression, phrasing, the use of the sustaining pedal, and so on, and indeed every detail of performance, properly depend upon insight into the tonal structure. Of course the ability to compose music of one's own depends on exactly the same thing. It can be given without teaching rules or grammar, as has clearly been shown by the work of Schenker, and its applications here and abroad. Mere grammatical harmony is an almost total loss, musically and educationally.

3. Our third requirement will be that the student have a wide knowledge of musical literature. No one is fully fitted to teach music unless he is familiar with the great masterpieces and knows the work of the great composers. This may be gained both by listening and performance. The student should be given organized opportunities for running through great compositions on the piano as a part of his musical education.

4. Lastly, we shall desire our student to have effective and

directed ensemble experience. This should include work both in the vocal and the instrumental fields, and he should have opportunities to act as director from time to time. We regard this as important, not so much for its own sake, as for the musical-mental values which it can engender.

THE PREPARATION OF THE MUSIC TEACHER: WORK IN EDUCATION

There are two outstanding criticisms of the work in the field of education commonly offered to prospective teachers of music. The first is its extraordinary narrowness. Very often the chief emphasis seems to be upon classroom method, and not infrequently only one method seems to be taught. This is represented as the unique and, consequently, narrow way of salvation,—a claim which is altogether preposterous. Occasionally one encounters people who react violently against the whole subject of method by saying that no knowledge of methods is necessary at all and that the only thing needful is competency with music. Neither is this proposition defensible. Clearly what we need is a creative and flexible grasp of method,—a comprehension of it in the light of broad principles.

The second criticism is that many courses in education which the prospective music teacher is required to take are organized to a flagrant degree on the cold storage principle. This is often true, for instance, of the courses in educational psychology, and principles of education. Such courses are practical, so to speak, in theory; that is, they contain all sorts of useful stuff, but they are not organized in such a way as to make it really effective and usable. On the contrary, they are organized in such a way that the student is supposed to learn the material, to store it up in his mind for several years, and then to find out how to apply it. Obviously this lack of effective practicality is most serious. It is a specific case of our general error of teaching knowledge for its own sake. Such work fails to enable the student to understand the educative process either in himself or others. It is no proper part of a program whose central aim must be the shaping of action through enlightenment.

What we want is an approach through a broad psychological and philosophical interpretation of education, focussed more and more specifically on the classroom and teaching situations with which the student will have to do. The "why" rather than the "how" of method must receive our chief emphasis.

In connection with this view you will notice two things. (*a*) First, consider the place of practice teaching in the scheme. In the literal sense there is no such thing as practice teaching. There can be no rehearsing of situations to be dealt with or learning of tricks by repetition. Practice teaching of this kind can only be practice in applying some rule-of-thumb method. The real purpose should be to give the student contact with concrete situations in which the general principles and theories he is learning become realized and through which he appreciates their meanings. (*b*) Second, note that the study of education so conceived will throw light upon musical experiences and development. It will seek to interpret musicianship as a phenomenon of the human mind and of the social order. It will deal with the way in which the mind apprehends music and with what music does to the individual who apprehends it. Between the study of the educational problems involved in music and the study of music itself there should be a true and close affinity. The thought is as old as Plato that to know properly how to convey anything to another is to appreciate and understand it better one's self.

SUGGESTED SUPPLEMENTARY READINGS

MURSELL, JAMES L., *Principles of Education*, W. W. Norton Company, 1934, ch. 21.

ZANZIG, A. P., *Music in American Life*, Oxford University Press, 1932, ch. 14.

CHAPTER ELEVEN

Music and Interest

THE PLACE OF INTEREST IN MUSIC EDUCATION

No subject can exemplify the proper treatment of interest more perfectly than music. In this, as in so many other respects, our music program constitutes a potential object lesson of what can and should be done. It reveals to us in a concrete situation the errors, both theoretical and practical, which beset us in dealing with interest, and also the ways by which those errors may be avoided.

Purely as a matter of theory, this problem of interest is fascinating, for in considering it we come face to face with some of the most striking dilemmas of educational thought. Moreover, it is a problem of the highest moment for the working teacher. Yet it is not, in general, very clearly understood, although an intelligible and enlightening interpretation can readily be had. Nor does the proper line of constructive action with regard to interest seem apparent to most people engaged in school work, although it can be quite definitely laid down.

Should school work be interesting? If so, why? How may we set about to make it interesting? Ought we to do so? What methods of promoting interest should be avoided? To what extent and in what respect should our planning of school activities be determined with reference to interest? What are the chief barriers to its proper development? These are some of the questions which we must ask and which it is the task of this chapter to answer. They are questions concerning which every teacher and every school administrator may well desire more light. Nowhere shall we find a more illuminating illustration of the proper principles in dealing with interest than that afforded by the undertaking of teaching music to children.

In order to clarify our thinking about the true place of interest in education in general and music education in particular, I propose to advance four propositions which, I think, embody the essence of the doctrine we must accept.

1. Interest is absolutely essential to the educative process. It is not a sort of bonus, or extra. It is not something without which we can manage quite nicely, even though we welcome its presence. We must secure it on pain of failure. This is imperative. *The pupil who is not interested is not being educated.*

This proposition can be almost painfully evident when we confront certain kinds of practical situations. For instance, we set up music as a requirement in the seventh grade, in junior high school, but we often find a certain proportion, and perhaps quite a considerable proportion, of the pupils who are either quite indifferent to it or even actively hostile. Immediately this lets us in for a peck of disciplinary and administrative troubles which are bad in themselves. Such troubles, however, are only symptoms and results of a much deeper and more serious defect, because these children are not getting any educative or human value out of their required music. Is it possible to believe the contrary? Music is to them a distasteful experience, to be resisted rather than accepted, and the moment the coercive pressure of the school requirement is relaxed, they escape from it with relief. Surely any dispassionate observer would immediately say that this spells educational failure. Negative rather than positive attitudes are being acquired. The art means nothing in their lives but boredom.

Interest is thus essential,—for the obvious reason that education is not merely learning. Always it is learning in a certain context and for a certain purpose. It is not an affair of forming habits, but of forming habits which one is disposed to use. Repetition, in and of itself, has no educative effect whatsoever. Everything depends upon the inner, spiritual quality and purpose of the repetitions. "Exposure" to any subject is no more than opportunity, whereas educative process turns on using that opportunity. John Dewey has defined interest as the "identification of one's self with an object." That is to say, one is interested when one identifies one's inner self and one's inner purpose with an undertaking. Without this no educative effect is possible at all.

2. The second proposition contrasts with and almost seems to contradict the first in a manner positively dramatic. *The content of education cannot be determined by interest.* Many people accept the claim that interest is essential in education, and then leap to the conclusion that we ought to find out what things are interesting to the child and teach him those and only those. But this is a capital fallacy. If we try to apply it, we arrive at quite preposterous results. The reason why a child *must* learn to read and to multiply is not at all that these things are more interesting than anything else in the world. The reason is that without them he cannot possibly become an effective member of a civilized society. They are necessary elements in an adequate scheme of educational content, not

because they are interesting but because they are important. Moreover, interest may attach to anything and everything. There is no human pursuit, no matter how remote, or trivial, or useless, which is necessarily and essentially dull. A person may become absolutely fascinated with working at chess problems, but this is no argument for including courses in chess in the school curriculum. You will notice in the argument I presented on behalf of an important curricular place for music that I said nothing about its possessing a unique intrinsic interest. This would have been quite an impossible line of defense, simply because many other studies can have an intrinsic interest just as great. It is true that we cannot be educated without being interested, but it is also true that we can be interested without being to an important degree educated, because we are interested in the wrong things. Interest may mean no more than the merest whim, and in that case it is an educational will-o'-the-wisp.

3. At first sight we seem to be involved in a contradiction. Interest is necessary, but it cannot determine the content of education. The contradiction, however, is apparent rather than real. We determine the content of education by its importance. We build our curriculum out of materials which seem to us so necessary, so worth while that everyone should learn them. But who recognizes the importance of our educational content? Naturally the people who make the curriculum must do so. It is desirable for the people who do the teaching to recognize it. But surely the pupil also should be led to understand, to feel, to believe in the value of the things we provide for him to master. If a study is really worth while at all, it should be made to appear so to the learner. This is the true secret of educational interest. If we can reveal the life sig-

nificance of a study, interest is likely to take care of itself. Suppose we require a pupil to study something which has no immediate life significance. He may not put it quite so clearly, but he is very apt to come to us with the question: "What is the use of my learning all this?" No question is more fatal to interest. A doubt as to the ultimate value of doing something or mastering something cannot but disintegrate the working morale on which the educative process essentially depends. When we are dealing with subject matter divorced from life, interest becomes an insoluble problem. This is exactly the reason why so many teachers entirely fail to deal with interest, and why they attempt to camouflage their failure by saying that it does not matter. Under these conditions, everything in education becomes an insoluble problem, in as much as no one can get blood out of a stone. *Our constructive principle is to base interest upon manifest importance.*

4. *The arousal and promotion of interest on such a basis requires a conscious, organized, and coherent program.* We cannot possibly leave this objective to the tender mercies of mere chance. In order to see clearly what planning for interest means, let us return to our seventh grade situation where a considerable number of pupils are not interested in their required music. What principles should guide us in trying to overcome the trouble? What can we do about it?

(*a*) In the first place, it will not help much merely to tell the pupils that music is extremely interesting, that it occupies an important place in life, and that they ought to like it. This reminds us of the famous jingle in *Alice in Wonderland:*

> Speak roughly to your little boy,
> And beat him if he sneezes;

For he can thoroughly enjoy
The pepper, if he pleases.

True enough, music is interesting, and it does occupy an important place in human life. Even so, we must convince our pupils of this, not by our words but by the way we organize their musical opportunities. It is not the slightest use to tell our class that listening, performing, and creating music are delightful occupations when we have set up our class patterns and our teaching procedures in such a way as to make them boresome.

(*b*) In the second place, we should remember that the source of the difficulty may not lie in the immediate teaching situation. For instance, our groups may be so very large that effective and diversified musical projects become almost impossible. Or again, our groups may be ill-selected or ill-organized in some way. I know of one case where a music class of well over fifty pupils was made up entirely of pupils of both very high level and very low mentality, with none of medium ability included. Then the administrative officials were surprised to find a lack of interest evinced by many of the children, and were inclined to blame the teacher, when it is evident that the root of the trouble was the management of the schedule. One can always create impossible obstacles for even the finest teacher, if one's total program is badly adjusted.

(*c*) In the third place, one must take into account what has gone before. What kind of musical experience did these pupils have in the first six grades? Was their work pointed towards really effective and satisfying musical living in the seventh grade? If not, then it is evident that we are impoverishing our seventh grade undertakings by factors over which the teacher of that grade has no control.

(*d*) In the fourth place, we must obviously examine the seventh grade procedures themselves, for perhaps we shall find there our real difficulties.

The analysis which I have brought to bear on this specific problem is of universal application. Organizing for interest in education means far more than giving the class teacher some practical hints. The individual teacher alone cannot do it. What we must have is a setting up of our whole subject from the kindergarten to the twelfth grade in such a way that the pupils are always led to respond to it as having life significance. We must think of our enterprise as an enterprise in selling. We must understand that there are many obstacles, both administrative and pedagogical, which, if permitted to exist, may wreck that enterprise.

Organizing the Music Program for Interest

It follows from the argument just presented that our entire music program must be organized from the kindergarten onwards to create, sustain, guide, and develop the pupil's interest in music. In other words, we must have a determination of the program which is dynamic, and which aims at a will to learn and a will to be musical, rather than one which depends upon the logic of the subject itself. To some minds this may seem extremely radical, yet it is the conclusion towards which all our contentions point. The great, the indispensable necessity is to have music seem to the learner serious, significant, and worth while. We wish to reveal music to him as playing a part and having a value in his life, and our plans must concentrate upon "selling" it to him on its merits. I shall not spend many words in explaining the characteristics of the music program as so conceived, for they are already familiar to the reader. The only novelty here involved is the focussing of many of our findings up to this point upon the well-known problem of interest.

The general principle to be observed is that our music program must turn upon genuine musical projects. Nothing else will serve. It gives us at once the appeal of an immediate and obvious return. All experience attests the great dynamic possibilities of such projects. *A cappella* groups from junior and senior high schools of Kansas City, invited to sing each semester in various churches, have so "sold" the idea of big chorus choirs that there is hardly a church in the city that hasn't developed its own chorus choir.

Many an instrumental director finds that his pupils are willing, nay eager, to practise and rehearse after school hours, or during vacations, for the sake of being able to take a more effective part in joint performances. These, to be sure, are outstanding cases, but they show us where we must turn in organizing our music program for interest. We must set it up as a program of varied musical projects.

Musical projects also must be planned along dynamic lines if they are to give us this momentum. Their power is potential rather than inevitable. Hence we must ask: What are the great and characteristic sources of interest and motive in a musical project?

(*a*) First of all, a musical project makes possible for the pupil a genuine and authentic sense of achievement. There is a definite undertaking before him,—a composition to be performed adequately or a piece of music to be composed.

He has a limited and specific objective. All that he learns ties in to a result which he can grasp and appreciate. This is one of the chief motive forces in all teaching. It is sharply in contrast with a situation where all we have is a series of lessons that never transfer into actual practice or the attainment of some palpable goal. It makes everything real and, to that extent, appealing. (*b*) Then the musical project constitutes an opportunity for self-expression,—for making one's own contribution. This should be definitely fostered. Music properly handled offers splendid and almost unique opportunities for pupil initiative under guidance, all the way from making comments on a piece of music which one has heard, or deciding upon the proper nuance in performance, to the creation of original melodies. (*c*) The musical project offers opportunities for social action in a great many directions, as we have seen. This too should be definitely cultivated. (*d*) Lastly, the dynamic appeal of a musical project depends upon the beauty of the music itself.[1]

Our musical projects must be set up with these aims and values constantly in mind. We should understand that anything, whether in our classroom procedures or in the general administration of the schools, which makes it hard to do this is antagonistic to proper interest. It threatens our work as an educational sales-program, because that work depends precisely upon its being possible to arrange for a diversity of musical undertakings, organized through and through in terms of the dynamics of the mind.

[1] MURSELL, JAMES L., and GLENN, MABELLE, *The Psychology of School Music Teaching,* Silver, Burdett and Company, 1931, pp. 93-96.

INTEREST AND "SUGAR COATING"

The term "sugar coating" is a designation for certain ways of working for interest in education. Usually it is employed in a somewhat contemptuous manner. Those who regard interest as unessential so refer to all attempts to arouse and direct it, and they tend to designate all teaching which concerns itself with dynamic factors as "soft pedagogy." Surely there are some methods of endeavoring to build up interest to which the term cannot appropriately apply. Furthermore, some people explicitly believe in "sugar coating." They pertinently ask what is wrong with it and quite rightly refuse to be deflected by mere sarcasm from what they consider proper. What then is the truth of the matter? Should we allow ourselves to use "sugar coating" or not? How does the conception fit in with the doctrine of interest which we have propounded? Here we have a question which is very important and also highly practical.

1. First of all, it will be well for us to try to understand exactly what we mean by "sugar coating" in education. I take it to indicate the attempt to arouse interest by means which are essentially irrelevant to the learning or undertaking in hand. A great many ingenious devices have been developed for such purposes. For instance, we may assign animal names to each of the notes, perhaps calling C a duck, and G a swan, and so on. Or we may work out a game for finding *do* from the key signature. Or we may introduce a highly competitive form of motivation by dint of our seating arrangements. Or we may institute conditions under which certain pupils are given the privilege of being designated to teach others. All of these devices, and many others besides, come under our defini-

tion. All of them may be, and very often are, irrelevant to the musical undertaking itself.

2. Second, it is clear that "sugar coating" is a matter which can exist in varying degrees. The extent to which any given device is irrelevant to the actual musical project may differ. Invariably the important thing is the way in which a device is used in practice, rather than its character on paper. The use of animal names for the notes is clearly an irrelevancy. So also is a game for finding *do*. Yet it is possible to arrange and use them in such a way that they really do favor musical learning. In the same manner, seating arrangements in which the best singers are placed at the back of the room may be made for the sake of a good group tone, rather than for competitive purposes, and in this case they are legitimate enough, for we then have an essentially musical, rather than an essentially competitive situation. This, again, would hold for the competitive tests for ranking at the National High School Orchestra Camp, which, on our principle, are not to be classed as irrelevant or extraneous devices because there is no deflection of the mind from musical achievement. By such analyses we win a further insight into the true nature of our processes. Our criteria in education must never be mechanical. The device itself is not the determining factor. Used in one way it may be definitely "sugar coating," but not so when used in another. Everything depends upon its effect on the mental processes of the pupil and upon its directive influence on his attention.

3. Perhaps the most obvious weakness of all kinds of "sugar coating" is that its effect is transient and its use quite limited. The most typical and patent case of "sugar coating" would be to tell a child that if he learns to sing or play a piece well we

will give him a dime. While this might be quite effective in the studio situation, it is not practical in school work for the very good reason that we don't have enough dimes. In much the same way, a well-devised game or a clever but irrelevant visual device may serve us not too badly on occasion. It is clear, however, that we cannot use such procedures regularly. If we try to, we shall turn all our teaching into a sort of continuous vaudeville. Even though no other objections could be found, this alone would make it manifest that "sugar coating" and the use of irrelevant devices cannot solve for us the problem of interest.

4. Furthermore, other objections emphatically do exist. One of them is that it is bound to be dangerous to base our educative processes upon anything other than the thing to be learned. Interest must depend ultimately upon the learner's own perception that what we want him to do is worth doing. It must consist in his identification of himself with the undertaking in hand. It cannot satisfactorily be engendered by tricking the pupil into swallowing our dose by the employment of adventitious inducements.

Here we find a part of the real weight and force of criticisms of all schemes for arousing interest by means of "sugar coating." The most trivial and useless activities can be made interesting if we engineer them into the right dynamic setting. What could be more futile than flipping counters with one's index finger? Yet it is attractive enough when made part of the game of crokinole. Is there really anything very fascinating in kicking and carrying a large inflated leather ball, or hitting a small hard one? Yet football and golf seem to please and interest considerable numbers of people. One might take these as perfect examples of highly successful "sugar coating." They show us very clearly and beautifully just why we do not want it in education. "Sugar coating" frees us from the necessity of building up our program on the foundation of significant, appealing activity and experience. Its essential purpose is to make anything just as pleasing and interesting as everything else, irrespective of its value and importance. This means that it frees us from the need of really educating.

All this applies with great force to music education, for it is noteworthy that most attention is paid to the use of irrelevant devices in those systems which are most mechanistic and didactic. Suppose we wish to teach the musical score. We cannot sell this to the child on its merits because those merits are too doubtful, too limited, and too remote. Hence we invent all sorts of clever subterfuges. All kinds of sugar must be used to get the child to swallow the dose. If, on the other hand, we have provided for significant and appealing activities, then extraneous and irrelevant motivational devices will be far less in demand. Musical projects do not need to be introduced with all kinds of irrelevant vaudeville camouflage. Their tendency is to sell themselves. All we have to do is to help the good work along, and see to it that nothing interferes. So it is that the use of "sugar coating" tends to warp our program away from valid educational issues and outcomes and to make us tolerate the trivial and the relatively worthless.

5. Another great danger in the use of "sugar coating" is that it leads us to quite wrong conceptions of the nature and place of interest in education. One often hears enthusiastic teachers commend some scheme of procedure by saying that "the children just love it." So far as this goes, it is clear gain, but it does not go nearly far enough. What is it that they love?

Ought they to love it? It is our painful duty to insist upon these questions.

Whenever interest is absent, we may be perfectly sure that things are going wrong. Whenever interest is present, we cannot by any means be perfectly sure that they are going right. Everything depends upon the object towards which that interest is directed and the outcomes achieved through its agency. All too readily can a teacher completely deceive himself. He finds cause for self-congratulation in the fact that the children seem to like what he wants them to do. But what if the things he wants them to do are not the most important, the most worth-while that could be chosen? Then their interest and liking is based upon foundations of sand. What they enjoy may be the chance for competition, or for playing a game, or for looking at pretty pictures or seeing someone write on the board, or for even the teacher's own pleasing personality. What they ought to be enjoying is the musical undertaking itself. Here, undoubtedly, is one criticism which applies to creative music in the sense of making toy instruments. It also applies to much work with inferior musical media, such as harmonica band activities and the like. The fact that children are interested in such things is far from being proof that we ought to continue them. Perhaps we should; but again, perhaps not. For we should desire children not merely to be interested in something or other, but to be interested in what is valuable, because they are being brought to perceive and feel its value.

6. Coming down to a specific and practical issue, we must always use irrelevant devices and "sugar coating" with great care and discretion. Perhaps such things cannot and should not be wholly abandoned. Nevertheless, they provide most

admirable opportunities for self-deception on the part of the teacher. Our question always is whether the children are doing worth-while things and learning worth-while things, and we cannot be too rigorous with ourselves in insisting upon it. To use clever irrelevant devices now and then may help, just as it may help to offer a child a dime if he will learn something, but the essence of our work must be the organization of musical projects which will seem to the child significant and appealing, and which need no bolstering up by an extraneous scaffolding.

7. One solid element of truth in the idea of "sugar coating" is the great importance of positive attitudes in any educational situation. Learning should indeed be made a pleasure, not a task. The engagement of the will is wholly essential for genuine education, but to secure this, we do not need "sugar coating," though the proponents of irrelevant devices have grasped a most important truth.

INTEREST AND EFFORT IN MUSIC EDUCATION

As I have already intimated, there are many people who regard interest as unessential and insist that educative effects depend simply upon hard work. In such views there is an important element of truth. Very little progress is possible without intense and directed effort. This is most certainly true in the case of music which is a supremely difficult art. Moreover, a certain grievous misinterpretation of the doctrine of educational interest is all too common. This is made by those who suppose that the business of a good teacher is to remove all difficulties and to make everything easy so that the pupil can learn without trying. Here we have an influential interpretation of progressive educational principles, but it is an entirely false one. We must never ignore the need for hard work. We cannot have any education worth the name without effort, in music or anywhere else.

At the same time to insist upon effort as somehow distinct from or inconsistent with interest is to fall into a fallacy. Between the two there is no incompatibility whatsoever. Only when we regard interest as mere whim, or unregulated liking, can we set it off from hard and educative effort. Whenever we do so, we run counter to the whole meaning and value of interest in the educative process.

1. Hard work, as such, is not educative at all. Merely to exert one's self, merely to force one's self to do something one does not wish to do, has no intrinsic value and guarantees no return. Long ago Goethe exploded this doctrine in the field of morals. In reply to those who would identify virtuous action with unpleasant and unwilling action, he pointed out that we willingly love our friends and hence, on such an hypothesis, loving our friends could not be counted a virtue. The same absurdity exists in connection with learning. (*a*) In the first place it has been demonstrated many times that one may work hard, in the sense of going over and over an unpleasant and unappetizing task, and get absolutely nothing out of it. A pupil drudges despairingly over an assignment in mathematics or history, and a week later he has lost even the little which for the moment he may have acquired. Old-fashioned instrumental practice is an almost perfect instance of a routine which went very much against the grain, and so was very hard to endure, and yielded a minimum of educative result and human value. (*b*) The worship of difficulty for its own sake is one of the most perverse of all educational fallacies. The business of a teacher is certainly not to remove

all the hard parts of a subject, but it most assuredly is to facilitate, in part at least, their mastery to the utmost possible degree. There is certainly no need to do anything to "make" music difficult. Under the most skilled direction it will still call for all the effort our pupil can muster. (*c*) Almost always we find that the claims of mere hard work as possessing some unique, intrinsic educative effect and potency are supported by an appeal to formal discipline. It is said that working hard at something has the same effect upon the mind that calisthenics have upon the body, but this, as we have seen, is an exploded conception. It is practically a very dangerous way of thinking because it reduces all subjects to the level of so much intellectual gymnastics and treats their content as indifferent.

2. Only self-initiated hard work is educative. What is necessary is for the learner to set out on his own motion to master this or that. He must adopt a purpose as his own. He must identify himself with a task. This is precisely our definition of interest. Restated it is this: *Only hard work coming from interest can be truly educative.* The contention has many far-reaching implications.

First of all, it warns us—and teachers need such a warning—that we cannot effectively make another person work hard. All we can do is to make him unhappily go through the motions. We can force a child to practise his scales for an hour each day, but we cannot force him to practise them with the kind of directed, self-critical, analytic attention upon which rapid and assured progress depends. Mere pressure is very little good. Teachers often disbelieve this and admire the martinet who sets heavy assignments and ruthlessly checks up on their fulfillment. Yet the effectiveness of such attempts

is more than doubtful. The interested pupils learn a great
deal, but they would do so anyhow. Under such a régime
the proportion of interested pupils is quite likely to be reduced
to a minimum. Mere pressure is more or less useless. The
human mind is so very ingenious that it will escape our exac-
tions and defeat our plans. The pupil simply works to please
us and to get round our requirements, and, by and large, he
has no insuperable difficulty in succeeding.

While we cannot make another person work, this is very
far indeed from meaning that we cannot incite and guide his
effort. We incite his effort precisely by interesting him in what
we want him to do. Instead of telling him that he must learn
such and such an assignment, or suffer sundry penalties, we
present to him an appealing and significant undertaking. We
still, of course, exert some pressure. We do not wholly abandon the imperative mood in dealing with him, but the pressure is directed entirely toward getting him into a project
which, once entered upon, will provide its own momentum.
Once this has taken place, effort is still further promoted by
revealing to him the standards demanded by his enterprise,
up to which he must measure if he is to achieve any reasonable self-satisfaction. We support him in his endeavors by
showing him how to tackle and overcome difficulties which
might readily turn into impossibilities without our guidance.
All this is the task of the teacher as contrasted with the task-
master.

3. If we organize music education properly for interest, we
also organize it properly for effort. This is so for two reasons.
First, the mere degree or intensity of effort which may be
called forth by a musical project is often far greater than
anything a teacher would dare to impose. It is no uncommon

experience to find that children who have the right kind of instruction will practise with a fervor, an intensity, and a persistence that is positively alarming. Here we have a particular instance of a very general educational principle. Some commentators have said, paradoxically yet not without seriousness, that it is really a very good thing for schools to have a number of inferior teachers on their faculties; for, if every teacher in a school were a first-rate exponent of progressive ideas, the pupils would be over-stimulated into a series of nervous break-downs. The second reason why interest and effort belong together in music education is that the real difficulties in music, as I have said before, are terminal rather than initial. It is not so hard under expert direction to gain some sort of facility with the voice or an instrument and to learn to write music of a sort. What is always exceedingly hard is to rise to the heights of artistic perfection. No driving from behind will ever take anyone there. To reach those heights demands courage, self-sacrifice, and loving toil. Musical beginnings are not difficult, though often they are made so. Musical progress is extremely difficult and it can be attained only by the sort of effort which arises out of, and is concomitant with, effective interest.

INTEREST AND EDUCATIONAL OUTCOMES

So far we have dealt with interest simply as a motive force in education. In fact, many discussions of the topic do not go beyond this, but it is a great limitation. Such a treatment is not adequate, and makes it impossible to understand the full significance of interest, or to perceive the impelling and commanding necessity for deliberately arousing and directing it. Interest, properly understood, is indeed a great and necessary educational dynamic, but it is something more. It is the supreme educational outcome. *The great result of education must be the creation of interests.*

1. The range and nature of a man's interests determine the scope and usefulness of his personality and the breadth and effectiveness of his life. If his interests are limited and narrow, if they do not extend beyond his job and one or two occupations, then he is a narrow and limited person. If they are trivial, he is a dilettante. If they are broad and concerned with important matters, he is a significant personality. *A man's interests are those things to which he gives himself of his own accord.* They are those elements in the environment to which he responds, which he thinks about, and with which he deals. They are, indeed, his most intimate and important possessions. Taken as a whole, they constitute the working philosophy by which he lives. *Hence, to mold interest is the most essential of all educational tasks.* And for music education this means that its supreme mission must be to arouse, sustain, and direct an interest in music. Towards such interest everything in our school program must be aimed.

2. *Interest is the factor which chiefly determines whether the things learned in school shall be used in life.* History which consists of nothing but facts, and names, and dates is quickly forgotten. If its study means nothing else, then it will never function in the learner's life. However, details may still be forgotten, and yet a vital interest remain, which can express itself, for example, in reading more history or in interpreting present events in the light of the past. Much of the content of factual courses in literature may depart from the mind, and yet there may still be a permanent disposition to read and to read more significant material. Exactly the same

is true of music. If our music program can arouse the pupil's interest, this is the best guarantee we can have that he will apply elsewhere what he learns in school. If our music program succeeds only in boring the pupil, this is the best guarantee we can have that he will turn away from music as speedily as he can.

Therefore, whenever we say that a school subject should be "made interesting," we mean that it should be handled and presented in such a way that the learner will desire to continue with it on his own initiative. We mean far more than supplying some sort of tricky device to help us over the rough spots in our teaching. Interest is the great motive force in the classroom, and it is the great motive force which carries the learner's education beyond the classroom. Here once more we see the superficiality of the idea of "sugar coating." Our aim should not be to "make" a subject interesting in this limited and highly artificial sense. Rather we must seek to help the learner to discover the power and appeal of the material we provide for him to learn. Once he has discovered this, we have set all the probabilities in favor of his finding uses for it out of school, when he is not under tutelage. *Always we should remember that transfer to life, which is the very heart of all educational effectiveness, does not depend on the use of some special array of devices, but on the aroused and active purposes of the learner.*

3. *Interest is the factor which largely determines whether education shall stop when the pupil leaves school or shall continue throughout life.* Education which stops when the pupil leaves school is of doubtful value at the best. The school is a starting point, an agency for orientation. What is done in school, if it is well done, should be paying larger and larger

dividends as life goes on. Because of it a man should be a better and fuller personality at forty than he was at twenty, and at sixty than he was at forty. Often this does not happen. A man gets into a rut and grows steadily less rather than greater, narrower rather than broader, more restricted rather than wider in vision, less and less able to learn. Whenever this happens, the school, in large measure, has failed. But it need not happen. Continuous growth is eminently possible. It is possible, however, on one condition. *Education must succeed in arousing the individual to genuine, personal interests. This is the basis for all continuous mental and personal development.*

Here we see the true contribution of general to vocational education. Pre-professional training often involves a most serious defect by becoming premature training. The result is narrowness. Professional activity, no matter how expert within its range, becomes a prison to the spirit. The man is lessened by his work; and if that work partakes of the nature of creation, it surely suffers. *The true foundation of all specialization is living and broad interests.* The great need, particularly for the creative worker, is to see his own particular activity in its wide setting in the scheme of human life. This is most certainly so in the case of too many a professional career in music. Many a professional musician hardly seems to have an interest in music; rather he is only a practitioner of its techniques. This is a shocking defect, and often it is traceable to his early training, which should not be approached in terms of a premature specialization. To do so involves an apparent saving, but a real and tragic loss.

In closing this chapter let us turn to consider some of the more specific practical applications to education in general, and to music education in particular, of the thought that interests are the great and imperative educational outcomes.

First, it means that we must conceive of our whole curriculum as representing the essential interests of a civilized human being. The great problem is not to determine what items of knowledge and skill we must mediate to our learner so that later on he will find them ready to his hand. The questions which we must ask are rather these: What interests is it desirable that he shall have? Which of many possible interests shall we seek to arouse? The claims of music to an important place in the curriculum depend precisely upon this principle. In order to validate them, the principle must be applied, first to the curriculum as a whole, and second to our organized music program, which, again, must be primarily a program for the arousal and direction of musical interests.

Second, we must plan our teaching for the sake of arousing and sustaining interests. Our business is not to compel the learner to cram facts, or form habits, for their own sake. Rather it is to reveal the subject as worth mastering, using, and thinking about. If this is not done, the characteristic educative and human values of teaching vanish.

Third, we may ask what is the relation of the tool studies to our account of interest. What of reading, writing, and arithmetic? What of the mastery of the musical score? They are to be regarded as techniques which must be mastered if we are effectively to identify ourselves with significant and cultural undertakings. They are the gateways to interest. For instance, reading English is not important for its own sake, but it is enormously important because it opens the way to innumerable interests. In our modern schools it is taught with this emphasis and not just as a skill. The same is true of writing and of arithmetic. It holds true of all tool studies, and decidedly this includes also the reading of music. To be able to read the musical notation has in itself not one whit more significance than to be able to read any other cipher or arbitrary symbolism. Only in so far as it makes possible more effective musical interests and more significant musical activities does it have any place whatsoever in our scheme. The more definitely we organize the teaching of it with this thought in mind, the better that teaching is likely to be.

SUGGESTED SUPPLEMENTARY READINGS

DEWEY, JOHN, *Interest and Effort in Education,* Houghton Mifflin Company, 1913.

KILPATRICK, W. H., *The Foundations of Method,* The Macmillan Company, 1925, ch. 10.

MURSELL, JAMES L., *Principles of Education,* W. W. Norton Company, 1934, ch. 13.

CHAPTER TWELVE

Music and Standards

THE SIGNIFICANCE OF STANDARDS IN EDUCATION

When we say that the characteristic medium of education is experience and that its great aim may properly be conceived as the development and guidance of interest, it may seem to render standards unimportant; or at least they may appear to be purely individual. We may think it a legitimate inference that whatever the pupil does must be regarded as satisfactory just so long as he is having some sort of experience and is feeling some sort of interest. Clearly this would make all education directionless and spineless. It is a wholly false interpretation of the account offered in these pages, but it is very true that our conceptions lead us to think of, and to try to establish, standards very differently from the conventional manner. It gives us a much more sound and fruitful approach to the problem than that ordinarily taken. Here again we shall find the music program an ideal field in which to exemplify just what standards in education ought to be, what they ought to do, and how they ought to be administered.

The problem of standards in a scheme of education aiming at human values rather than mass results is admittedly baffling, but it is also exceedingly important. There are few matters about which clear thinking and wise planning are more necessary and more practically valuable. In such a case, a very illuminating mode of treatment is to simplify the whole issue down to its fundamentals. Let us, for the time being, banish from our minds a whole mass of confusing and essentially irrelevant detail. Let us forget about schools and schooling, courses, and marks; about the twelve grades and what are alleged to be their appropriate levels of achievement; and indeed about the whole ponderous mechanism of education. Let us consider only the individual human being and the conditions of his intellectual and personal development. Let us ask two questions. What does it mean to say that a person has standards? Why is it important that he should have them?

1. What does it mean to say that a person has standards? (*a*) It means that he is able to recognize excellence and to distinguish it from mediocrity. The higher and the more effective his standards, the better he can do this, and the finer become the shades of difference apparent to him. This is true of every field,—science, mathematics, art, literature, sport, music, and so forth. (*b*) It means that he is not easily content with his own performance and achievement. He is capable of recognizing its defects. Those defects will not necessarily discourage him, but the possession of standards will prevent a premature or fatuous self-satisfaction. (*c*) It means that he will have a guiding principle within himself for achievement and effort. He has a goal by which to steer. He sees the need for effort and improvement, and knows, at least in general, the way he must take. The higher and the more effective a person's standards, the better they serve him in all these respects. We should notice that one thing which having standards does *not* necessarily mean is an anxious comparison of one's self with others. Of course judgments of value, judg-

ments of better and worse, are involved. The possession of effective standards means that a man cannot think himself as good a pianist as Paderewski, or a mathematician of the calibre of Einstein, or a stylist equal to Lytton Strachey. Moreover, he may make such men his models and exemplars, but the essential situation is not competitive. The influence of standards, effectively entertained, is to make a man seek and appreciate excellence for its own sake, rather than for the sake of beating someone else.

2. Why is it important for anyone to have standards? What we have said furnishes us with a ready answer to this, our second question. (*a*) Without standards no one can make effective educational progress. The surest of all barriers to such progress is satisfaction with mediocrity in one's self. An ideal of excellence is a most important and necessary condition for becoming educated and for improvement and growth. (*b*) The ability to discriminate excellence is a most important factor in high human quality. This is the second great reason why standards are important. The person who is easily pleased may be popular, but he will not be effective. He will not accomplish anything important himself; nor will his influence on others lead them towards high achievement. Absence of standards means a sort of feckless amiability, a toleration of anything as good enough. Of this we have far too much, both in music and elsewhere. The educated person—the person who is really to achieve something—must have about him a certain intolerance of anything less than the best, either in himself or others. Living at a high level does not mean a harsh, grouchy, critical attitude, but it does mean a recognition of high excellence, a disposition to honor it, and a capacity keenly to distinguish it from mediocrity.

So we may clinch the argument of this introductory section with a definition. *A standard is a desirable level of skill, achievement, insight, appreciation, or attitude.* This applies to every field of human interest and activity, including music. It makes the importance of standards in education perfectly obvious. Indeed, without such ideals of excellence, education itself would be virtually inconceivable. The practical general problem is to see how schools can organize themselves so as to impart to their pupils such ideals of excellence. The specific problem of this chapter is to see how it can be done in connection with our program of music education. How may the teaching of music present an example of what the setting and inculcation of standards in humane and constructive terms should mean? What conditions must be met, if standards are to fulfill the purposes which we have just discussed, i.e., their true purposes in human life? These are the problems to which we must now address ourselves.

Standards Must Be Organized in Terms of the Learner's Purpose

Our definition of standards as "desirable levels of skill, achievement, insight, appreciation, or activity" at once suggests the question: Who desires these things? Perhaps the first reply which comes to our minds is that they are desired by the curriculum builder, the administrator, the supervisor, and the teacher. So far we are right enough, but there has been an essential omission. The pupil must be the center of our entire educational picture. Moreover, he must not have the status of a patient upon the operating table. Until he himself desires a certain level of attainment or a certain standard, he will not achieve those important and beneficial effects which we indicated in the preceding section.

Very often school standards are set up and administered without regard to the purposes and desires of the pupil. They are treated as indications of what we ought to desire for him, rather than as what he ought to desire for himself. A certain body of content, skill, technique, and so forth is laid out, and it becomes the business of teaching to see that this is acquired. This way of handling standards is pushed to the limit of its logic in Europe, where the central educational authorities of the state set up a series of public examinations to which all pupils in all schools are subjected. The questions are made out and the papers are marked at headquarters, and all the teacher has to do is to coach his classes well enough so that as many as possible may pass. In this country educational tests are sometimes used in a somewhat similar manner. Even when this is not done, we very often find essentially the same philosophy of standard-setting in vogue, though it may be less rigorously applied. We have it also in programs of music education where each grade is supposed to master a certain list of songs and to learn certain intricacies and details of musical notation, determined in advance. The whole business constitutes a very serious educational fallacy, and that fallacy becomes particularly glaring in connection with music.

When we think of and administer standards in this way, they become only incidentally educative. We create a complex and impressive machinery, but the essence of the matter escapes us. We have put on a performance of *Hamlet* without including the Prince of Denmark. What we must try to do is to lead the *pupil* to want to know more history, or to write better English, or to sing, or play, or listen, or create music more effectively. Obviously this is the only sensible meaning which can attach to standards in education. They must create in the learner a dissatisfaction with his present level of attainment and a desire for a better one. They must reveal to him an ideal which he adopts as his own. A body of standards, conceived as a sort of blueprint list of accomplishments, to be drilled into the pupil whether he will or no, is more or less of an absurdity. We have here little that promises an awakening in him of a recognition of possible and desirable masteries.

The doctrine that educational standards must be ideals of attainment desired by the pupils may strike the reader as true, but also as "idealistic" and impractical. Certainly it is very difficult to attain in most subject-matter fields. How can we lead the pupil to desire more effective masteries in history, in arithmetic, in science, and so forth? The practical thing seems simply to block out what we think he ought to learn and then to take measures to compel him to do so. Now this is a very real difficulty and I have no disposition to minimize or slight it, but I think it is entirely possible to indicate the conditions out of which it arises, and then, perhaps, a better way may not appear so impossible. The trouble lies in this, that most subject-matter fields are not readily organized in terms of significant undertakings which can engage the active purposes of the learner. On the contrary they are most readily organized into lessons. Let us say that our history has been blocked out into units or topics in accordance with some plan of grade standards of the ordinary type. Suppose one of these topics to be assigned on a certain day. Why should the pupils want to master it? Why should they

want to learn it well? Is it not clear that no inner, personal
reason at all may be found? Will not the true motive force
be simply the compulsion, or the coaxing, which the teacher
is able to exert? Nearly all of them will be perfectly satisfied
with half learning, or even less, except in so far as they fear
a scolding or perhaps anticipate some kind of reward. We
have done something called setting standards, and we have
built our lesson plans upon those standards. As a matter of
fact, we have only deceived ourselves, for no functioning
inner standard is present at all, simply because there is no
significant, purposive undertaking.

The point which I am making may be clinched by a simple
and familiar illustration. Compare learning a lesson in history
with learning to drive a golf ball. In the former case, any
standards which may exist are imposed by the school and the
teacher. In the latter, everything is very different. There is no
assignment and no compulsion. The teacher is a helper, not
a dictator. A very strong and definite purpose is present, and
it is this which creates and defines standards of achievement
and makes them effective. At first the learner's working ideal
is humble and low. About all he wants to do is to hit the
ball cleanly and to send it tolerably straight. Little by little
his ambition grows. He tries for more distance, and then for
yet more. At last he gains the supple strength and delicate
mastery of the expert, and only a perfect drive contents him.
Here we have a prototype of the true educative situation.
Without such directing, inner purpose we must resort to
blueprint standard-setting.

Now music offers most admirable opportunities for maintaining standards which shall be drastic and genuine and yet
shall function in terms of the purpose of the learner, because,

as we have already seen, it naturally organizes itself in and through purposive undertakings. Musical learning, properly directed, resembles learning to drive a golf ball far more than learning a history lesson under compulsion. Musical projects must be the heart of our program, and musical standards arise out of those projects.

1. First, this means that we should set up every project, whether it be of the nature of listening, performing, or creating, for the sake of engaging active purpose. The most serious disaster which can befall us is to have our pupils indifferent to the undertakings which we propose, for the educative effect of those undertakings depends upon their dynamic appeal. Always we must do all that in us lies to incite the pupil to desire to produce, or recognize, or enjoy musical effects.

2. We should encourage initiative and self-criticism. The teacher should not be forever telling the learner what to do, and how to do it, and in what respect he may improve his work. Rather the teacher should forever be helping the pupil to find out these things for himself. When a musical project is turned into a game of follow-the-leader, it has gone seriously astray. It should be a chance for the learner to discover the demands of the music and the means of fulfilling them.

3. We must use musical materials which foster high standards, fine workmanship, delicate discriminations. Here again we find our justification for selecting many types of music which will foster a variety of appealing projects. On the other hand, poor, trivial, cheap music, or that obviously included for only technical and not musicianly purposes, is definitely antagonistic to the setting of standards in terms of inner purpose. If it cannot be avoided, there is little to be done with it

save to run through it quickly and go on to something else.

4. Our whole music program must be organized as far as possible to evoke and foster genuine and effective musical purposes. The more we can do to provide a diversification of real situations, situations where music is actually used rather than merely learned, the more effective our standard-setting is likely to become. Again we may notice the effect of superior chorus and orchestra groups at the high school level upon the entire situation from the first grade onward in such cities as Cleveland and Kansas City. The tendency of such organizations is to reflect backwards through the entire graded system and to integrate musical purposes with life aims.

Standards Must Exist for the Sake of Functional Masteries

Again, our definition of a standard as "a desirable level of skill, achievement, insight, appreciation, or attitude" suggests the question: Desirable for what? School standards, as often set up, seem to exist for their own sake or for the sake of further work in the field under consideration. Once more, however, a deep, far-reaching fallacy is involved. In the abstract, we cannot make a list of the things a person should learn in order to become an "educated man," and call these the standards of the perfect or adequate education. Neither can we, in the abstract, make a list of the things a sixth grade child should know or the skills he should possess. We can set up standards only when we know what kind of things an "educated man" or a sixth grader needs to be able to do. Hence a standard as a "desirable level" of attainment is desirable for the sake of functional mastery.

Within the last few years there has been a widespread attempt to put this principle into practice in American education. It has taken the form of what is known as the "Unit Plan" of organization.[1] On this plan, any given subject—history, for example—is not subdivided into a number of lessons of the conventional type. Instead, it is subdivided into a number of "mastery units." A mastery unit differs from the ordinary lesson in this particular respect, that it is not a topic which contains a stated body of content, but rather a topic so organized that the pupil can achieve a "mastery level" in it as a whole. Moreover, the attempt is made to arrange conditions in such a way that the pupil himself is aware whether or no he has "mastered" the unit before him. This immediately banishes that half learning which is the curse of the ordinary lesson and the nemesis of every educational scheme that defines its standards in terms of pre-determined blocks of content. The task itself becomes the controlling factor. Standards exist with reference to the task. The pupil must learn well enough and rise to a level high enough to achieve an effective grasp of each topic he undertakes.

The music program offers us a series of almost ideal "mastery units." Every musical undertaking has exactly this character. *Our standards must be set by our musical projects and for our musical projects.* Whatever it is that we want our pupils to learn, whether it is something very elementary or very advanced, whether it is the capacity to indicate the beginnings and ends of phrases, or to write from musical dictation, or to find *do,* or to play a scale,—that learning must never be carried on for its own sake or because it is a conven-

[1] MORRISON, HENRY C., *The Practice of Teaching in the Secondary School,* University of Chicago Press, 1931.

tionally accepted part of music education. Always the thing must be learned for the sake of an improved musical mastery in the way of listening, or performing, or creating, and the pupils must see the connection. This is vitally important. The benefit must be immediate, not prospective. It must reveal itself in an immediate musical undertaking, going on here and now. It must result in better enjoyment and better achievement; in better playing or singing of this particular composition; in better listening to this particular piece; in a more effective molding of this particular melodic line or harmonic sequence. Such learnings as I have cited above are not the stuff of our standards. The true standard is the functional mastery with music.

Schemes of music education constantly run counter to all this. They define their standards in terms of topics rather than in terms of better musical achievement. We have this when grade aims are formulated as a sequential knowledge about the score, turning on such matters as key signatures, note names, note lengths, time signatures, rest lengths, and so forth. We find the same thing at another level, as in the ordinary course in harmony, where a series of lessons deals with primary and secondary triads, first inversions, suspensions, six-four chords, the dominant seventh, and so forth. No one will be foolish enough to deny that a musician ought to be familiar with such things. My point is that gaining mastery of them should be directly contributory to a growth in musical power, which is the only thing in the world that makes them worth knowing at all. Therefore, putting our doctrine in other words, *the achievement of a standard should always mean a conscious release of power.*

Standards Must Be Learned

The point that standards must be learned is obvious enough; yet in school work we constantly overlook it. How does one gain fine discriminations, or the ability to recognize excellence, or to criticize one's self? Certainly not all at once. Nothing is more futile than to tell a pupil to do better when he does not know what "better" means. Nothing is more futile than to tell a pupil he has failed, when all he can do, in his bewilderment, is to take your word for it. To know what excellence means and to be able to value it aright comes only through long and directed experience. It is the result of learning. Indeed, in a sense, it is the supreme result of learning. If, on the one hand, we may say that all effective education is a shaping of interests, on the other hand we may also say that all effective education is a building of standards. Thus, whenever we set up anything for our pupils to learn, we should think of it as an agency through which they may learn standards. Each piece of music, each musical undertaking, is at once a goal and a stepping stone. It should be a part of a slow revelation of what it means to be a musician and of the power and appeal of fine music.

Standards Must Be Organized in Terms of Individual Achievement

School standards are usually organized in terms of average achievement. A line or level is established which seems feasible for the average of the group. The problem of the teacher then becomes to bring everyone up to it, if possible; and the problem of the pupil is to conform. Instantly the individual becomes a difficulty, unless he happens to be right on the line.

This is true whether he rises above the average or falls below it. It is quite enough to warn us of a very grave error, for the individual and his progress, rather than the average, are the crux of education. Standards so conceived and administered most certainly do not function as inspiring ideals. They are only mass conveniences.

The great and characteristic means of expressing standards, based upon averages, is the marking system. The very essence of all marking is the relating of each pupil to an average level. It is a demonstrated and very elementary fallacy to think that there is such a thing as "A" work or "F" work, as such. "A" work means, or should mean, work considerably above the average; "F" work means work very considerably below it. All grading is essentially relative. The use of the so-called probability curve, according to which a certain percentage of each grade is given, and which, as a matter of fact, really does improve a teacher's work to a certain extent, is nothing but a recognition of this. No one with any competent familiarity with statistical technique will question the relative, rather than the absolute, character of grading. Everything turns on the reference of the individual to the average. When we turn away from mass standards and insist that the individual rather than the average ought to be our point of departure, we are immediately forced to give up marking. Putting it quite baldly, our claim is that *we ought not to mark in music*.

Elsewhere I have argued that the marking system constitutes a pernicious influence in the organization of our schools.[1] Whether or no this general proposition finds acceptance, it is abundantly clear that the sort of program of music education

[1] MURSELL, JAMES L., *Principles of Education,* W. W. Norton & Company, 1934, ch. 19.

which has been envisaged in these pages is very ill-adapted to furnish any basis for the assignment of marks, and that it is apt to become weakened and distorted if we try to use it in such a way.

1. First of all, if we are to work out a mark for a pupil in any course, we must have a series of more or less uniform test situations. Such tests may be oral or written, but they must be given. They must be constructed and administered in such a way that everyone has about an equal chance at them. In fact, the conventional course is built about just such a series of tests, and the resultant mark is an index of how well the pupil has done. But the essence of our music program is precisely not such a series of uniform situations. It is a series of musical projects which are diversified so as to appeal to varied interests and needs. This in itself is enough to warn us that they cannot possibly furnish any proper basis for marking. How much credit towards the final grade should we give for listening to the Egmont Overture? Or for suggesting the topic for a poem to be set to an original melody? Or for inventing the first phrase of that melody? Or for indicating where a *crescendo* should be placed? Or for enjoying a rhythm game? Such questions cannot be answered because activities of this kind cannot be properly evaluated as contributing towards a figure which serves as an index of average achievement. If, however, we have a series of lessons on notation, accompanied by a series of tests, then indeed we can work out an intelligible mark, but we would sacrifice the educative and human values of our work. It is precisely because we wish to operate in terms of significant, diversified human experience, rather than uniform lesson learning, that marking is wholly incompatible with our enterprise.

2. If we are going to mark, our chief interest in the individual as a unique phenomenon must turn simply on how far he diverges from the average. I know of teachers, required to grade "on the curve" and to assign a certain percentage of each mark, who actually hope that some of their pupils will do badly enough to justify a failing grade. This reveals, at its very worst, the false attitude towards individual achievement which is created by the marking system. Our music program should exemplify a precisely contrary attitude. Let us say that we are dealing with a so-called "monotone," who is enjoying his music, who is making progress, who is in some important respects doing well, but who cannot show up very effectively in vocal performance. What ought we to do with him? The logic of the marking system requires that we give him a failure, or at best a very low grade. Certainly that logic absolutely forbids us to give him a high mark. If we do this, we cannot deal fairly with children whose immediate level of achievement is superior to his. What is the way out? Surely not to mark at all. Or what shall we do if certain children dislike a song which we have given them or a composition to which they have listened? Are we to penalize them for daring to have their own musical preferences and for being sincere about them? This seems an odd way of promoting musical development. The whole spirit and philosophy of our enterprise demands that we respect the artistic purposes and preferences of others, even when they do not coincide with our own or seem to us wholly desirable, and also that we provide opportunities rather than tasks. But the marking system, under which every variation is evaluated with reference to an average, treats individuality as the basis for rewards and penalties and calls for uniform and exacting tests.

3. Furthermore, the marking system introduces a competitive motivation which is destructive in its effects. This, again, is part of its inevitable logic. Unless we wish to make it quite absurd, we are bound to give the higher marks sparingly. This, in turn, leads our pupils to compete for them more or less openly. Assuredly, degrees of excellence will continue to exist, but the whole question is how we ought to treat them. Certainly we should not play them up, as the marking system does, so that they become an incentive to a rivalry which often grows quite bitter. The whole trend of our work should be in the direction of coöperation rather than competition.

4. Lastly, consider a more specific point, namely, the significance of the failing grade. What can it mean to say that a pupil has failed in his music? If we have a series of content or achievement tests, uniform in character, we can answer precisely enough. We mean that he has fallen a certain distance below the average level of attainment. We can attach a definite statistical meaning to the concepts of failing and passing. But suppose we ask for their educational meaning, what then? Taking it in this sense, to say that a pupil has failed in his music can only indicate that he has gotten nothing out of it. In this case should we entirely blame the pupil? Should we attach to him a humiliating badge of misfortune because he has dared not to profit by our distinguished instruction? May there not be something the matter with the instruction? In any rational scheme of education the failure of a pupil must be regarded as the failure of the school and of the teacher, but the grading system elegantly shifts the entire responsibility to the pupil.

As a matter of working practice, the marking system does not lead quite as inevitably as one might think to all these evil consequences. The reason is that teachers greatly mitigate it. Rarely do we find it applied in accordance with its rigorous inner logic. Instead of marking simply on demonstrated achievement, which is the recommendation of every treatise on the subject, teachers take into consideration all sorts of factors in determining the standing of their pupils. However, this is no argument in favor of marking. On the contrary, if an instrument is so very clumsy and promises to do so much damage that sensible people can never be persuaded to use it as it should be used, the clear indication is that we ought to throw it on the junk heap.

The proposal to do away with marking, however, is likely to suggest two very cogent and pertinent questions.

Our first question will be: Is it likely that our pupils will work without marks? This can be summarily answered. Any teacher who is dependent on the grading system to compel his pupils to work should be deprived of his pedagogical crutch just as soon as possible and made to hobble along as best he can. There is something positively perverse in the idea of systematically forcing children to toil at music because they fear a low mark or desire a high one. If our music program really depends on such a dynamic, we had better stop deceiving ourselves with the fiction that we are doing worth-while things and look for jobs breaking stones.

Our second question will be: Should we have any substitute for marking? Most decidedly we should. No school, and no department of any school, can be managed in an orderly and proper manner without records and a scheme of pupil accounting. What the registrar's books should show against each pupil's name is not a mark indicating his position with respect to an average, but an account of his own actual achievements, interests, and activities. It is important to know, for instance, that he has become a member of the junior high school orchestra, that he has contributed to a significant creative project, that he has performed on occasion as a soloist, that he has sung certain songs and has improved in his singing, and so forth. If we build our program out of significant undertakings, then our records should reflect the fact. This general plan of pupil accounting is coming more and more widely into use. It is found to be a greatly superior substitute to the marking system.[1]

Standards Must Be Organized for a Sequential Advance

The whole argument of this chapter may seem to tend against any planning of a sequence of grade aims or standards. This, however, is not so. What is inconsistent with the positions we have taken is a rigid scheme, conceived as a statement of abstractly and intrinsically desirable average achievements. It is very necessary indeed that we plan our program as a whole, from the kindergarten to the twelfth grade, and that we chart our direction definitely and clearly. Such a plan should have the following characteristics.

1. It should be regarded as a working blueprint of a feasible sequence of individual development. If we think of it in these terms—that is, as indicating a sequence of advance in musical skills which we could recommend for continuous individual growth—we shall often find it most illuminating. Our temptation is always to think of grade averages rather than individual progress. This militates against flexibility and leads us to worship the letter of the law we have laid down.

2. Our statement of grade aims should be broad and inclusive. It should not be limited to items of knowledge about

[1] Morrison, Henry C., *The Practice of Teaching in the Secondary Schools,* University of Chicago Press, 1931, ch. 30, and Mursell, J. L., *The Psychology of Secondary School Teaching,* pp. 418-9, W. W. Norton & Company, 1932.

music, or to items of skill in reading. It should include, and indeed treat as paramount, such factors as personal attitude, musical discrimination, and feeling for rhythmic and tonal patterns.

3. It must be intimately related to functional musical masteries. As I have insisted, it is in such masteries—in actual listening, and performing, and creating—that our standards find their entire significance and reality. Therefore, in organizing a scheme of grade aims, we should always consider it as a formulation of those factors which a child will need to improve his actual work with music, and which he can gain in and through such work.

4. We do well always to formulate our grade aims in terms of growth. The really important factors in musical development are not end points, but processes. For instance, we can set up the ability to recognize and write down the treble clef as an aim for a certain grade. So far so good,—but not very far. It is one of the things a child should no doubt learn incidentally, but it should not be represented as a paramount aim. Contrast this with the aim of bringing about an increase in the child's power to discriminate phrase patterns when heard, or to indicate a complex rhythm. Such things are far more important as factors in musical effectiveness. They cannot be treated as termini. We are always approaching them, but we never reach perfection in them.

Suggested Supplementary Reading

Morrison, Henry C., *The Practice of Teaching in the Secondary Schools,* The University of Chicago Press, 1926.

Mursell, James L., *Principles of Education,* W. W. Norton & Company, 1934, ch. 19.

CHAPTER THIRTEEN

Technical Aspects of Music

GENERAL SIGNIFICANCE OF TECHNIQUE IN MUSIC EDUCATION

The three chief technical aspects of music are as follows: first, the motor skills involved in performance; second, the mastery of the notation; and third, expertness in dealing with tonal structures and relationships, which is called—and improperly called—theoretical music. Various other correlative techniques exist, as, for instance, *solfège* and the use of the baton, but the three which I have named are the most important. We are now to consider their significance and proper treatment in music education.

It may surprise the reader to find them lumped together in a single chapter. Of course they differ enormously in detail. They involve very varied specific problems of learning and teaching. This is quite obvious. If this book were chiefly concerned with the application of psychology to musical instruction, we would be obliged to consider them separately, but the educational principles which determine their proper management are almost exactly the same in each case. It is with these general educational principles that we wish to deal in the present connection. The reader will find it very enlightening to think about them in conjunction as three aspects of a single massive and important problem,—the problem of the place of technique in a scheme of music education organized for hu-

man values. Our constant aim has been to present a general
philosophical interpretation of music education and its values,
and the question of technique is certainly one which we cannot shirk. In this section I shall discuss the common significance of the three primary techniques in relationship to our
central doctrines. Then I shall go on to consider them one by
one, though the suggestions I shall make in regard to proper
modes of teaching will be for the sake of illustrating and rendering more concrete and intelligible the central position
taken.

The musical techniques have exactly the same place in the
economy of life as any other skills. They are agencies for individual transformation, release, and growth. This, as I say, is
true of all skills. When a child develops expertness in the use
of table utensils, a transformation of personal and social attitudes takes place. He becomes less dependent on his parents
and better able to participate in various group situations.
When a child gains the skill of reading the English language,
exactly the same kind of thing happens, though on a larger
scale. He qualifies for a vast range of significant social enterprises; he gains in independence; he is able to entertain and
instruct himself; he becomes a new and more effective person. In the same way the acquisition of a musical technique
means a personal transformation and a broadening of cultural
and social outlook. A person who becomes able to sing is definitely more of a person than before. He is able to enter into
a whole range of social contacts from which he was previously excluded. The person who can play an instrument possesses far more than one single new avenue of self-expression.
He has a key which can unlock many doors. So also the
ability to read the score breaks down barriers to participation

in many life activities. Professional men, including nationally
known leaders like Charles Dawes or Harold Ickes, who are
composers in their own right, gain definitely from this power
in their quality as human beings. This notion that the essential life value of a technique consists in its being an agency for
personal transformation and social development is a most
fruitful principle. It shows us many things about music education which are essential for us to understand.

1. First of all, our principle makes quite evident the sheer
nonsense of teaching any skill merely for its own sake or
in isolation from its functional applications. Yet, as we all
know, this very thing is constantly done in music education.
Direct drill on the notation is the core of many a program.
It is excused and defended by saying that such drill trains in
quickness, or accuracy, or power of comprehension, or ability
to concentrate, and so on. Again, we constantly find technical
exercises in vocal and instrumental music entirely divorced
not only from any musical application but also from any
social use to which the new skill might be put. The clear purpose behind such procedures is to develop a technique for its
own sake as a sort of battery of motor abilities. Occasionally
an attempt is made to defend such practices as educationally
valuable by saying that it is good for the brain to have neural
patterns formed in it. No more nonsensical idea has ever been
promulgated by desperate pedagogs. Or again, we very often
find theoretical music taught without any reference whatsoever
to any valid musical activity or to any social situation which
might call for musical expression. This situation likewise is
preposterous, for expertness with tonal structures and relationships, like any other technique, is significant only in terms
of its actual uses and its influence upon life. We may even

go further than this and say that a technique only *exists* in its applications. What shall it profit a man to be able to play the F major scale at a rate of six hundred tones a minute if he goes to pieces in a scale passage in the cadenza of a concerto; or to be able to write an exercise in four-part harmony according to rule, but utterly incapable of arranging effectively a folk melody for a glee club? A technique is not something which we *have*. It is something which we *use*. In a very real sense it has no existence at all, independent of its applications.

2. Our principle shows us how equally disastrous and non-sensical it is to regard techniques and specific skills as unimportant in music education. Relatively few teachers will try to push this fallacy to the limits of its logic. I know of one case of a violin teacher, in another country, who does so with most unfortunate results. His theory is that children should just try to make music on their instruments without any technical instruction at all, which he regards as cramping to the creative impulse. Obviously this practice is to ignore the fixed conditions of personal growth and educational transformation which depend precisely upon the acquisition and effective use of skills. The outcomes of this teacher's work show the magnitude of his error. No real musical capacity is engendered. His teaching does not constitute a constructive and broadening social force in the lives of his pupils, though most of them enjoy it well enough.

While few would go as far as this, a great many music educators, particularly in the vocal field, feel a strong suspicion of technique. There is, indeed, some genuine reason for this, since technique is all too often badly taught and not brought into relationship with expressive activities and social opportunities, but always we are compelled to say that such an attitude indicates a false idealism and a most unfortunate refusal to face facts. Education certainly depends upon experience; but it is a great deal more than a casual ramble through delightful pathways. Effective experience, indeed, cannot be had without effort and concentrated learning. Education, again, means personal and mental growth, and the techniques are the tools of such growth. Our great educational problem is how to make the mastery of a technique humanly significant, not how to dodge it altogether.

3. Our principle that all skills should be regarded as mechanisms for personal transformation and release gives us a most important hint with regard to the musical techniques, which our further discussions will justify in detail. Not one of the primary musical techniques exists which cannot be far more easily acquired than we ordinarily suppose. A great many of the difficulties of technique are the artificial and avoidable results of bad teaching. This is certainly true of expertness with tonal structures and relationships. When we watch conservatory students wrestling desperately and blindly with their harmony exercises, we may be quite sure that something is very far wrong and that a psychologically inept mode of teaching is destroying educative and human values. A working mastery of the score, again, is commonly made far more difficult than it should be. The arduous labors endured by students in the effort to acquire instrumental techniques and vocal controls cannot but strike one as very largely a pathetic and reprehensible waste,—and a needless weariness of the spirit. In general, a businesslike and sane ordering of the educative process on sound principles will overcome many of the obstacles which make the musical techniques seem so formidable a problem in music education.

So much for our broader comments. Now we shall go on to discuss more in detail each of the three chief technical aspects of music. To repeat, what is said in regard to matters of detail is not presented chiefly for its own sake, but with the purpose of illustrating and rendering concrete our general proposition that the same educational principles are controlling in each case.

EDUCATIONAL PRINCIPLES INVOLVED IN ACQUIRING MOTOR TECHNIQUES

The following are the fundamental principles which must guide us in building motor skills in the way of vocal control or instrumental manipulation.

1. Every technical problem should be taught in close association with a musical situation. (*a*) It should arise out of a need felt and recognized by the learner. The problem itself should be created by a functional musical situation, and its cogency should arise out of the pupil's desire to deal with that situation. The right moment to practise scale passages on the piano, or trills on the violin, or the forward placement of the voice is when one or another of these skills is demanded in the creation of a musical effect. (*b*) The ability to create the musical effect required should be our criterion for determining the success of a technical development. (*c*) Technical problems should be set up in connection with actual musical *expression*. Our aim should not be to compel the pupil to drill on a dry, formal set of movements. His whole mind-set should be towards the creation of beauty and the shaping of a specific tonal pattern into intelligibility. Very often a technical difficulty is quickly and surely resolved if the pupil will concentrate upon the expressive effect he desires, when

otherwise it has refused to yield to a great deal of painful drilling. (*d*) The connection between technical problems and their immediate application can certainly be less intimate with the advanced than with the elementary pupil. The reason is that such a connection must exist in the learner's mind, and so long as he is able to perceive the relationship between working on the motor adjustment and creating musical effects, our condition is satisfied. Furthermore, the mind of the mature pupil can compass a wider span without the contact breaking down, but the connection must still be there. Even with the most advanced music student it is a fallacy, and a sure source of weakness and waste, to try to build a technical repertoire by formal drill alone. (*e*) In concluding, we must insist upon one point not often clearly understood: To teach technical problems in actual contact with the learning of a piece is clear gain; but, if possible, we should try to go even further. Technical problems become most cogent, most gripping, and are organized for the most effective learning when they are associated not merely with a piece of music but *with a piece of music to be performed somewhere and for or with somebody.* We should try to relate them, not just to music in general, but to music in its total social and personal setting.

2. It is exceedingly important to approach all manipulative problems in terms of intimately thinking the musical pattern. When we fail to do this, we render all such problems far more difficult and refractory. The ordinary pianistic approach, adopted by many private teachers, is very bad in this respect. It attempts to deal with technique as mere key juggling. The essential thing is to think the notes and to feel their relationships before one tries to play them, and to return again and again to our musical thinking and our controlling musical

imagination. The method adopted by Eitz and Bennedik, to whose works I have already made reference (see p. 192), becomes relevant here. It will be recalled that Eitz is the originator of a system which differs from the tonic *sol-fa* of Curwen in that a separate name is associated with each step of the chromatic scale. This renders a transfer from the vocal to the instrumental medium much easier than when the *sol-fa* syllables are employed. What is done is this: They recommend beginning always with vocal experience. This experience is made specific, and the attention of the learner is drawn to the tonal relationships in their detail by the use of the tone-names. Next, the pupil reads and sings the instrumental melody, using the tone-names, before he attempts to play it. Then he proceeds to transfer to the instrument the precise, directed musical impression he has gained. I do not say that this is the only possible effective procedure, but clearly it is a good one, as its results show. It could certainly be applied in our own school music, as it is in parts of Germany. It would help greatly to bridge the gap between vocal experience and instrumental class work and would tend to make the musical apprehensions which the pupil has developed in his vocal experience function in the business of acquiring an instrumental facility, something for which intelligent provision is all too rarely made. The essential thing is to create in the pupil an attitude of careful and discriminating listening and imaging, rather than one directed merely to mechanical manipulation. Instrumental teachers often *talk* to their pupils about listening, but they rarely try systematically to teach them to do so. This can certainly be done in our school music, where we have just the conjunction of vocal and instrumental experience which favors the listening and imaging attitudes we

desire. Very infrequently do we think of general mental atti
tudes as an element in motor technique, but here is an attitude of the highest importance in its proper up-building.

3. We should approach technique, in part, through motor
rhythmic experience. This is done by Jaques-Dalcroze, who
gives beginning pupils a year of eurythmics before starting
them on the instrument. In this procedure we have much of
the secret of the enormous facilitation of technical learning
which he claims to be able to bring about. The reason is intelligible enough. The proper movement pattern for actuating
an instrument and producing on it a tonal sequence flows
with the rhythmic flow of that tonal sequence. When the
pianist or the violinist fails to move with the rhythmic swing
of the music, he creates many difficulties. When he succeeds
in doing so, those difficulties tend to vanish. Hence this
rhythmic response should be made an important factor in
the acquisition of technique. However, the movements required to actuate an instrument are, in themselves, not very
suitable for the apprehension of rhythm. They are small, confined, and conventionalized. The learner who uses only such
movements is apt to come out lacking a keen sense of the
rhythmic demands and intimations of the music. If we can
feel those demands and intimations in terms of large, free
movement, then it is not difficult to write it small in the
movement-language of the instrument. The reader may try
this for himself by selecting a passage and then stepping, beating, or even clapping or counting its rhythm. He will find
that even such rudimentary devices will very often clear up
a technical difficulty. A wise scheme of music education will
deliberately base much of its approach to technique upon this
idea.

4. We should determine what I may call the alphabet of movement demanded by the instrumental medium in question. The number of different unit movement types involved in any instrumental technique is usually not very large. It is much smaller than we might suppose from the ordinary books of exercises. In his book *The Physiological Mechanics of Pianoforte Technique,* Ortmann has supplied this alphabet by making elaborate photographic studies of the action of expert and clumsy pianists. He finds only five fundamental movement types; namely, arm legato, tremolo, staccato, finger stroke, and scale. The same kind of analysis could readily be applied to other instruments, such as violin, woodwind, drum, brass, and so forth. It is familiar enough in connection with many techniques and skills outside music. Properly used, it leads to a great increase in efficiency in learning such techniques, because it shows us exactly on what we ought to concentrate, and saves great waste of time and effort. Such a movement analysis, revealing to us the ultimate components, or alphabet, of the skill we are trying to establish, furnishes us with a picture of the true constitution of the technique in question. It is much simpler, much less encumbered with irrelevancies, than the material found in conventional books of exercises. Of course I am not suggesting that all we need to do is to have the pupil practise each one of a small number of movement types, and that the outcome will immediately be a full-fledged technique. Nevertheless, it is immensely helpful to know the precise physical adjustment which must be made in order to produce a desired musical effect.

As a general comment on these proposals for a rationalized approach to technique, note how it tends to integrate instrumental instruction with the entire program of music education. This is not often done. There is frequently no definite, well-planned carry-over from vocal experience, rhythmics, listening, and creative music to instrumental music. Our school work tends to divide itself into two departments of music, one of which dominates the other according to the personalities of the directors. This is manifestly wrong and anti-educational. The reason is clear enough. The instrumental work is set off by the constant problem of specialized techniques. Our proposal is to approach instrumental technique in terms of general musical experience, all varieties of which are relevant and valuably contributory. We evolve our instrumental approach from rhythmic feeling and from the kind of directed listening and tonal imaging characteristic of well-organized vocal experience. All such procedure makes the acquisition of technique definitely educative in the musical sense and also far easier than it is ordinarily considered.

EDUCATIONAL PRINCIPLES INVOLVED IN MASTERING MUSICAL NOTATION

We have already said something concerning the use and mastery of the score in a scheme of music education, but our discussion was incidental to our analysis of the nature of method and of the values and limitations of various methods now in use. Here we propose to deal with the problem of notation directly, asking what principles we must apply in order to solve it.

1. It is obvious enough that, essentially, the score is a representation of a tonal and rhythmic pattern. Moreover, it has grown into a very elaborate one. In part it is a direct graph of the tone, for the lines and spaces indicate visually the rise and fall of the pitch. In part it is an intricate, conventionalized

symbolism; this being true of sharps and flats, time signatures, durational symbols, measure lines, rests, and the indications of key and clef. A person can readily have a very highly organized musical experience without any knowledge of the score at all. Music, when all is said and done, is an affair of the ear rather than the eye, and the notation is nothing but a system of labels. Nevertheless, labels have a great value. They tend to make experience more exact and specific. One can certainly appreciate and enjoy the beauty of a range of mountains without knowing the names of any of the peaks, but a knowledge of their names seems to add a subtle something to our pleasure. So with music, the psychological and educational value of the score is to clear up and guide musical perceptions and images.

2. From this argument it would seem to follow directly that the score should be developed in connection with a wide variety of musical experiences and activities. (*a*) The score has a valid place in connection with listening, where it offers certain definite values. It can be used to render listening more specific and more significant musically. (*b*) The score should be used in connection with performance. What we should seek here is a gradual development of the power to sing or play independently from the notation. Often this accomplishment seems the only use to which the score is put in music education, but such should not be the case. (*c*) The score, developed quite informally, can be a valuable adjunct in rhythmics. One can indicate a required rhythmic figuration of movement by a modified notation upon the board, or one can graph and symbolize on the board a movement experienced and felt as correct and desirable. (*d*) Lastly, the score

should, and indeed perhaps must, be used in connection with any extensive and ambitious creative project.

3. Specific efforts should be made to control and direct eye movements with maximal efficiency. The proper use of the score turns on the ability to look at it properly. A surprising number of complex skills involve such expert eye movement as a very necessary element. When one learns to drive a car safely over the road, one learns, among other things, to *look* properly. The efficient reading of language, as we all know, depends upon glancing at the right places on the printed page. When we add a column of figures quickly and accurately, we run our eyes along it at properly spaced intervals; and if we fail to do so, we make an error. Finding one's way in the woods requires that, instead of gazing vaguely all about us, we direct our scrutiny towards certain crucial indications. The same is true of the use of the score. It depends upon the proper eye movement response.

We know, with considerable certainty, how the eyes should move in reading English, with various other languages, and even with some mathematical symbolisms. Sufficient research has been carried out to make this reasonably clear, but we can only conjecture how they should move in interpreting the score. Two considerable experiments have been carried on, dealing with this problem. However, the data are far too scanty to make possible anything but the haziest of generalizations. One presumes that the learner must gain the ability to apprehend at a glance such factors as phrase structure, rhythmic structure, and harmonic sequence. One is tolerably certain that he ought not to be taught to look at each separate note. Rather he must learn to see the significant musical patterns, just as the automobile driver must learn to see the total shifting pattern of the traffic, rather than gazing anxiously at each separate car, pedestrian, and dog. Doing this is strictly a motor problem, and we should attack it as directly and economically as we can, although, in advance of better and more precise knowledge, this suggestion is not saying so very much. For instance, we have no data in the first steps of elementary music reading for determining whether efficient eye movement is best promoted by scale-wise passages or passages based upon the tonic chord. The probability is that it does not greatly matter. Those who contend that pattern songs are not necessary in teaching the score have an argument here. Of course pattern songs can be used effectively, but no human being has the knowledge necessary to prove that they represent an optimum procedure. About all we can say for certain is that the score ought to be approached in and through the medium of musical experience, and that we should make every effort to help the child to see what he hears and to hear what he sees.[1] This in itself may well be an argument for the use of tonic chord figurations, for reasons that have already been explained, but we have no conclusive, direct evidence on the point.

In closing we may mention certain fallacies connected with the proper teaching of the score, the error of which stands revealed by our analysis. (*a*) First there is the fallacy of approaching it directly through a study of the grammar of its logical construction. This at once cuts it off from music, and its vital relationship is not saved by introducing a considerable amount of "pre-experience." (*b*) Second, there is the fallacy of thinking that we ought not to teach the score at all, be-

[1] McConathy, Osbourne; Miessner, W. O.; Birge, E. B.; Bray, Mabel E., *The Music Hour*, Elementary Teacher's Book, 1929, ch. 4.

cause any kind of technique impedes the creative impulse and stifles musical interest. Clearly, if the above suggestions are followed, mastery of the score becomes a tool for the mastery of music. Moreover, we do not first master the score and then apply it in music. We gain in musical power actually through our increasing grasp of the notation. (c) Third, there is the fallacy of supposing that the musical score is something exceedingly difficult. We can make it so, if we set it up in formal lessons and teach it in terms of its logic rather than in terms of its use. But if we make it an incidental support to musical experiences and activities, most of the looming difficulties will be circumvented. (d) Lastly, there is the astonishing fallacy that the score cannot be taught. How such an idea ever arose is beyond my power to imagine. About the best answer might be that a great many teachers have failed to impart it and have then excused themselves by saying that it could not be done. If the musical notation is not teachable, if instruction cannot promote a mastery of it, then nothing in this world is teachable and we had better close up our schools and quit. If, in the past, the teaching of the score has been a failure, we can very largely attribute it to the fact that the technical approach was the only one tried. The procedures which have been recommended will obviate a repetition of such failures, provided that teachers are able to adjust their formalism to accord with the new emphasis in education.

Educational Principles Involved in the Mastery of Tonal Structure

Music education exhibits no more destructive fallacies than those which arise in connection with what is called "theoretical" music. What should one be supposed to learn when one studies "theoretical" music? Clearly, a mastery of tonal structures and relationships, and a power to handle them. But evidently, if one learns music properly, even from the most elementary level, it is precisely this power which one ought to gain. Music *is* tonal structure. Gaining a feeling for it and a facility with it is exactly what we ought to mean when we talk about musical development. What else is there to learn? Yet what do we ordinarily find? Absolutely no emphasis upon all this, right up to the conservatory level,—a mere teaching of blind manipulations, and then courses which deal with tonal structure as an abstract science; a sudden insistence that the student learn the rules of harmony and counterpoint. This abstract science is abruptly imposed upon a mind which, up to now, has had absolutely no inkling that all of it was really in music all the time.

Such a scheme has two evil results. (*a*) The study of harmony and counterpoint is made virtually meaningless in terms of actual musical experience and activity. It is just so much textbook science to be learned by rote. It does nothing to improve the students' powers of musical self-expression. (*b*) All other work in music is treated as chiefly manipulative. Its central aim is not directed towards a mental grasp of and inner feeling for music as a tonal structure. These two weaknesses are implied in the common curricular distinction between theoretical and applied music,—a distinction against which we cannot too vigorously protest. All music is applied, and all music is intellectual. What then ought we to do?

1. From the very first, in musical projects of every kind, we should teach the child to attend to the tonal pattern and relationships. This need not, and should not, be done gram-

matically or formally. What we want is the progressive education of the ear. Always our purpose must be to increase the feeling of the pupil for the expressive and æsthetic values of music. These values consist and realize themselves in the tonal pattern. From such work come two benefits. First of all, our musical projects become musically significant, rather than mere projects in manipulation. They become agencies for the development of musical intelligence, and the pupil finds that increasing intelligence makes it possible for him to recognize opportunities for, and to achieve, finer and more satisfying musical effects. Second, a continuous musical-mental development is initiated, so that if, later on, he takes up the formal study of harmony, counterpoint, and form, he comes upon things he has always known, and recognizes these subjects as particularizations of his past experience.

2. Formal work in harmony and counterpoint should be greatly postponed. Such studies have a dubious place, even as electives, in the senior high school. However, if our music program has been properly organized, by the time the pupil reaches the twelfth grade he should already have achieved an inner apprehension of their essence, even though he is not familiar with their technical terminology and formal generalizations. Work in harmony and counterpoint can be significant only when projected on a foundation of very extensive directed musical experience. The kind of feeble illustrations which are introduced into the ordinary conservatory course can be called nothing better than a bad joke. The time to begin the study of the rudiments of harmony and counterpoint is ten years before a formal course is ever undertaken. Long ago Plato propounded the famous doctrine of *anamnesis,* or recollection, according to which all true learning is really

a remembering of things which have always been part of us, and which we have always known, but which we now, for the first time, make clear to ourselves. This is exactly what should happen in courses in harmony and counterpoint. A democratic program of music education can point towards them in just this way, because it can really teach *music*. Hence, the rules should come as a summary or explication of things already well known. The grammar of music, taught on such a background, actually functions.

3. The formal teaching of harmony and counterpoint needs thorough and drastic revision. The essence of such a study is simple enough. What we are aiming at is to give the pupil a feeling for the trends of tonal pattern in a tonal environment or tonality. He must develop a feeling for the rightness of a proper treatment and for the wrongness of an erroneous one. This is quite different from learning a rule and then puzzling over the visual symbols of the score to find out how to apply it. The ordinary and sacred rules need not be taught at all if we will only have the faith to attack directly the problem of giving the learner an apprehension of tonal trend and relationship. The work is now being approached in just this way in some of our leading university departments of music and conservatories, largely under the influence of Schenker. The ordinary teaching of harmony and counterpoint is thoroughly bad, because it is so perversely indirect, dealing with generalizations about music, instead of actual musical experience and analysis. Rightly taught, "theory" is vastly easier than we ordinarily find it to be. Also it is far more interesting and inspiring, for it really ceases to be "theory" at all and integrates with every type of musical activity. Of course it is true that, to become an expert com-

poser, one must subject one's self to arduous self-discipline and drill on contrapuntal devices. But what the advanced student, whose basic orientation is already well established, can do with benefit is entirely different from what the elementary student must do in order to acquire such an orientation.

SUMMARY

The three primary types of musical technique exhibit the same educational principles. The reader may have noticed the broad similarity of the discussion in each case, but I wish to make the idea quite clear, for it is the central thought of this whole chapter. The principles we have brought out in each case are these:

1. Always teach techniques in and through their use. The more completely and intimately they are associated with life situations the better.

2. Never formalize or generalize in advance of concrete apprehension.

3. Teach simply, directly, and economically, aiming straight at the ability it is desired to evoke and putting resolutely aside every irrelevant factor, no matter how conventionally venerable or how traditionally accepted.

These principles are also of very wide application to education outside music. They indicate the means whereby any formal tool study can be rendered significant and educative. Everything turns on the *three requirements of application, concrete experience, and economically directed learning*. This is the secret of success in reading, in arithmetic, in algebra, in science, and everywhere that a body of technique must be mastered. When we import our principles into music education, we lay the bogy of technique. Technical development comes to play its true part as the core of a solid, significant, and serviceable musical development. We see that to pay attention to technique is in no way inconsistent with the ideal of a program of music education organized for human values.

SUGGESTED SUPPLEMENTARY READINGS

MURSELL, JAMES L., *Principles of Musical Education,* The Macmillan Company, 1927, ch. 8.

MURSELL, JAMES L., and GLENN, MABELLE, *The Psychology of School Music Teaching,* Silver, Burdett and Company, 1931, chs. 9 and 12.

ORTMANN, OTTO, *The Physiological Mechanics of Pianoforte Technique,* Ortmann, publisher; Peabody Conservatory of Music, Baltimore.

CHAPTER FOURTEEN

Musicianship and Human Quality

AIM OF THE CHAPTER

Although it is the aim of the present chapter to sum up and bring to a head the entire argument of this book, more is involved than a mere summary. Our central thesis—that music education must be organized for human values and that it lends itself very readily to such treatment—is to be brought into relationship with a question of the highest importance which has not yet been considered. This is the question of the nature and distribution of musical ability. It is a problem with which we must reckon before our exposition can be regarded as complete.

Perhaps the reader may have found himself more or less in agreement with the chief positions which have been taken. He may be prepared to admit that music does indeed possess the potential human values and the developmental possibilities which have been indicated, but still he may be inclined to ask whether it can have such values and possibilities for everybody. Are not a very considerable number of people unable to benefit extensively by musical opportunities? Is not musical talent an ability manifested by only a certain proportion of human beings, perhaps even by relatively few? If this is so, then certainly we cannot advocate music education for everybody. Here we have an essential point. Such questions are raised, either explicitly or implicitly, by music educators, by general educators, and by all intelligent persons who do any thinking about musical matters. They are entirely reasonable questions and we must face them. We must ask whether our claims are not largely vitiated by human nature itself; whether they do not hold only for a certain proportion, perhaps a small proportion of children in school. So it becomes essential for us to consider the nature of musical ability and its relationship to the entire educational program. The values of music may be admitted for those who are able to benefit from them, but are those values for the few or for the many?

In advance I shall sum up the argument which I shall endeavor to present. It is divided into two parts. First, I shall try to show that we may properly regard the aim of music education as the *evocation of musical ability*. Second, I shall try to show that the evocation of musical ability depends on the raising of a person's cultural level and on the development of his personal values and spiritual sympathies. In our discussions these two points cannot be kept entirely separate from one another, but they represent the essence of the present chapter.

The Nature and Distribution of Musical Ability

Let us begin by offering a definition. *Musical ability is the capacity to discriminate and respond effectively and significantly to tonal patterns.* This may be considered valid as far as it goes. Music is clearly the art of tonal design. However, our definition involves many distinctions and calls for considerable exposition. We are now to seek to develop it and to show what it implies.

1. Musical ability is not an inherited special sensory ca-

pacity or an array of such capacities. This is not always clearly understood; yet it seems to be true. The musical person is not necessarily one who has a much finer auditory mechanism than the general run of human beings. According to our definition he is, first of all, able to *discriminate* tonal patterns. This may seem very much like calling musical ability a sensory capacity, but such is by no means the case. Of course, if a man has such very defective hearing that he cannot discriminate a tempered semitone, music can never mean a great deal to him. If, however, he can differentiate pitch changes considerably less than quarter tones, it will serve him adequately for most musical purposes, though probably he will not be able to become a good violinist or woodwind performer.

The reason is that musical discrimination does not turn upon the ability to distinguish very small differences of pitch. *It turns upon the ability to recognize the quality and the tendential effect of intervals.*[1] This is quite a different thing. An interval, say a major third, may be very considerably mistuned, and yet it still has all the musical functions—that is, the tendential effects—of a major third. It is a scientific fact that every one of the intervals we use, except the octave, is more or less "out of tune" with reference to the just intonation. Nevertheless, they serve as the basis of a valid and intelligible tonal language. The power to recognize and discriminate the quality of thirds, sixths, fifths, or octaves, and the tendential values of the dominant, the subdominant, or the leading tone is not a sensory capacity at all; although, obviously, without a proper sensory foundation this power can-

[1] OGDEN, R. M., *Hearing,* Harcourt, Brace and Company, 1924; and WATT, HENRY J., *The Foundations of Music,* Cambridge University Press, 1919.

not be developed. And this is the characteristic power of the musical mind in dealing with tonal patterns. I have been asked from time to time by music teachers how to get children to sing "in tune." There is no specific. The ability to sing in tune is a resultant of increasing tonal discrimination. One can only say that it is brought about by helping the child to listen for, recognize, and expect tonal trends and interval effects. This is exactly what we ought to mean by ear-training. The fundamental sensory capacity itself cannot be trained.[1] It depends upon the mechanics of the ear, which are fixed by heredity. But musical discrimination results from the use to which we put our fundamental sensory capacity, and this is most certainly susceptible of education. A person may have an exceedingly refined sense of relative pitch and yet absolutely no musical apprehensions. On the other hand, a person may have a mediocre sense of relative pitch, but may have gained very valuable musical apprehensions. And, as Seashore's results show clearly enough, the great majority of human beings can discriminate within the range of a quarter tone, which suffices to render tonal patterns potentially meaningful for them.

2. Our next proposition is much more serious. *Musical ability is not an hereditary special talent.* This flies in the face of many of our common preconceptions, and yet there are strong reasons for maintaining it. The argument on which this claim depends is partly general and partly special.

(*a*) In general, the status of special ability is extremely dubious and uncertain. Can we legitimately say that various people are born with mathematical ability, or literary ability,

[1] SEASHORE, CARL EMIL, *The Psychology of Musical Talent*, Silver, Burdett and Company, 1919.

or artistic ability, or executive ability, or military ability, and so on? We constantly hear such statements made, but they seem to involve us in a very old fallacy, long ago exploded by scientific psychology. This is the belief in faculties. Pre-scientific psychology accepted the doctrine that the human mind is made up of a number of special subdivisions or pow-ers, known as faculties. This provided the basis for that form of charlatanism called phrenology, because it was thought that the shape of a person's head indicated which faculties he pos-sessed and how highly developed they were. Faculty psychol-ogy is universally discredited, but it lives on in the guise of a belief in special inherited abilities. Special abilities are merely faculties under another name. All the arguments against the existence of faculties also apply here. First, it is pointed out that the human mind always works as a whole. Executive, or artistic, or musical, or military, or mathematical, or literary activity is not the outcome of a single part or division of the mind but of the entire personality, functioning in a certain direction. Second, it is pointed out that the lists of faculties which have been proposed have no empirical basis whatsoever. They are mere guesswork. We simply invent a faculty when-ever we happen to need it. The same contention applies also to the doctrine of special abilities. Thirdly, it is pointed out that the doctrine of faculties explains nothing. When we say that a person succeeds or fails in mathematics, or literature, or music, or executive work, because he either possesses or on the other hand lacks a faculty in this regard, we have offered no real explanation whatsoever. We have just applied a high-sounding label and have run a most imminent risk of self-deception. This criticism applies also to the doctrine of special ability. When one child succeeds with music and another fails and we account for the difference by saying that one possesses musical ability while the other lacks it, this appraisal gets us precisely nowhere. It is merely saying, in other words, what we already know. It does not even begin to tell us why. It is like the famous definition of an archdeacon as "one who performs archidiaconal functions." So much for our general argument which shows, at any rate, that the belief in musical ability as a special innate talent involves most serious difficulties.

(*b*) Our special argument is based upon the fairly considerable body of research which has been carried on with respect to musical ability.[1] By and large we may say that the investigators accept as their criterion of musical ability our notion of "effective and significant response" to tonal patterns. The general outcome of their work is distinctly unfavorable to the idea of musical ability as a unit trait or hereditary special ability. Of course they find that it differs in different people, but even where both parents are unmusical, their offspring tends to show a fair measure of musical responsiveness, although the child of two unmusical parents is never, within the scope of the investigations, found to manifest outstanding talent,—a result which might easily be attributed to the environmental influence of an unmusical home. Moreover, Copp in particular has insisted that we rarely come upon a child wholly lacking in musical ability, which we might presumably

[1] Particularly COPP, E. F., "Musical Ability," *Journal of Heredity*, 1916, vol. 7, pp. 297-304; HAECKER, V. and ZIEHEN, TH., "Über die Erblickheit der musikalischen Begabung," *Zeitschrift für Psychologie,* 1921, vol. 88, pp. 265-307, and 1922, vol. 89, pp. 273-312; KOCH, HANS and MJOEN, F., "Die Erblickheit der Musikalität," *Zeitschrift für Psychologie,* 1926, vol. 99, pp. 16-73; MJOEN, JAN A., "The Inheritance of Musical Ability," *Child Study,* April, 1928, vol. 5, no. 7, pp. 3-18.

expect if it were a special talent possessed by some but not by others.

The argument for a special hereditary musical endowment is strongest, of course, when we deal with the outstanding genius. Even here it is not conclusive. For one thing, we know comparatively little about the nature of creative genius, and it is dangerous to argue from ignorance. For another thing, the typical first-rate musical genius usually appears to have been a man capable of outstanding achievement elsewhere, though perhaps of not such outstanding achievement.[1] Furthermore, the great musician has almost always been the product of an environment which, if not specifically musical, was at least sympathetic to music.

3. It is highly significant that musical ability is closely associated with many other abilities. This is more or less implied by the point which has just been made. Investigations have shown it to be true in fact.[2] Thus we find that outstanding musical talent typically goes with linguistic, artistic, and mathematical ability. It is associated also with general intelligence. This is somewhat contrary to the findings of Seashore, but we must recall that his test battery does not give an adequate index of musicality. When the criterion is effective and significant response to tonal patterns, a much closer relationship to intelligence manifests itself than would be suggested by correlations between the Seashore Tests and standard intelli-

[1] Feis, Ostwald, *Studien über die Genealogie und Psychologie der Musiker,* Wiesbaden, J. F. Bergman, 1910.

[2] In addition to the studies cited, see also Miller, Richard, "Über musikalische Begabung und ihre Beziehungen zu sonstigen Anlagen," *Zeitschrift für Psychologie,* 1925, vol. 97, pp. 191-214; Pannenborg, H. J. and W. A., "Die Psychologie des Musikers," *Zeitschrift für Psychologie,* 1915, vol. 73, pp. 91-136; Schüssler, H., "Das unmusikalische Kind," *Zeitschrift für angewandte Psychologie,* 1916, vol. 11, pp. 136-166.

gence tests. Further, we have ample evidence that musical talent is associated with general success in school work. Miller has demonstrated this on the level of a training school for teachers. Schüssler, working with some hundreds of cases, reports that 41 percent of the unmusical, 57 percent of the "half musical," and 87 percent of the musical "achieve the goal of the school." The common finding that conservatory students do less well in their academic courses than college students means nothing in regard to the relationship of musical talent to other abilities. We do not know to what extent our conservatories select musical ability. The music student is one whose vocational trend has already manifested itself, and who may regard other interests as secondary, particularly as those interests are presented to him in the typical academic course. Lastly, we find that musical ability is associated with admirable traits of personality and physique,—leadership, sympathy, extroversion, and so forth.

The educational implications of all this are clearly most important and far-reaching. Musical power is associated with general high grade traits of mind, cultural interest, personality, and physique. The typical musical personality certainly should not be the narrow specialist.

4. The conclusion which it seems to me reasonable to draw from the argument as presented so far is that musical ability is not a special, inherited talent but a specialization of general ability. Consider the whole range of living creatures, all the way from the paramecium to the genius. In what essential respect do they differ? They differ fundamentally in ability to deal with structure, in power of mental organization. At the lowest level, about all that we have is a power to tell the difference between two things and to respond differently to

them. The paramecium which fumbles its way round a drop of acid in the water manifests this power, which is the dim beginning of mentality. As we go up the scale, this capacity to deal with structure becomes more and more comprehensive and complex. A monkey lacks sufficient mental organization to untie a simple knot. A man can untie a fairly simple knot, but is baffled by a tangled fishing line. To a super-man the tangled line might seem just as obvious and simple as a single bow to you and me. Intelligence tests deal with a small segment of the vast range of mentality, the segment bounded at one end by the low grade idiot and at the other by the genius, but within this limited segment, it is differential power to deal with structure which they reveal.

Musical ability is simply the ability to deal with structure embodied in tone. In this respect it is precisely analogous to every other kind of mental ability. The visual artist deals with structure in terms of form and color and line. The dramatist deals with structure in terms of human situations and motives. The mathematician deals with structure in its most abstract and general aspect. The soldier, or the executive, deals with structure in terms of military or business conditions. All mental ability is capacity to deal with structural elements and to give an organized response. Musical talent is simply this general capacity running in a special channel and working through a special medium.

What, then, determines whether a man shall be a musician or not? I am not inclined to deny that some hereditary factors may affect the situation, but, in general, the significant forces would seem to be *the direction of interest and will.* To become a musician means the concentration of general ability in a special medium.

5. Musical ability is natural to man. Indeed, in a very real sense, it goes far below the human level. Responsiveness to tone is a very general vertebrate characteristic, and there is sound reason for believing in the existence of a sub-human form of musicality.[1] This is far more than a matter of hearing. A creature might have efficient auditory apparatus and yet not be susceptible to anything which could properly be called a musical type of response. But in many sub-human forms of life, and surprisingly far down the scale, we find a most impressive, massive, apparently emotional response to tonal patterns which it is hard to refuse to recognize as the root of musicality.

There is no doubt that musical talent is very widely distributed among human beings. Schüssler, using a rather rigorous criterion, came to the opinion that from five to ten percent of all children were probably "unmusical"; but he hastens to qualify this statement by saying that even most of these can benefit substantially from musical opportunities and music education. Copp, applying a less satisfactory criterion, concludes that very few children indeed are insusceptible to musical influences or incapable of responding to musical training. Of course, as I have said before, there are great differences in the excellence of musical ability as among different persons. How such differences distribute themselves throughout the population we do not know.[2] However, we have not the slightest argument for denying that all but a very small minority of children can benefit as much or more from music, up to the

[1] DISERENS, CHARLES, *The Influence of Music on Behavior,* Princeton University Press, 1926.
[2] There is increasing reason to believe that we do not know as much as we have supposed even about the distribution of general test intelligence in the population.

eighth or ninth grade, as from any other subject which could be presented to them. The evidence for this proposition is not, of course, conclusive. But how many of our educational policies are built on conclusive proofs? What we have is a strong and cumulative body of testimony, without countervailing arguments founded upon empirical research. We can certainly proceed in reasonable confidence that music has an exceedingly general appeal and that at least ninety percent of human beings can derive marked benefit from the right kind of musical opportunities.

The Evocation of Musical Ability

The clear implication of the position taken in the foregoing section is that we may properly think of the entire course of music education as the progressive evocation of musical ability. We have defined that ability as the capacity to discriminate and respond effectively and significantly to tonal structures and relationships. This power is natural to man. In a measure it is possessed by almost everybody. Thus it becomes our educational task to arouse and develop it; to enable the individual to possess his possessions and to realize himself musically. This is very different from many of our ordinary notions about teaching music. What we want is not to impose music upon the child, but rather a creative release of natural musical capacity. Let us follow out some of the rich and striking implications of our idea.

1. We may regard the first great task of music education as the discovery of musical ability. The meaning, possibilities, and *modus operandi* of this undertaking are often grossly misunderstood. The discovery of musical ability is often taken to mean finding out whether or no a child possesses it in advance of training. Let us suppose we have before us a six-

year-old child who has had no music education at all. We look
about for some prognostic test, or other index, which will reveal to us how well he will respond to musical opportunities
and music lessons. This seems like common sense. Is the
child a promising subject for musical training, or is he not?
If we can find out, it seems to hold out the prospect of a wise
economy of effort, and also to indicate proper lines of ad-
vice and treatment. But our search for a reliable test ends in
failure, for no good prognostic index of musical ability exists.
Surely, though, we think one might be created. However, our
whole approach is thoroughly fallacious. The child's musical
ability is in him, but it is nascent. We cannot know a great
deal about it until it has been evoked by appropriate treatment. We cannot tell how far his interests may be shaped
and his purposes directed towards musical ends until after
the event. A prognostic test, valid prior to all training and experience, is probably a mere myth. It can measure only static
factors, whereas musical ability is dynamic through and
through and depends upon the molding of purpose and will.
What then does it mean to say that music education ought to
serve as an agency for the discovery of musical ability?

A. First and foremost, the discovery of musical ability must
begin as self-discovery. The important discoverer is not the
teacher but the child himself. We must seek to bring about
a situation in which the child finds out something outside
himself and also something inside himself.

(*a*) The child must be led to discover something outside
himself. That is to say, he must be led to discover music as a
great and endlessly fascinating pursuit and an opportunity for
rich and varied experience and activity. An essential factor
in the discovery of the child's musical ability is his awakening to this world of magic beauty and interest. It is part of

his heritage as a human being, and to show him the riches of this heritage is the first great task of music education. (*b*) The child must be led to discover something within himself. Music must be presented as something appealing, something to which his inner nature can naturally respond. This is why early music education should be highly informal and the very opposite of a series of arbitrarily imposed tasks. The discovery of a part of our cultural heritage always means the discovery of unsuspected but real powers and possibilities within himself. He finds out, by direct experience, his kinship with the race and his essential sympathy with its achievements. He finds out that to become musical is not at all to learn something alien but to be most fully and essentially one's very self.

B. The second thing to notice is that only through this progressive self-discovery can the child reveal his capacities to others. If musical ability existed as a kind of mental faculty or special department, which was either large and strong, or small and weak, or somewhere in between, then perhaps we could probe, explore, and find out all about it, quite in advance of any musical opportunity or evocation. However, this is precisely not the case. There is only one sure way to find out about a child's capacities for music. Give him the right kind of musical experience and opportunity and see what he does with them. Only be sure it is the right kind. Very often music teachers handle young children very badly indeed, trying to force upon them technical masteries as yet inevitably meaningless, drilling them on the most abstruse aspects of music, and, in general, carrying on a program of formal lesson learning. Then, when the children do none too well, the teacher excuses himself by complaining that they lack musical capacity. Quite obviously, the lack is on his part, and it is a lack of educational insight. Set up a music program calculated to lead to musical self-discovery, and it will also lead to musical self-revelation.

C. What should we do in attempting to bring about such self-discovery and self-revelation? We must have an educational program of a very definite kind, and we must vigorously avoid certain modes of approach. The essence of the matter is contained in an intimate piece of autobiography, once given to me in conversation, by one of the most eminent of American composers. He said that his interest in music and his will to be musical and to express himself musically were generated in the atmosphere of a musical home life. This very simply gives us the key to our problem. We cannot provide all our pupils with such homes, but we should approximate to their conditions as closely as we can. We must have a music program, carried on in terms of significant and unforced life experiences, which consists of musical activities, rather than of lessons to be learned and tasks to be done. We must make music a natural part of the child's environment. We must regard techniques as very secondary, indeed, at the outset. By such means we assist the individual to discover in himself, and to reveal to others, his capacity to respond effectively and significantly to tonal patterns.

2. We spoke of the power of tonal discrimination as one element in musical ability. The course of music education, from its earliest beginnings, must be towards a refinement of this power. The methods frequently used represent wrong ways of bringing this about. So far as such succeed at all, it is accidental and by indirection. They consist in emphasizing the external, mechanical means of rendering tonal discrimi-

nation more accurate and precise. They turn on teaching the score, teaching technique, and insisting, at all costs, upon the right notes. All this involves a half-truth in music education. Precise tonal discrimination is, indeed, essential. Moreover, these are among the agencies by which such precision is assisted. But always they are only the means; and the discrimination, the power to hear and image better, is the true end. When such things are taught as tricks, or tasks, or arbitrary requirements not intimately connected with musical experience and not consciously contributing towards the improvement of musical activity, they fail of educative effect and do not contribute what they should towards the evocation of musical ability.

Remember always that what we want is an increasing capacity to discriminate tonal patterns and relationships, not an assemblage of external tricks or skills. Feeling for interval, for tonal tendency and trend, for rhythm, for tone quality,— these are among the essential elements of musical ability, and the development of musical ability means progress in capacities such as these. We cannot be too clear about our essential aim, which is to inculcate clear, firm thinking, recognizing, and feeling of the relationships and patterns of tone. Towards this all the agencies of music education must be consciously and deliberately directed.

Through directed listening the child may discover what it means to discriminate phrase structure, form, tone color, harmony, and so forth. Through rhythmics he enters into the meaning of rhythm and discovers the natural response of the body to music. Singing should always be regarded as a primary agency for revealing the inner appeal of tonal structures. Instrumental experience adds a significant factor of added precision and exactitude. The visual experience of using the score can help to make all musical impressions more definite, and contribute immensely to creative interests. And motor technique should be handled as exemplifying the physical expression of definite musical thinking.

3. Musical ability, as we have defined it, involves not only discrimination but also significant and effective response to tonal structures. This also can and should be evoked by appropriate educational processes. We must help the child to discover that a musical composition is an opportunity for emotional experience and response and for conveying something which one has felt and apprehended one's self to others. We must help him to find out that every worthy composition is a cultural phenomenon of great significance; that it is the output of a human personality and the resultant of many circumstances; and that an awareness of such things makes it vastly more interesting to work at and creates a vastly more effective and complete response to it than is possible if we take it in a sort of vacuum. It is along these lines that music should be taught for the sake of evoking musical ability.

Notice particularly how this transforms our whole attitude towards the problem of the child whose musical endowment is meager. We know perfectly well that some children are sure to go much further in music and do far more with it than others. But we do not conclude from this, as is so often done, that the proper course is to discover the poorly endowed children as soon as we can and then limit their opportunities in advance. On the contrary, we believe that it is our duty to take everyone along, just as far as he is able to go. We do not believe that there is any considerable number of pupils who will be unable to respond to musical opportunities or to learn to appreciate fine music. Moreover, the proper treatment of the relatively unmusical child will not consist in applying some special devices, such as those recommended for dealing with the "monotone." Such devices may have a certain use in helping a child to find his singing voice, but they are a very small detail in all that should be done. What we must have is a humanized program of music education, aiming at the evocation and establishment of musical ability, and, through this, at the building of better, happier, more effective personalities.

OVERCOMING MUSICAL DEFICIENCIES

Another valuable way of thinking about music education, closely cognate with what we have been saying, is to regard it as aiming to overcome and prevent musical deficiencies. When we say that a person is "unmusical," we may mean one or more of many different things. Perhaps all of us, even the most highly endowed, are unmusical to some extent and in some sense. It is very likely that the absolutely perfect response to tonal structure never, or rarely ever, takes place. Therefore, to call a person unmusical is by no means to label him a hopeless case from the standpoint of music education. Quite the contrary in fact; for, while there may indeed be some hereditary defect, yet nearly always there turns out to be some defect due to training and opportunity, which is also a defect in human quality. And this is exactly the kind of situation which music education exists to remedy. We overcome the musical deficiency by overcoming the human deficiency. Let us consider the most important types of musical deficiency and see how they may be overcome.[1]

[1] I adopt here the classification of unmusical types presented by RICHARD MUELLER-FREIENFELS in his book, *Erziehung zur Kunst,* Leipsic, Quelle und Meyer, 1925.

1. First, we have the type lacking in general emotionality, so "dry" in respect of cultural life that tones are nothing but so much sound and not emotionally appealing stimuli. This type is often taken as the characteristically unmusical person. Clearly this defect renders "significant and effective" response to tonal patterns impossible. In the great majority of cases it is due to environmental and educational influences and not to heredity. To avoid it we must seek to set up the right kind of emotional orientation from the very first, which is always the proper preparation for more specialized musical learning.

2. Then we have a type, not readily distinguishable from the first, whose difficulty consists of special inhibitions, such as nervousness or excessive tendencies towards self-criticism. Defects of this kind may be actually engendered by the wrong sort of music education, where tasks are rigidly imposed and severe drill measures much in evidence. For their obviation we need a music program carried on through natural, expressive, and social situations and opportunities, where the emphasis is constantly upon creative contribution.

3. Yet another type is that which lacks a feeling for rhythm. We should notice that rhythmic feeling is natural to man, simply because it depends upon the natural physical action of his body. At the same time, it must be evoked by the proper kind of training. No expertly directed program of music education need leave any considerable number of children devoid of a very definite feeling for rhythm.

4. Still another type is that which lacks what Mueller-Freienfels calls "musical hearing," which means the sense for intervals and tonal trends. Such a defect, he pointed out, may exist without any physical aural deficiency whatsoever. Most

certainly it is not then due to heredity. Any well-directed sequence of musical projects should build up in the child this capacity for "musical hearing." The child who lacks it is apt to reveal this deficiency, among other ways, in an inability to "carry a tune," and so becomes classed as a monotone. What he needs is directed general musical education rather than special ingenuities of treatment.

5. A still further type is that which is deficient in motor coordination, and so fails to sing in tune or properly to control the voice. It is readily confused with type four, because in both cases we have what seems to be a monotone. Yet the whole line of treatment must be different. Here the defect is much less deep-seated. What the child needs is assistance in securing the right vocal placement.

6. The final type is that which is defective in musical memory. By this Mueller-Freienfels means to convey something different from what we might ordinarily understand. He points out that our sense of musical form depends upon remembering the constituent elements of the composition, so that we can recognize them when they appear again, either with or without modifications. Now such lack of musical memory, which renders it impossible that a composition as a whole shall produce an integrated effect upon us, is really due to defective *noticing*. That is to say, a person of this type has not found out how to listen as he should. He may learn this, not only through experiences in the way of listening, but also through intelligently directed performance and creation.

Music Education as Cultural Awakening

The argument of this chapter, and indeed of this entire book, now returns upon and amplifies itself. We have contended that musical ability is a specialization or canalization of general ability. In itself it typifies mentality and is intimately associated with many other human capacities. When we speak of evoking it, what we mean, in the widest sense, is rendering tonal pattern a significant and influential element in the life of the individual. To bring this about requires, above all, breadth of treatment, as we have seen. Music needs to be taught in its broad cultural and emotional setting if it is to be rightly apprehended. We must concentrate upon the human and affective aspects of tonal structure primarily and only secondarily upon its technical aspects. But it should be quite clear that to do all this means making music an agency for cultural stimulation and awakening. The truly striking consideration is that it becomes exactly this, when it is taught best for its own sake. To teach music as a sort of special though very complex trick is to do violence to its place in the individual mental make-up and also in the cultural order of things. Music is an art with endless ramifications, with endless psychological and cultural affiliations. It is not learned properly save in a broad setting and it does not have a tithe of its full potential value in human life unless apprehended in such a setting.

When we learn music as we should, we also learn a great deal more. First, we gain a respect for the emotional and æsthetic aspects of life. We learn that man does not live by bread alone and that a narrow practicality does violence to human nature. Second, we gain a respect for creative activity, which is no mere spectator's respect, for it is gained by a participation, however humble, in such activity. Third, we gain a respect for, and an understanding of, fine workmanship, because we ourselves have learned how desirable and how difficult it is. Fourth, we learn to desire self-expression and to be willing to submit ourselves to the discipline necessary for the mastery of its means. Fifth, we are brought closely and vitally into contact with a wide range of culture, with art, and with literature, with biography and science, with the characteristic products of exotic life.

It is in such ways as these that music education can subserve human values. It will not do so by chance, or by magic, or by a superstitious clinging to deadly though traditional routines. It is one phase of our school work where all things may be made new. It can, when properly directed, exemplify what education should be at its very best. *And it can discharge the great and central mission of all education, which is to raise the level of human quality.*

SUGGESTED SUPPLEMENTARY READINGS

HUGHES, C. L. "Environmental Influences on Musical Taste," *High School Journal,* 1933, vol. 16, pp. 175-178.

KWALWASSER, J., *Problems in Public School Music,* M. Witmark & Sons, 1932.

MUELLER-FREIENFELS, RICHARD, *Erziehung zur Kunst,* Quelle und Meyer, Leipsic, 1925.

MURSELL, JAMES L., and GLENN, MABELLE, *The Psychology of School Music Teaching,* Silver, Burdett and Company, 1931, ch. 2.

Symposium: "Music from the Standpoint of the General Educator," *Teachers College Record,* 1927, vol. 28, pp. 663-678.

Symposium: "Music and the Child," *Child Study,* 1928, vol. 7, pp. 3-18.

Index

383